Giving Kids the Business

GIVING
KIDS
THE
BU$INESS

The Commercialization of
America's Schools

Alex Molnar

Westview
PRESS
A Member of the Perseus Books Group

34926770

Copyright © 1996 by Alex Molnar

Published in 1996 in the United States of America by Westview Press, 5500 Central Avenue, Boulder,
Colorado 80301-2877, and in the United Kingdom by Westview Press, 12 Hid's Copse Road, Cumnor
Hill, Oxford OX2 9JJ

A CIP catalog record for this book is available from the Library of Congress.
ISBN 0-8133-9139-3

The paper used in this publication meets the requirements of the American National Standard for Perma-
nence of Paper for Printed Library Materials Z39.48-1984.

10   9   8   7   6   5   4   3   2   1

For Helena Kraemer

Contents

Acknowledgments

*G*iving Kids the Business would probably not have been written without the encouragement, criticism, gentle prodding, good humor, and patience of Barbara Lindquist. She listened to my ideas, offered suggestions, commented on rough drafts, and steadfastly refused to let me forget that this was a story worth telling—or that I was the one who should tell it.

Educators such as James Caradonio, Foyne Mahaffey, and Charles Kotulski; parents such as Karen Miller, Jacquelyne Souders, Lorrie Kennen, Jenny May, and Jack Price; and activists such as Arnold Fegge of the PTA, Marianne Manilov, Robin Templeton, the staff of UNPLUG, and Peggy Charren, Founder of Action for Children's Television contributed ideas, examples, and leads along the way. They were models of what concerned citizens can accomplish when they set their minds to it—even against what sometimes seem to be overwhelming odds. They are an inspiration.

The women and men of the press—both print and electronic—covering the business and education beats shared as much information as they received when they called on me for interviews about various aspects of this story. Without exception, they were generous, helpful, and professional in their dealings with a poor academic trying to learn how to cover a story like a journalist.

George Kaplan, Peter Finn, Charlotte Baecher, Anita Holmes, Marianne Manilov, Robin Templeton, and Jerry Benjamin all took considerable time and care to provide detailed comments on draft chapters. Gerald Bracey was always available for questioning on what the research said about issues of concern to me. Joel McNally listened closely as I explained my ideas and suggested text revisions. He helped me meet what seemed an impossible deadline in the last hectic months. And Jennifer Morales preserved my sanity by making sure all the endnotes were in proper form, all the facts were checked, and all the i's were dotted and t's crossed before the manuscript was submitted.

Gordon Massman, my editor, who took a risk on what was sure to be a controversial project and let me take the time necessary to do the job right, was a steady support throughout the process.

Finally, thanks are due to the many others who gave their time to provide information, who sent me materials, and who offered suggestions that helped me turn *Giving Kids the Business* into a reality.

Alex Molnar

The marketplace will take care of children.

—Mark Fowler,
chair of the Federal Communications Commission
during the Reagan administration

1

Marching As If to War

I f an unfriendly foreign power had attempted to impose on America the mediocre educational performance that exists today, we might well have viewed it as an act of war," proclaimed the *Nation at Risk* report in 1983.[1] *A Nation at Risk* was commissioned by Reagan administration secretary of education Terrel Bell, and it represented the voice of America's education establishment. However, it was quickly embraced by business leaders, and it provided the underlying justification for over a decade of corporate involvement in the reform of America's public schools.

The enthusiasm with which executives and their political allies responded to *A Nation at Risk* was not surprising. Its underlying logic cast America's enduring economic crisis as primarily a symptom of the failures of public education. Its self-assured, bombastic tone helped direct public attention away from any careful assessment of the extent to which the economic problems facing the United States were a function of structural problems in the economy, the consequence of deliberate corporate strategy, or a result of government policy toward business. It also helped create a political climate in which the pronouncements of business leaders assumed preeminent status in the debate over educational change.

Although you would never guess it from the corporate public relations handouts, corporate involvement in the schools is nothing new. The contours of public education in the United States have been, in large measure, shaped by a wave of business involvement in education policy and practice that began a century ago. Throughout the history of American public educa-

1

tion, businesspeople have dominated virtually every aspect of the enterprise, from national and state policymaking bodies to local school boards to the boards of grant-making foundations. In the 1980s, they turned on their creation with a vengeance.

After the publication of *A Nation at Risk,* the alleged catastrophic failure of public schools became an article of faith in boardrooms, policymaking circles, and the media. The economic importance of public education became the most potent argument for education reform in the 1980s and 1990s. If schools didn't do better, executives shouted, the economy would continue to crumble. Again and again, business leaders told the public that international competitors were beating American businesses because foreign schools did a better job of educating their young.

Corporate America mobilized, preaching the gospel of school improvement as a matter of national economic survival. All over the country, businesspeople took the lead in collaborating with politicians and educators to promote a grab bag of reforms intended to improve the performance of America's public schools.

Business leaders contributed political muscle to the fight to raise teachers' salaries, promote greater professional accountability, institute more stringent high school graduation requirements, and reform the school curriculum to make it more rigorous. Higher standards for teachers and students, curriculum more relevant to the world of work, and more accountability for everyone associated with public education were, executives argued, essential if America was to regain its competitive edge in a global marketplace.

Soon, it seemed no area of school life was beyond corporate scrutiny or without business involvement. Corporations helped train teachers and administrators, offered scholarships to deserving students, provided instructional materials, subsidized school programs, and cosponsored the activities of professional organizations. Businesspeople toiled as tutors, served as mentors, and offered their organizational knowledge to schools willing to learn the lessons of the corporate management "revolution." Correctly applying the principles of Total Quality Management—a business restructuring fad of the 1980s and 1990s— became the professional aspiration of a generation of school administrators.

The number of school-business partnerships increased dramatically. In 1984, such partnerships existed in only 17 percent of the nation's schools.[2] By the 1989–1990 school year, according to the National Association of Partners in Education, corporate enthusiasm for conjugal ties had established partnerships in 51 percent of America's school districts, involving 2.6 million volunteers and 29.7 million students.[3]

Corporate America was bursting at the seams with reform zeal. In 1989, RJR Nabisco chief executive officer (CEO) Louis V. Gerstner Jr. announced the creation of the company's Next Century Schools program to provide "venture capital" to help stimulate the "visionary thinking" of the "front-line troops" in America's schools.[4] In 1989, shortly before becoming secretary of education, Lamar Alexander told a conference of Wyoming's corporate movers and shakers that companies such as Federal Express and Burger King should set up schools to show educators how the private sector got things done.[5]

Perhaps Alexander had heard of the Corporate/Community School, which was opened in Chicago in autumn 1988 and funded by a coalition of fifty companies determined to demonstrate how schools should be set up and run. According to Joseph Kellman, president of the Chicago-based Globe Glass & Mirror Company, the game plan was "to change the system—the massive, obsolete, ineffectual system."[6] In what would become a familiar refrain, Kellman also proposed to usher in the dramatic changes he sought without spending more money per pupil than the Chicago public schools did. Similarly, Ray Harris, a Minneapolis real estate developer, promised that his Chiron School would be "revolutionary." And General Mills helped create the Public Academy, a school granted waivers from regulations in order to try new approaches to learning.[7] By 1995, all three "revolutionary" schools had been absorbed into the public education system. However, that was still in the future at the dawn of the 1990s, a time when there was little American business thought it couldn't do.

The Business Roundtable committed itself to a ten-year effort to improve public education, and the U.S. Chamber of Commerce announced it was developing its own proposals to reform the schools. In 1991, at the urging of President George Bush, the New American Schools Development Corporation was formed to channel business money to educational projects that corporate America considered worthy. In 1992, Whittle Communications Corporation announced that it had hired Yale University president Benno Schmidt to head up its Edison Project, a plan to create a nationwide chain of for-profit schools. And, somewhat more modestly, Education Alternatives, Inc. (EAI), offered to contract with school districts to manage their schools for the same amount of money the district spent per pupil and to do so with such efficiency that it would be possible to return a profit to investors. No one, it seems, thought to ask why anyone would want executives who commonly describe each other as "aggressive" and "ferocious" and as "firebrands" and "terrorists" with an "attack mentality" anywhere near schools or children.[8]

Stalking the Elusive Skills Shortage

In the popular press as well as in business and education journals, corporate educational reform efforts have been covered extensively. With few exceptions, reports of corporate involvement in education adopt a celebratory and uncritical view of corporate motivation and a dim view of the performance of the public schools.

In spring 1990, Xerox CEO David Kearns was featured on the cover of a special issue of *Fortune* magazine devoted to "saving our schools." Kearns, pictured sitting at a student desk in front of a chalkboard, was, the cover promised, going to "speak out" on educational reform. Inside, readers learned that Kearns "came at the education problem as an economic and global competitive issue" and that it hit him "that by the year 2000 we'd be out of qualified workers."[9]

Kearns (soon to be appointed an assistant secretary of education) may have based his comments on the conservative Hudson Institute's *Workforce 2000* report, published in 1987.[10] *Workforce 2000* predicted a disastrous shortage of skilled workers in the 1990s. Its author, William B. Johnston, called for increased immigration to make up for the shortfall.[11]

A few months after the publication of *Fortune*'s special issue, the Commission on the Skills of the American Workforce issued a report entitled *America's Choice: High Skills or Low Wages!* This report drew far different conclusions than *Workforce 2000*. Outlining what would become the Clinton administration's education and employment premises (Ira Magaziner, a Clinton policy adviser, chaired the group), the commission's research found that "only five percent of employers feel that education and skill requirements are increasing significantly" and that most of the so-called shortages of "skilled" labor were in "chronically underpaid 'women's' occupations and traditional craft trades."[12]

The language of corporate school reform is the language of "human resources" and "human capital." A 1992 Labor Department report, "Learning for Living," is a good example of "human resources" logic at work.[13] The report accepted without reservation the claim that there is a jobs crisis in the United States because high school graduates lack the skills necessary for employment in what it calls a "high performance" economy. Despite its advocacy of some sound teaching principles, the report gave no consideration to the aspirations and dreams of children. In fact, a person searching through corporate reform literature would, in general, have little hope of finding concern about educational equity for girls or minority group members or about the simple justice of spending at least the same amount of money to educate each child. Nor do corporate-sponsored reforms consider the possibility that perhaps we should provide decent, humane schools for all our children because we love them and because childhood in the United States should be a rich and rewarding time during which children learn to care for each other through the example of adults who care for them.

Two *New York Times* stories, published five years apart, expose how ephemeral the so-called skills crisis was and is. On September 25, 1989, the headline on a front-page story was "Impending U.S. Jobs 'Disaster': Workforce Unqualified to Work." The story went on to quote business executives complaining that schools were lagging behind the needs of employers. Brad M. Butler, former CEO of Procter & Gamble, feared America was creating "a third world country within our own country." James E. Burke, CEO of Johnson & Johnson, commented that it was "the American dream turned into a nightmare."[14]

On March 10, 1994, another *New York Times* front-page headline read: "Low Pay and Closed Doors Greet Young in Job Market." This time, the *Times* reported on the plight of young, qualified workers who were "finding that 'McJobs'—that pay $6 an hour or less, and offer little in the way of a career path—are about the only openings around."[15] It did, indeed, seem as if a third world country was being born inside the United States—and that American corporations were the parents of this unwanted child.

By the mid-1990s, no skills crisis was in sight. In Milwaukee, for example, an analysis of the labor market not only found no evidence of a skills shortage—most of the full-time jobs available were in minimum-wage occupations such as short-order cook, custodian, and security guard—it also found that the real shortage was in the number of jobs available. In the ten poorest zip code areas of Milwaukee, the study found 2,000 full-time jobs and 9,600 people in need of work. To make matters worse, Wisconsin governor Tommy Thompson put himself in the forefront of the national welfare debate by proposing the Wisconsin Works program. This welfare "reform" would add another 18,000 to the number of people seeking employment in 1996,[16] meaning that about 28,000 people would soon be chasing 2,000 jobs.

The *America's Choice* report concluded that the road to salvation for American workers was through a reorganization of the workplace to emphasize continuous worker training, closer coordination between school and work, and higher standards for student academic performance. When applied to public education, *America's Choice* articulated what amounted to an illogical supply-side labor theory. It might best be described as "Milton Friedman in a field of dreams" or "give them the training and the jobs will come." Applied to the workplace, however, the report was on to something. Despite all the

high-toned rhetoric about the importance of education coming from corporate executives, American corporations invest less in worker training than
their foreign rivals. Furthermore, what money they do invest in education
goes disproportionately to the upper ranks of employees.[17]

Dueling rhetoric and anecdotes aside, there was little evidence by 1995 of
either a skills crisis or a general movement by business to reorganize the
workplace and treat workers as investments worthy of continuous training
rather than, as Bruce Springsteen put it in a song, spare parts.

A front-page article in the *New York Times* on August 28, 1995, "Skilled
Workers Watch Their Jobs Migrate Overseas," painted a very different picture than either the *Workforce 2000* or *America's Choice* reports. According to
the *Times* story, increasing numbers of U.S. corporations were hiring skilled
foreign workers overseas—not because of a shortage of skilled American
workers (whom they were laying off by the thousands)—but because foreign
workers were cheaper. The story went on to say that the high-tech tools of
the information age, far from being the salvation of America's workers, were
often used to reduce their wages.[18] Given this reality, if American schools
produced more highly skilled workers, the chief consequence would likely be
to elevate the level of discourse at unemployment offices.

It is impossible to know how many business leaders believe their own reform rhetoric. Whatever their individual beliefs may be, the false connection
drawn between the alleged crisis in American public education and the real
economic crisis facing working people assures that the education reforms
sought by corporate America can never succeed. The logic of corporate education reform sets up the country for a continuing "manufactured" crisis in
education that cannot be resolved, no matter how much schools are changed.

The simple truth is that no school system, regardless of how "reformed" it
may be, can deliver on the implicit promise of corporate-sponsored reforms:
the creation of a full-employment economy with an expanding number of
well-paying jobs. Fulfilling that promise requires a dramatic change in U.S.
economic and political strategy and tactics. That is something U.S. corporations seek to avoid at all cost because if such strategies were effective, they
would necessarily transfer wealth from corporations and well-to-do individuals to working people.

Corporate Schizophrenia

Throughout the 1980s and 1990s, business leaders endorsed educational reform as absolutely imperative for the nation's survival. But by and large, they

saw no reason to change the probusiness spending and regulatory policies they had lobbied long and hard to put in place.

As a result, during the 1980s and into the 1990s, corporate leaders' actions had a schizophrenic quality. After the publication of *A Nation at Risk*, most executives seemed to embrace reforms supported by the education establishment. Some business groups (the Business Roundtable, for example) even took a fairly progressive view of the issue of creating more equitable funding for rich and poor school districts (albeit without quite taking a position on the matter).[19] For the most part, however, the tax and social policy priorities championed by corporations made it more difficult for public schools to succeed and reduced governmental resources to help achieve a more wholesome and safer environment for poor and working-class children outside the school.

Senator Howard Metzenbaum saw the problem and argued for measures that would discourage businesses from exacting from communities preferential tax treatments that undermine the local school tax base:

> In speech after speech, it is our corporate CEOs who state that an educated, literate work force is the key to American competitiveness. They pontificate on the importance of education. They point out their magnanimous corporate contributions to education in one breath, and then they pull the tax base out from under local schools in the next. Businesses criticize the job our schools are doing and then proceed to nail down every tax break they can get, further eroding the school's ability to do the job.[20]

As a result of corporate success in setting the social and economic policy agenda, public schools, particularly those in the most rural and the most urban areas of the country, found themselves serving larger numbers of children who were poor—and more intensely poor than at the dawn of the 1980s. At the same time, the ballyhooed increases in education spending during the period went overwhelmingly to augment funding for children with exceptional educational needs and for costs such as food service, transportation, and building maintenance.[21]

Instead of supporting an adequate tax base for public schools and an equitable division of educational resources, corporations such as the Bank of Boston apparently preferred private philanthropy, such as endowing the Boston Plan for Excellence in Public Schools, to paying their fair share of taxes. The Bank of Boston, for example, paid no state taxes at all in 1987 despite posting a profit of $19.7 million.[22]

The much praised contributions of business and industry to public schools are minuscule in relation to the needs created by cutbacks in social spending. In 1989, total corporate contributions to public elementary schools totaled $156 million. Corporate contributions to private schools and to colleges and universities totaled $2.4 billion in the same year.[23] Considered from another angle, $156 million is a tiny fraction of the $1 billion plus in tax breaks that Wisconsin corporations alone received each year from the state of Wisconsin in the 1990s.[24] By one estimate, total corporate contributions to kindergarten through twelfth-grade (K–12) education in 1990 would run the nation's schools for less than two hours.[25]

As for the highly touted school-business partnerships, a 1989 study of 450 partnership programs conducted at the University of Chicago found that in urban school systems, most of the partnerships covered capital outlays that districts with adequate tax revenue easily could have provided for themselves. The partnerships did little to advance meaningful educational reform.[26]

By the end of the 1980s, despite all the attempts to obscure the issue, it was becoming harder to avoid the conclusion that the United States would be unable to pay for the public education system to which it was theoretically committed—a system capable of providing equal opportunity for every child to receive a high-quality education—unless there was a radical change in the economic and political decisions being made in corporate boardrooms, in statehouses, and in Washington.

In 1990, the business community's support for *A Nation at Risk*–style reforms came under direct attack in *Politics, Markets and America's Schools.* The book's authors, John Chubb and Terry Moe, argued that the overly bureaucratic public education system, responsive as it was to the political process, could only be reformed by transforming it into a market-driven system based on government-funded vouchers that allowed parents to choose the schools their children attended. Chubb and Moe criticized the business community, contending that when it came to school reform, the corporate world's ideas would do little to make the changes in the overall structure of the system they felt were necessary. As a result, Chubb and Moe argued, corporate reform proposals were almost impossible to distinguish from those of the education establishment. It was time, they contended, to let the market reform the schools.[27] Although Chubb and Moe's assumptions, methodology, and conclusions were all seriously flawed,[28] their criticism found a large corporate audience that was ready to repent.

The desire to keep public attention away from business-backed economic and social policies that were undermining the job security of American workers and swelling the ranks of the nation's poor made it all but inevitable that a growing segment of corporate America would shift to the right. While stepping up their attacks on public schools, many business leaders embraced tax-supported vouchers for children attending private and religious schools, so-called charter schools that would be exempt from many state regulations and especially union contracts, and for-profit schools run by private entrepreneurs rather than educators.

Vouchers, charter schools, and for-profit public education are actually variations of old educational ideas that had been tried and found wanting. When the ideas were tested previously, they had run into serious problems, ranging from the unconstitutional to the criminal. Now, repackaged with a lot of flashy new rhetoric about high-tech computer technology and educational innovation, they have become the "visionary" educational reforms of the 1990s.

Each reform has its own twists and nuances. But the reforms have many things in common as well. One overriding theme is that problems in the schools have nothing to do with the amount of money provided for K–12 education and the unequal distribution of that money. Instead, each reform supports the fiction popular with business leaders that, if the system were made more efficient, there is no reason Americans couldn't maintain a universal system of public schools and provide every child with a high-quality education without spending more money. In other words, unleash the market and stand back as thousands of entrepreneurs create better schools.

Despite the fact that, by the mid-1990s, American public schools were, against all odds, actually educating a more diverse and more impoverished student body to a higher standard of academic performance,[29] many corporate leaders have supported renewed attacks on public schools for costing too much, achieving too little, and not providing the highly skilled workers whom, despite all evidence to the contrary, executives continued to claim the country needed.

As wave after wave of corporate downsizing sent thousands of more skilled workers to the unemployment line, disrupting the lives of children and their families and communities outside school, business leaders loudly confessed their failure as school reformers. Louis V. Gerstner Jr., now at the helm of IBM, claimed the problem was that business was not given enough control over school practices in return for the enormous amount of money it was contributing. It was time for radical reform.[30]

Declaring their reform efforts had been defeated by an overly bureaucratic system dominated by special interests, especially teachers' unions, executives announced that it was impossible to reform the nation's public school system, particularly in large cities. The only thing left to do was to dismantle it.[31]

Button-Down Revolutionaries

The revolutionary upheavals preferred in the corporate boardrooms of the 1990s are private school vouchers, charter schools, and, even better, privately owned, for-profit schools. The available evidence from the United States and other countries strongly suggests that the market will not provide solutions to America's education problems.[32]

However, besides allegedly being able to improve education at no additional cost, these reforms offer a public-spirited justification for introducing public education to the profit motive and giving educators a healthy dose of the "real world" in the form of competition. Most important, they keep the focus on schools and off the failure of business to promote the well-being of most of the country's citizens.

Many executives continue to support government-established curriculum standards, vocational training, and more widespread use of computer technology. For example, an education "summit" hosted by Louis V. Gerstner Jr. and Wisconsin governor Tommy Thompson at IBM headquarters in Palisades, New Jersey, on March 26–27, 1996, was billed as an effort to put academic standards and technological innovation back at the top of the school reform agenda. Long on rhetoric and short on concrete proposals, the "summit" seemed like little more than an opportunity for IBM's Gerstner to create an opening for his company's products and for media-savvy governors like Thompson to grab headlines for a few days.

The support provided by the CEOs of major corporations, like Gerstner, and the education establishment is what drives the Clinton administration's agenda of national education goals, youth apprenticeship programs, technology initiatives, and school-business partnerships. Like just about every other domestic policy since the New Deal, however, that agenda has come under increasing attack since the congressional elections of 1994.

With conservative "free marketeers" ascendant in Congress, calls for "revolutionary" free-market solutions to educational problems and rhetoric about the catastrophic failure of America's public schools have become even more feverish. Many business leaders have seen the opportunity to seize the moment and further reduce their financial obligations to public schools.

Although they grab a lot of media attention, the attacks on the education system are no threat to corporate plans to exploit an education market that business leaders think may be bigger than military procurement. With the Cold War defense-spending bonanza winding down, a fresh, young domestic market looks inviting in many executive suites and investment houses. Of course, corporate proposals to make public education into a profit center are pitched with ringing language about good citizenship and public-spiritedness.

The nominal political struggle between proponents of traditional corporate-educator-government collaboration to reform the schools and the more radical advocates of market-based proposals has attracted lots of media attention. However, this battle is, in many respects, superficial. The more profound underlying conflict, although couched in educational terms, is not fundamentally about education at all. In this conflict, corporate supporters of traditional business-government collaboration and advocates of market-based school reforms are on the same side. Both tend to favor imposing the kind of job "restructuring" that was the hallmark of the private sector during the 1980s on public education in the 1990s. This restructuring is the key that is to unlock the education market.

The stakes are enormous. The public schools are the country's largest, most costly, and most pervasive civilian institution. If America's public schools cannot be made over in the private sector's image through massive downsizing and wage cuts, the nation will be forced to confront an idea that is the worst nightmare of the executive class: a downward redistribution of wealth. Taking more money away from wealthy individuals and corporations to pay for the education of poor and working-class children is precisely what corporate-led school reforms, above all else, are designed to prevent.

It is obvious to anyone who cares to look closely that the public schools can no longer be sustained primarily by working-class citizens whose incomes have been dropping for more than two decades. Given the alternative of spending more of their own money, business leaders prefer to pretend it is possible to have both higher-quality, universal public education *and* lower costs by letting the market work its wonders.

The consequences of such market-driven changes on the private sector throughout the 1980s are obvious. The United States now has the most productive workers in the world. At the same time, American workers work longer hours, have fewer benefits, and earn less than their counterparts in many industrial countries. The United States also can boast the largest gap in wealth between the rich and the poor of any industrial country and the highest rate of childhood poverty.[33] The stock market now soars every time a new wave of corporate layoffs is announced. The real wages of American workers continue to stagnate or decline despite record corporate profits. Whoever else may be benefiting from the wrenching economic changes of the 1980s and 1990s, it is not the majority of American citizens.

If the experience in the private sector is any indicator, market-based reforms in public education will harm not only most of the people who work in the schools but also the children and the communities that depend on them. At the same time, a relative few will benefit a great deal.

One of the roles of government, particularly as defined by the democratic vision of President Franklin Delano Roosevelt, is to serve as a buffer protecting the citizen majority from the bloodless machinations of the market. In this vision, public institutions, including the public school system, are vehicles for the peaceful redistribution of wealth and opportunity. They help secure the social contract and provide the foundation for a stable democracy.

But the promise and vision of government has become so limited that so-called neoconservatives in both major political parties now argue seriously and publicly that the only role of government is to get out of the way so the market can do its job. The confusion of market and civic values has become so profound that the Clinton administration has floated "market democracy" as a catchphrase to describe its political vision.[34]

Wisconsin Turns Right and Becomes a National Model

The political journey of Wisconsin under its three-term Republican governor Tommy Thompson provides a good example of how the corporate-led restructuring of the American economy has defined the terms of the current national debate over school reform. Thompson took over as chair of the Education Commission of the States and the National Governors' Association in 1995, making him an influential voice on education and welfare reform nationally. He is also a hotdog political surfer riding the biggest wave of his career.

In 1994, for the first time in over twenty years, the Republican party took control of both houses of the Wisconsin state legislature. And Thompson promptly responded with a budget that included the whole laundry list of market-based education reforms: an expansion of Milwaukee's private school voucher plan to religious schools, a sweeping charter school law, and lots of opportunities for the privatization of school activities.

Thompson has come a long way since a conservative *Milwaukee Journal* business editor lamented in a 1984 column that the agenda of the state's corporate leaders was threatened by the emergence of a rough-edged, cartoonish figure as a potential Republican gubernatorial candidate.[35]

As soon as he took office, Thompson began to methodically put in place a political agenda designed by and for the Metropolitan Milwaukee Association of Commerce (MMAC) and the Wisconsin Manufacturers & Commerce (WMC), the state's two most powerful business lobbying groups. Two videotapes tell the story. The first, *Choices*, was produced by MMAC, the Council of Small Business Executives, and the Independent Business Association of Wisconsin.[36] It was shown in factories and businesses all over the state in a successful effort to influence the 1986 election. Narrated by a retired Milwaukee TV anchorman with the contrived earnestness of a local newscast, *Choices* called for cuts in unemployment compensation, inheritance taxes, and capital gains taxes, accompanied by reduced spending on the University of Wisconsin, reduced aid to local governments and schools, and reduced aid to individuals (especially in the form of Aid to Families with Dependent Children [AFDC] and medical assistance payments).

Choices did not mention that Wisconsin state spending in the 1980s had, in large measure, been increased to offset steep reductions in federal assistance to states and localities during the Reagan administration—the so-called new federalism. Instead, it argued that Wisconsin was "overspending" because of misplaced priorities and that the result was killing the ability of businesses to create jobs.

In 1987, having successfully helped elect Thompson, the *Choices* team elaborated further on how Wisconsinites should go about saving their jobs in a video sequel called *Choices II*.[37] This time, the producers not only called for reductions in income taxes, capital gains taxes, and inheritance taxes, they also argued that state employees (in the lower-paying job categories) were "overpaid" compared to their private sector counterparts in terms of wages, fringe benefits (read medical insurance), and "especially pensions."

In one particularly telling scene, an actor portraying a secretary faces the camera and says angrily: "I've read the newspapers and I get mad when I hear the state pays people who do the same amount of work I do 20 percent more than I get. That's unfair!" The possibility that the real unfairness on display involved the low wages and benefits of private sector workers like the secretary in the video was apparently not an alternative the producers of *Choices II* were interested in having viewers consider.

Choices II also called for the elimination of Wisconsin's binding arbitration law (for which teachers had given up the right to strike), the consolidation and privatization of government services, and enrollment reductions, tougher admission standards, and higher tuition for the state university system.

According to *Choices* and *Choices II*, the way to create jobs was to let low-wage taxpayers spend the few dollars they might realize from proposed tax cuts on things like car payments and vacations in northern Wisconsin (both of which they would presumably need in order to escape from neighborhoods deteriorating around their ears because of reductions in government services). *Choices II* failed to mention that affluent Wisconsinites would be traveling to more exotic destinations with their much larger tax savings.

The people paying for the *Choices* videos were smart enough to realize that Wisconsin could not keep providing the tax giveaways to corporate interests that were passed during the 1970s and 1980s and still provide the level of public services enjoyed by the majority of Wisconsin citizens. That was especially true given federal spending priorities and dramatic reductions in aid to state and local governments initiated by the Reagan administration.

Anyone with an eye on state revenues could see that as corporate Wisconsin and the federal government continued to pay less, state taxpayers would have to pay more. Homeowners particularly bore an ever greater share of the cost of governmental services that depended on property taxes—most visibly, public schools. By 1994, corporate tax breaks were taking over $1 billion out of the state treasury every year. Data showed that between 1973 and 1993, the contribution of residential property taxes to total state and local property taxes had increased from 51 percent to 62 percent. During the same period, the contribution of manufacturing property taxes to the total decreased from 15 percent to 5.6 percent. And despite the claimed importance of corporate tax reductions in job creation, Wisconsin's manufacturing employment remained flat.[38] It was obvious that with the real wages of most Wisconsin workers falling and their tax load increasing, something had to give.

Mirroring national business groups and the Reagan and Bush administrations, Wisconsin's business establishment and thus the Thompson administration itself made it a primary political goal to ensure that, whatever else might change, corporate tax breaks would be maintained—hence the *Choices* videos and the direction of the Thompson administration's economic, social welfare, and education policies.

To carry out the *Choices* agenda, the Thompson administration adopted a three-part strategy that anticipated the Contract with America unveiled by Republicans during the 1994 congressional election campaign: first, anchor in the public mind the belief that the services provided by all levels of Wisconsin government were the primary reason for high property tax rates; second, construe any attempt to raise corporate tax rates or to make the state income tax more progressive as job-destroying folly; and third, package reductions of governmental services and the shift to the use of private contractors as "new thinking" that would magically provide more for less.

These strategies have been enormously successful in Wisconsin and Michigan and are being pursued in other states with more mixed results. They constitute the key elements of the Republican-led political "revolution" on display in Congress. That's why Wisconsin's experience provides a window on the politics of education reform nationally.

All the *Choices* recommendations have now become law or state policy in Wisconsin—thanks to Thompson's political skill, enormous amounts of business money, the rise of an effective conservative political and public policy apparatus, and cheerleading media that, for the most part, share the corporate point of view. All those components play on the escalating frustration and anger of private sector workers over massive job dislocations, wage cuts, and benefits reductions, on the one hand, and tax increases to support government services, especially public schools, on the other.

During the first ten years of Thompson's reign, Wisconsin has nearly completed a twenty-year transition from a low-unemployment/high-wage state into a low-unemployment/low-wage state. Corporate tax giveaways are now politically sacrosanct. In the corridors of power in Madison and Milwaukee, it has become a firmly entrenched, bipartisan article of faith that the only way out of an ever tightening financial box (constructed by corporate and political economic policy) is to reduce governmental services or turn them over to the private sector.

As a result, Wisconsin's well-off citizens have never been better off. They have plenty of extra cash to spend on such things as minimum-wage rent-a-cops to protect their property, private health clubs where they can keep themselves fit while being served by minimum-wage workers, and private schools for their children where, if all goes according to plan, the wages of public school teachers will no longer be putting so much pressure on them to increase the pay of their own kids' teachers.

It's quite another story for the people who wear the rent-a-cop uniforms, wait on the tables, labor for reduced wages and benefits hauling garbage and emptying bedpans, and struggle to make ends meet on inadequate or nonexistent private pensions and social security. They have watched public services in their communities deteriorate and educational opportunities for their children shrivel.

Logically, the interests of those workers should create political pressure to change the destructive downward spiral in which they are caught. Instead, large numbers of them—abandoned by a Democratic party now firmly wed to corporate interests, egged on by a daily dose of high-octane nonsense on AM talk radio, and seeing no constructive way out of their predicament—have allied themselves with those responsible for their plight. They have turned on government employees, especially teachers, as if they were the enemy. Much like the secretary depicted in the *Choices II* video, many low-income workers all over Wisconsin and the United States now join corporate executives in demanding that government employees get the same treatment as that dished out by private sector employers. It's a kind of social-class version of the battered-child syndrome.

Since the question of why private sector workers have derived so little benefit from the productivity increases of the last twenty years is rarely asked,
much less seriously debated, many Wisconsin workers apparently are convinced that their only hope for survival is to destroy the livelihood of other
workers. With neither Democrats nor Republicans offering politics or policies that would ensure that the nation's wealth and financial burdens are
shared more justly, it is small wonder that civil servants are out and contracting out is in, that the market reigns triumphant, and that the race to the bottom for working people continues apace.

Thompson's success in achieving the agenda of members of Wisconsin's
business elite has put a lot of money in their pockets and has assured that he
has no fund-raising worries. But preserving corporate tax breaks, reducing
governmental services, and even impressive employment numbers—given
the current stagnation in wages—are not long-term winners politically either
in Wisconsin or in the nation. However, just as massive layoffs produce a
short-term jolt in stock dividends, the important thing is to obscure the
long-range damage for as long as possible.

Children as a Cash Crop

The ability of education "reforms" such as privatization, charter schools, and
private school vouchers to cloud the issues goes a long way toward explaining
their political attractiveness. Besides that, such reforms are consistent with
the corporate economic agenda, and they hold out the promise of corporations making money. They also pull together corporate heavy hitters and
radical "social values" conservatives into a powerful, if unstable, alliance.

Market-based reforms trade on the assumption that the cost of public education can be reduced by increasing efficiency. Even better, they provide business leaders with alluring visions of turning children and the schools that serve
them into profit centers. The economic attractiveness and political potency of
these highly visible education "reforms" overwhelm the fact that none of them
has any educational content or any demonstrated or logical relationship to improving the quality of the public schools. Professional educators often seem
baffled by what appears to them to be the sudden emergence of market-based
school reforms on center stage. But in fact, the education establishment helped
sow the seeds that are sprouting today with its *Nation at Risk* report.

To be sure, the major education reforms promoted by corporations in the
1980s were not put forward as schemes to directly enhance the profits of individual corporations. Instead, executives argued that if an inadequate system of

public education was a threat to America's international economic competitiveness, it also was a threat to every citizen's well-being. Wrapped in this logic, the businesspeople who set out to help reform the schools could be characterized as discharging a high civic duty, not pursuing a narrow self-interest.

The wave of corporate criticism of public education during the 1980s, along with the flood of business-backed reform proposals and a relentlessly probusiness political environment, succeeded in opening wide the schoolhouse door for self-serving proposals, programs, and activities promoted by businesses. In a calmer, more balanced climate, these probably would have been recognized for what they were and rejected. Although cloaked in the rhetoric of school improvement and school-business cooperation, these corporate efforts were not attempts to create high-quality public schools better able to respond to the demands of a modern economy. They were attempts to turn the public schools themselves into centers of corporate profit.

Business efforts to gain access to public schools in order to sell products and establish name recognition, as well as to propagandize for corporate social and economic points of view, have been common for most of this century. However, in the 1980s, a Rubicon of sorts was crossed. Not only did the volume of advertising reach new levels of intrusiveness, marketing efforts were also often unashamedly characterized as legitimate contributions to curriculum content, as helpful teaching aids, and as a good way of promoting school-business cooperation. As a result, in homes across America, parents have since discovered that their sons and daughters are given "Gushers" fruit snacks in class, told to burst them between their teeth, and asked by their teachers to compare the sensation to a geothermal eruption (compliments of General Mills); that their sons are being taught the history of the potato chip (compliments of the Potato Board and the Snack Food Association); or that their daughters are discussing "good hair days" and "bad hair days" in class (compliments of Revlon). Tootsie Roll has provided a lesson on "the sweet taste of success," and Exxon has distributed a videotape to help teachers reassure students that the *Valdez* oil spill wasn't so bad after all.

The 1980s were not a time to say no to business. Educators were desperate to prove their willingness to cooperate. It is hardly surprising that as the 1980s wore on, it became more common and more acceptable for corporations to treat public schools as cash cows to pump up the bottom line. The calculus of narrow self-interest viewed through the rose-tinted glasses of market ideology seems to have led many business leaders to conclude that education reforms must fit handily into one or both of two corporate agendas: to cut costs and to find ways to profit directly from the schools.

The original economic justification for corporate leadership in educational reform has been turned on its head. The emphasis has shifted from the contribution good schools make to everyone's economic well-being to how public schools can be used to increase the profits of a particular business. This shift has paved the way for the commercialized reforms of the 1990s. If the profit motive was a stowaway carefully hidden when the corporate reform ship set sail during the 1980s, it is now at the helm.

The Shape of Things to Come

The problem of advertising in schools is at least a highly visible one. The "high-tech" innovations now being proposed by a growing number of corporations are more subtle and less examined, and they are potentially an even more dangerous step toward commercialized public education. In the 1990s, for example, telephone companies are promoting plans for high-tech "schools of tomorrow" that use a variety of electronic messaging, telephone, and information-processing services they are anxious to sell.

Corporate high-tech initiatives raise some serious issues. If information technology is indeed to be the key that unlocks the "world of tomorrow," it is worth considering whether a child's access to that information and the skills necessary to use it effectively should be governed by his or her school district's ability to meet the commercial demands of a profit-making, private corporation. If the information necessary for full citizenship is privately owned and sold only to those who can afford it, then the introduction of information technology may well usher in tomorrow's world of even more dramatic inequalities in our public school system.

K-III Communications's advertising-laced Channel One program, a twelve-minute news broadcast aimed at adolescents, offers the free use of TV monitors to every school that signs on to the program—as long as the school guarantees that 90 percent of its students watch the show almost every day. Channel One demonstrates how a relatively simple technology such as satellite broadcasting can be used to establish a connection between instructional innovation and corporate profit. Channel One uses technology as an incentive to entice cash-strapped schools to deliver students to advertisers.

Channel One is a flashier version of a kind of hucksterism in the classroom that has been perverting instruction to sell products and tell the corporate story for a long time. But in a political atmosphere in which business can do no wrong, the hucksterism has become ever more shameless. Even that venerable schoolhouse institution known as the *Weekly Reader* has taken

on a more insidious edge in its coverage of tobacco stories under the guidance of its corporate parent K-III Communications—a major shareholder in
RJR Nabisco.

The reason children are required to watch Channel One has nothing to do
with a school's curriculum or the channel's content on current affairs. It has
to do with the need to guarantee an audience to the advertisers who purchase
the two minutes of the broadcast devoted to commercials. Although there is
no advertising in textbooks (yet), commercials already have been built into
some "educational" software.

For-profit schools, along with other corporate-backed education reforms
such as private school vouchers and charter schools, have become useful vehicles for funneling tax funds into the hands of private entrepreneurs. If
widely adopted, they will most likely both concentrate the poorest children
in the remaining public schools and drain away the resources necessary for
those schools to function effectively.

Channel One's spawn, the Edison Project, is an attempt to explicitly make
high-tech systems in schools a mechanism for earning direct profits for investors. The financial contradictions underlying the Edison Project, which
proposes to run schools for private profit, are catching up with its founder,
Chris Whittle. The project may not survive, but it is not the only attempt to
use school reform as a cover for inventing new ways to generate corporate
profits—and it certainly won't be the last.

Charter school reform, originally proposed as a way of empowering teachers
to improve their own schools, has been transformed into a mechanism to dismantle teachers' union protections and to cut their wages. In the for-profit
scheme of things, cutting wages paid to teachers and school service workers
in a community has the happy result of producing dividends for stockholders—who almost always live elsewhere.

The other sources of private profit in the schools have repeatedly turned
out to be corruption and delivery of only a fraction of what is promised
under laughably grandiose plans on paper. Rather than bringing common
sense and simple decency to the task of improving the schools, all too many
corporate reformers now appear determined to aid and abet the charlatans in
their midst by fighting oversight and accountability in the name of market-
based school reforms.

An almost mystical belief in the power of the market has apparently led allegedly practical business leaders to ignore the total lack of educational standards or even educational content in proposals on so-called school reforms
such as private school vouchers or charter schools. And on the surface, it almost defies belief that bottom-line corporate America wouldn't be concerned

about the obvious potential danger that there may be an explosion in costs if taxpayers end up funding both a public school system and a private school system.

Commercialism in education wraps its motives of business cost-cutting and direct profits in dazzling rhetoric about high-tech classrooms "of tomorrow." This is the business dream of a "new, improved" American public education system as a marketplace filled with corporate vendors selling educational programs, support services, and the very latest model in school supplies.

If the current trend continues, the link between the provision of public education and the ability of schools to deliver corporate profits could be irrevocable by the end of the century. The chances of heading off this brave new world of commercial education are slim without a much greater public awareness of everything that is at stake for our schools, our culture, our economy, and our children if we allow private profit to become the motive force behind public education.

2

And Now a Word from Our Sponsor

There is no shortage of talk these days about how market-oriented education reform and private sector expertise could, given the opportunity, work wonders in the nation's schools. Before jumping on the bandwagon, it would be a good idea to take a close look at how a multibillion-dollar market that employs lots of high-priced corporate talent is already transforming America's schools and classrooms.

No doubt about it: There's plenty of gold in U.S. schools if you know how to mine it. According to Consumers Union, elementary-age children spend around $15 billion a year, and they influence another $160 billion in spending by their parents. Teenagers spend even more: $57 billion of their own money and about $36 billion of their families' cash.[1] It is small wonder that one business after another is rushing to exploit one of America's last marketing frontiers.

Whittle Communications (now Channel One Communications) captured headlines in 1989 when it announced plans to market a twelve-minute television program to schools that featured ten minutes of news and two minutes of commercials. Schools that signed up got the program free, as well as a control panel to pluck it off a satellite and VCRs and TV monitors on which to show it. All the schools had to do was guarantee that about 90 percent of their students would watch the program on almost all school days.

The uproar that followed the introduction of Channel One might have led many to think that advertising to children in schools and classrooms was something new. Actually, Channel One had only added a new twist to an old game. In 1957, one researcher estimated that approximately nine out of ten students saw a commercial advertisement in school each day.[2]

A legion of corporate hucksters ply their trade in schools across the country. Often using the language of school reform, teaching innovation, and curriculum improvement, these flimflam artists feverishly pitch products, services, corporate image, and a probusiness point of view to millions of students and their families every year. And more and more educators are jumping on the marketing bandwagon. The *Wall Street Journal* has reported, for example, that during 1991–1992 alone, Houston schools sanctioned over 100 different contests sponsored by a grab bag of firms, including Duracell International, Eastman Kodak, and McDonald's.[3]

Corporate whiz kids claim they can help save the schools by designing promotions that pitch products in the educational marketplace and offer real money or badly needed school equipment and supplies as promotional prizes. Until 1994, one company, School Properties USA, made its money lining up corporate sponsors for events such as regional high school athletic contests. It has since added a new angle. Now it offers to help schools raise money through corporate school "sponsors" providing "affinity credit cards" that give the school a cut of the profits, payment of royalties from the manufacture of officially licensed products, and licensing fees from manufacturers who want to advertise themselves as "official school suppliers." School Properties USA offers schools a share in the profits from catalog and direct-marketing sales of "official" school products.[4]

Needless to say, schools without much social cachet are not likely to realize significant money from such schemes. Neither are most schools serving poor students, which means that overall these kinds of market-based fund-raising programs are not "win-win" scenarios for public education. Inevitably, they work mostly to the advantage of the haves while the have-nots fall further behind.

Apples and Other Temptations

Despite concern among many parents and teachers that rampant commercialism is pushing the public interest out of public education, corrupting the curriculum, distorting the relationships between teachers and their students and between parents and their children, the schoolhouse sellathon goes on. Very often, the bait in today's marketing come-ons is technology.

The Apples [as in computers] for the Students promotion created by Service Marketing Group of Garden City, New York, is designed to be administered by local parent-teacher groups. The program is simplicity itself. Children, their families, their friends, their neighbors, and anyone else who might want to help earn computers and computer supplies for the participating school are urged to shop, shop, shop—at the sponsoring store. The school collects the cash register receipts and earns credit toward the award of coveted Apple computer equipment and supplies.

In what is probably a typical outcome of the Apples program, one participating Wisconsin elementary school proudly announced in the school bulletin that $500,000 worth of cash register receipts had been collected. The reward was two computers worth "more than $3,000.00."[5] In other words, for every dollar's worth of receipts collected, the school received a credit of about seven-tenths of one cent toward the purchase of a computer.

Why American public schools should have to rely on the collection of cash register receipts to gain access to computer technology is a question outside the scope of the promotion. There is little question, however, that the program is more efficient at delivering profit to the business that buys computers from Apple and sells them at up to a 40 percent mark up to participating grocery chains than at providing benefits for children.[6] Entrepreneurial school principals who see promotions as a free way to stock up on supplies for their underfunded schools could go even further and combine promotions to help their school earn even more goodies.

Campbell's Labels for Education program is promoted as "helping educators prepare our children for a changing world."[7] For 5,125 Campbell's soup labels, the company offers to provide schools with the filmstrip *Boyhood of Abraham Lincoln*; for 20,000 more labels, the school can earn a remote-control projector with which to show it; and for another 6,750 labels, a screen on which to show it will be shipped to the lucky school. Whether Campbell's soup offers the best nutritional choice or the best value for the families whose children are sent in search of labels is not part of the free equipment equation.

When they are not busy collecting receipts and peeling labels off soup cans, children may be asked to write personalized letters to friends and relatives pleading with them to subscribe to magazines so that their school can earn still more computers, this time from the MOM program.

The MOM program was created by Computers for Education, a unit of Freedom Industries of Murfreesboro, Tennessee. The program comes with a "teacher training video" featuring Raymond Berry, former receiver for the Baltimore Colts and coach of the New England Patriots. The video includes a lot of footage of Berry catching footballs and coaching people catching footballs as he delivers an upbeat message about hard work and dedication to the teachers who are watching. There is an interview with a principal extolling the virtues of a computer system his school is using in place of up-to-date maps that, he says, his school could not afford out of its own budget. There is also a pitch from the company president, Tom Crook, explaining that the MOM program was created as a way to help schools get what they really need: computers. It's easy: Get students to write six relatives and friends personalized messages asking them to subscribe to magazines so the school can get some computers.

As an educational assist in teaching letter-writing skills, a sample letter comes with the MOM packet and demonstrates the extent to which participating schools are expected to encourage their students to exploit friends and family members. Imagine some poor grandmother getting this plaintive request, courtesy of the MOM program:

> Dear Grandma,
>   My school needs more computers for our classrooms. You can help us by ordering some new magazines or extending your current subscriptions at this time.
>   You'll save money with the school prices and your magazine orders provide more "hands on" computer training for me. Order by the prize deadline and I can earn a school crew shirt.
>   Please help me if you can.
>   From: Amy
>   P.S. I love you.[8]

The letter accompanying the information packet sent to principals assures them that the MOM program is "directed at 'out-of-town' relatives and friends [and that] this program will improve your computer training program, yet will never interfere with any other school program or community event." Since teachers are expected to give up teaching time in order to pass out materials, collect them, and review the personalized letters students write, it can only be assumed that the "other school program[s]" referred to are other promotions, not the curriculum that students are allegedly sent to school to learn.

Harnessing Peer Pressure

In the upside-down world of school marketing, it is possible to imagine students with little energy or attention left for learning because they are kept so busy earning the equipment that is supposed to help them learn. To be sure, students and their families can't be compelled to participate in school-based promotions; however, they face considerable social pressure to join in and not let their school or classroom down. One Wisconsin school, for example, perhaps cursed with a laggard group of slow-spending parents, sent out a frantic message during the heat of its Apples for the Students campaign that pleaded with families to shop at the participating food store just one extra time to stock up on nonperishables prior to the deadline, so the school would be assured of reaching its goal.

Marketers strive to create this kind of pressure by suggesting that participating schools distribute classroom posters about the program, get teachers and student leaders involved in community outreach, make daily announcements over the public address system, set up contests between classrooms to see which can collect the most receipts, and kick off the promotion with a rally of the whole student body. Such gimmicks may be fun for some of the people involved, but it is hard to see how the time spent in pep rallies to fire up the troops to collect cash register receipts does much to lay a foundation for a "world-class" education system.

Although educational marketing advocates are loath to admit it, "free" promotions turn teachers into salespeople, require that they take time away from teaching to keep program records, and force them to push products that may not be the best value or businesses that may not be the best choice for many families. The true cost of these "free" schemes would become apparent if the loss of student learning time and the cost of staff time needed to administer them were factored into the calculation. School boards, principals, and parents might be startled to realize how much they're paying for all that "free" stuff.

Seal of Community Approval

Despite the obvious problems with using schools to make sales pitches to children and their families, it is rare to hear community leaders voice either ethical or educational objections to school-based marketing schemes. Instead, politicians and educators are apt to push the idea that they are legitimate "partnerships" between public schools and the business community that benefit everyone. That they benefit politicians and corporations is often obvious. It is less clear what they do for children.

For example, during fire prevention week in 1991, Ronald McDonald showed up at a Milwaukee school with Milwaukee mayor John O. Norquist.

The script for the event had Ronald McDonald introducing the mayor and asking the children: "You know what the O stands for? That stands for 'Oh, what a nice guy.' Let's hear it for our mayor." It might be argued that the children got a lesson in fire prevention from a clown who captures their attention. However, it could just as easily be asked why learning about fire prevention should carry with it a come-on for a restaurant chain, including a coupon good for a cheeseburger at participating McDonald's stores in return for filling out a safety quiz. Put another way, why try to save children from burning to death by encouraging them to eat a product filled with saturated fat that the school's own nutrition curriculum would tell them to avoid?

Political support for the Apples for the Students promotion is very clear. The program was awarded a Presidential Citation, and its information folder contains a page of impressive endorsements. President Bill Clinton, when he was governor of Arkansas, wrote, "I would expect parents and school officials to respond enthusiastically to this opportunity for children." Lauro F. Cavasos, former Bush administration secretary of education, stated: "The Apples for the Students program is a creative, free-enterprise solution for acquiring very valuable learning tools at no cost to schools and parents." Similarly, Sybil Downing, of the Colorado Board of Education, noted: "The project is particularly appropriate as schools and businesses reach out to each other as partners for the improvement of public education." Werner Rogers, Georgia superintendent of schools, echoed these sentiments as well: "This activity is an excellent partnership between our schools and the business community."[9] This is the sort of glowing praise corporations hope to obtain. They want their activities in the schools to evoke an image of civic-mindedness and sympathetic concern. Businesspeople want to be regarded as helpmates for schools that are having trouble making ends meet.

Robert Martin of the U.S. Chamber of Commerce hits all the right notes in an essay for school superintendents: "More skills are required from our workers than ever before. . . . Unfortunately, the level of support our schools receive has not kept pace with the added responsibilities. Local governments can't provide additional support. Voters are rejecting local referendums by wide margins. They're struggling to make ends meet as it is. . . . A helping hand from the business community makes a world of difference to school systems being forced to make tough budgetary decisions during lean economic times."[10]

Corporate apologists would never dream of acknowledging the link between schools' need for handouts and the success business lobbyists have had in plundering the public school tax base. They prefer to keep the focus on the corporate "helping hand" and encourage people to think that if business pitches in and helps schools out, there is no reason to begrudge them a profit and a little recognition out of the deal. After all, the logic goes, corporations have to make a profit in order to continue their good works. Too often, teachers, following the lead of politicians and policymakers, buy this claptrap. They will say it doesn't seem fair to question the use of corporate-sponsored materials or challenge school participation in corporate-sponsored programs even though they carry advertising messages.

But there are educators who argue that if businesses paid their fair share of taxes, schools wouldn't need special promotions to get necessary equipment and supplies. They note that corporations write off the cost of the "free" materials that carry their advertising messages as a tax-deductible expense. They ask why the public should help underwrite advertising campaigns in the schools for candy bars, deodorant, hamburgers, sneakers, diet soda, and virtually any other product a school-age child might conceivably want or be talked into wanting. And they question why schools, intended to promote the public interest, are being used to earn private profit for favored firms. However, those few voices are rarely heard above the choir singing the praises of school-business "cooperation." Not many people want to hear a discouraging word when "free" supplies and teaching materials are being handed out.

Well-Targeted Learning

It is difficult to track every sort of corporate material that is being sent into or used in classrooms at any given moment. What winds up in schools is very often part of a specific marketing campaign, and the targeted population and extent of the campaign may not be publicly announced. In its promotional materials for prospective clients, one marketing firm, Lifetime Learning Systems, claims that it reaches 63 million students from preschool through college every year and that over 2 million teachers "from every school in the United States, have requested that their names be placed on the Lifetime Learning Systems mailing list."[11]

However, the information available publicly is only what corporations, for their own purposes, are willing to share. A teacher in New Jersey might, for example, get a "learning" packet paid for by a snack food company because it is introducing a new sweet treat aimed at ten- to fourteen-year-olds and their test market is the eastern seaboard. In that case, only schools along the East Coast whose students are in that age group are likely to see the stuff. When the marketing campaign is over, the corporate material disappears. Something else will appear when another company wants to make a pitch.

When and where so-called learning materials turn up is based on some corporate need that usually has nothing to do with the school curriculum. To get around this problem, companies frequently bill their creations as "supplements" to the teachers' regular lessons. They encourage teachers to fit in some or all of the materials whenever and wherever they can. Some clever marketers try to make this into a virtue by claiming that the material is therefore controlled by the teacher, who can tailor it to fit the school's program. However, even a brief examination of this material would prove to most people that it is created to benefit its sponsor, not the teachers or the children.

There are many reasons why corporations try to put materials in schools. They may simply want to sell something to the kids. Companies that sell snack food, candy, clothing, and personal care products are often in this category. Other companies may want to develop a consumer base for their products down the line. These include computer manufacturers, credit card companies, and even car manufacturers.

Then there are the companies and industries with image problems. The mining, energy, plastics, and food industries crank out tons of propaganda aimed at schools, usually under the guise of "environmental" or "nutritional" education. The Plastic Bag Association, for example, has developed a program called Don't Let a Good Thing Go to Waste, and the American Forest Foundation has Project Learning Tree. After the *Valdez* oil spill, Exxon produced a video entitled *Scientists and the Alaska Oil Spill*. After watching the Exxon video, students might be excused for thinking that perhaps the massive spill wasn't really very harmful to the natural habitat of Prince William Sound at all. *Scientists and the Alaska Oil Spill* was exposed on the television program *60 Minutes* in 1993. However, for the most part, promotional materials flood into schools unknown to the general public and unmentioned by those who allow it to be used.

Exxon also produces a science program called the Energy Cube that includes a game in which students play residents of a planet that is warming up. The view conveyed to the game's participants is, in the words of one critic, not to "reduce fossil fuel use but to jack up air conditioning."[12]

Any of the estimated 70,000 teachers who have used Procter & Gamble's Decision Earth "environmental education" materials, if they were not very careful, may have taught their young scholars that clear-cutting forests is a good way to create new wildlife habitats. None of those messy questions about ecological damage caused by the practice are raised in the material. Decision Earth, aimed at students in grades 7 through 12, also has kind words about the impact of mining, disposable diapers, and waste-to-waste incineration (which, students are expected to learn, is "recycling").[13]

The American Egg Board (The Incredible Journey from Hen to Home) wants kids to know about the nutritional virtues of eggs and the positive side of the cholesterol story. When controversy erupted over the use of bovine growth hormone, Monsanto produced a videotape aimed at schoolchildren that assured viewers milk from cows using the chemical was indistinguishable from other milk. The Monsanto tape came as a shock to one Wisconsin dairy producer who was working as a substitute teacher when she saw scientifically disputed information favorable to the Monsanto product presented as fact.[14] In this case, a teacher with expert knowledge was able to spot the problem. However, no teacher can possess enough expert knowledge to sort out truth from distortion in every topic covered by the sponsored material that enters the schools. Since sponsored material is rarely subjected to the same review as regular texts, teachers are on their own. That's exactly the way many sponsoring corporations like it.

Free materials, at a time when teachers often have to spend their own money on supplies for their classrooms, are an irresistible lure for many. Even teachers who have qualms about going along find it hard to say no to businesses intent on pushing their way through the schoolhouse door.

Good Cop/Bad Cop

This is the era of school-business "partnerships." Such partnerships often involve the "good cop/bad cop" routine that many business executives have been playing to perfection for years. The smiling good cop says, "We want to help." The thuggish bad cop says, "Do things our way—or else." The bad cop's message can be fearsome. Executives deliver stern lectures about the need for higher educational standards as they point censorious fingers at test scores. The lack of educational accountability is destroying America, they snarl.

Again, this goes back to the rhetoric of *A Nation at Risk*, the rallying cry that got business involved in education reform in the 1980s and 1990s. *A Nation at Risk* put educators on notice that they had better cooperate with business in building a "world-class" system of public education. Again and again, teachers hear that outrage is stalking boardrooms across the land. Executives are fed up with a debased and trivial school curriculum that fails to provide children with the skills needed to compete with the Germans and Japanese. Business roundtables are being pounded and corporate heads shaken over the tendency of educators to "throw money" at their problems.

Schools don't need more money—they need reform, rant businesspeople whenever two or more gather to discuss the problems of public education. With their budgets cut to shreds and a hailstorm of criticism coming down around them, no wonder so many teachers, principals, and school superintendents anxiously look around for the hand of a corporate good cop to hold.

There may be innocent souls who believe that executives use the good cop/bad cop routine in a sincere effort to nudge school improvement along. Perhaps some executives are sincere. However, a jaundiced eye couldn't fail to notice that, very often, lurking behind the public act are businesses working for themselves and promoting their own interests.

How Junior Has Grown

Mark Evens, a senior vice president of Scholastic, Inc., began his 1988 essay in *Advertising Age* by playing up the good cop corporate image:[15] "The alarm bells rang and American business turned out in force. The American education system is in trouble, they heard, and we have become a nation at risk. In virtually every state in the union, companies of all kinds have been going back to schools, giving time, money and products to help meet urgent needs."

Evens continued, "Business involvement in education is hardly new, but there are new forms of expression. The education system can provide a unique opportunity for companies to support vital social needs while achieving basic marketing and public relations goals. Good will, good sales and good works may fit together perfectly in education marketing."

Evens managed to paint a picture of noble purpose and business need combined in perfect harmony to advance the welfare of American students. Perhaps not wishing to seem too self-serving, he failed to mention that at the time he wrote his essay, Scholastic was in the process of establishing its educational marketing division and was looking for corporate clients.

Early in his essay, Evens identified a few business-supported educational projects that, in his mind, illustrated how corporations, pursuing profits, and schools, trying to better educate their students, could work in tandem to advance the cause of social progress. Then he dispensed with the good cop fiction and came to the point: "More and more companies see education marketing as the most compelling, memorable and cost-effective way to build share of mind and market into the 21st century."

Evens then set aside any pretense of high educational and social purpose when he chose a model for all to emulate. "Gillette is currently sponsoring a multi-media in-school program designed to introduce teenagers to their safety razors—building brand and product loyalties through classroom-centered, peer-powered lifestyle patterning."

Nowhere did Evens mention how the Gillette program helps get youngsters ready to function effectively in the high-skilled "workplace of tomorrow" that businesspeople insist students must be prepared to enter. However, he did note that "earlier Schick had sponsored a similar in-school information program that was equally successful in generating requests for Schick (male) and Personal Touch (female) razors to be distributed to students through home economics educators."

And perhaps just to make sure potential clients didn't take his opening altruistic language too literally, Evens concluded with an educational challenge: "Can you devise promotions that take students from the aisles in school rooms to the aisles in supermarkets?" If a slow reader answers no to Evens's rhetorical question, the folks at Scholastic will no doubt be only too happy to help them out.

Exploiting the credibility it has achieved as a publisher of classroom magazines for over 75 years, Scholastic has become one of the most aggressive— and shameless—of the companies marketing to children. In its promotional materials, Scholastic brags about its clients: "These companies already experience the power of trust with Scholastic: AT&T, American Express, Apple Computer, Coca-Cola Foods, Discover Card, IBM, S. C. Johnson Wax, Thomas J. Lipton, M&M/Mars, Milton Bradley, Mott's, NBC, Nabisco, NYNEX, OXY 10, Procter & Gamble, Warner Brothers, Warner Lambert."

Scholastic also explains why it should be the marketer of choice for well-educated businesspeople: "[Scholastic is] the *only* publishing pipeline covering the entire pre-K to 12 grade marketplace. . . . Its products are interactive— teachers involve students by using Scholastic magazines and materials. . . . The classroom offers marketers a virtually non-competitive advertising arena."

For the right price, Scholastic will provide single-sponsor magazines, inserts, and special sections, contests, posters, teaching guides, videos, software, research, and books. The titles of its promotional pieces include: "*Discover Card* and Scholastic Give Teens Extra Credit," "*Minute Maid* Puts the Squeeze on the Competition with a Summer Reading Program," and "To Billy Joel, *CBS Records* and Scholastic History Is Hot."[16]

Scholastic is by no means the only educational marketer with dollar signs in its eyes. The increasingly blurry distinction between special interests and private profit, on the one hand, and public interest and the general welfare, on the other, has helped open the door to countless firms that market products in the classroom while pretending to promote student learning.

Learning Can Be Sweet . . . or Salty

Lifetime Learning Systems of Fairfield, Connecticut (owned by K-III Communications, the same company that owns *Weekly Reader* and Channel One[17]), supplies schools with bushel baskets of "free" materials sponsored by business interests and, in some cases, foreign governments. Teachers routinely receive materials from Lifetime Learning like the following pieces, sent out in a large white envelope addressed to the "Third Grade Teacher."

"OPEN IMMEDIATELY!" the envelope commands. "FREE educational program focusing on math, social science, and language arts skills enclosed." With this buildup, few teachers can resist tearing open the envelope to see what it contained to help them teach their students math, social science, and language arts. Inside, the teacher find an "educational program" entitled Count Your Chips. Under the heading "Lifetime Learning Systems, Inc. . . . an Experience in Dynamic Education" is an introductory letter. "Dear Educator," the letter begins, "February is National Potato Lover's Month and Snack Food Month. It's a great time to think about the vegetable that we all love to eat but too often take for granted—the potato."

It goes on to say, "Because February is National Potato Lover's Month as well as Snack Food Month, it is a great time to introduce 'Count Your Chips,' a free educational program created for the National Potato Board and the Snack Food Association by Lifetime Learning Systems. . . . Although the program is copyrighted, you have permission to make as many copies as you need for educational purposes." The letter concludes with a request to "please take a moment to fill out and return the enclosed reply card. This will keep your name on our mailing list and ensure that you continue to receive free educational kits in the future. As always, we look forward to reading your reactions to the program and welcome suggestions for future programs that will best meet your needs and those of your students." Perhaps Lifetime Learning has visions of teachers eagerly writing in and clamoring for lessons based on diet soda or candy bars.

The introduction to Count Your Chips advises, "Fun facts about potatoes and the ever-popular potato chip will be used to help your students sharpen skills in computation, problem solving, conducting research, and writing." The teacher learns that, in addition to teaching "computation, problem solving, graphing and other skills," Lifetime Learning wants "to educate students on the background of potato chips, including when and how potato chips were invented." The program provides worksheets, a teacher's guide, and suggestions for activities.

Activity One is "Be a Chip-e-matician!" In this exercise, students are supposed to learn math and potato chip facts. For example, students are given the fact that "each person in the United States eats about 6 pounds of potato chips in one year," then asked, "how many one ounce bags of chips would a person eat in a year?" Lifetime Learning is apparently not concerned that a third-grader might take the "fact" literally and imagine that every person in the country eats six pounds of potato chips every year. Indeed, a child's misunderstanding might be a potato chip company's gain. Suggested follow-up activities include encouraging students to create their own "chip math problems," then having the class compile their math problems to make them into a board game that, Lifetime Learning helpfully suggests, "could be called 'Be a Chip-e-matician!'"

Activity Two, called "The Chip Story," explains how the chip was invented and asks children to conduct research on the potato chip flavors people like best. Follow-up activities include a suggestion that students "make a time line to illustrate the potato chip story." The final activity, "A Chip off the Old Block," explains that the expression "chip off the old block" is an idiom and asks the teacher to help the students learn its true meaning. Among the follow-up activities is the suggestion that "students could also interview family members to determine the favorite family snack. They could then write a humorous family snack story." "Extended Activities" wrap up the theme with the thought that once the students have grown and harvested their own potatoes, they "might want to make some potato chips."

An earlier campaign by the potato chip industry called Make Room for Potato Chips was attacked by one critic as similar to "trying to portray Attila the Hun as a pioneer in urban renewal."[18] Apparently undaunted, Lifetime Learning stepped up to the plate and set out to convince teachers that the ingredients missing from efforts to improve student academic performance were fat and salt.

Count Your Chips is not a bizarre or isolated example of corporate marketing gone mad. It is only one of countless similar packets of materials sent free of charge and often unsolicited to teachers by firms such as Lifetime Learning Systems that have been hired to promote a product.

Gushers Wonders of the World is another Lifetime Learning classic. Lifetime's Gushers packet is addressed to "Dear Science Educator." The introduction begins:

> They are Earth's great geothermic "gushers": volcanoes, geysers and hot springs. For centuries, humans have been fascinated by these "wonders of the world." Now, your students can share in this fascination. Lifetime Learning Systems, in cooperation with General Mills, Inc., maker of GUSHERS fruit snacks, is pleased to present you with this free educational program, GUSHERS WONDERS OF THE WORLD, along with free samples of GUSHERS for your students to enjoy. . . . Targeted for use in the junior high school science curricu-

lum, GUSHERS WONDERS OF THE WORLD will heighten your students'
interest in Geology and the Earth Sciences, and motivate them to investigate
this interesting subject area on their own.

The packet then guides the teacher and students through three activities
("Thar She Blows!" "Popping Up All Over!" and "With a 'Gurgle' or a
'Whoosh'!") that are, more or less, the educational equivalent of boilerplate.
The creative punch of Gushers Wonders of the World is saved for the "Extended Activities" section. The real purpose of the Gushers program is most
clearly on display there. The teacher is invited to "distribute the samples of
GUSHERS supplied with this program, and suggest that students each place
a GUSHER in their mouths. Then discuss the process needed to make these
fruit snacks 'gush' when you bite into them." For those in the lucrative and
highly competitive snack food industry, finding teachers willing to almost literally put a product in their students' mouths must be a tempting prospect.

Many teachers still have reservations about being corporate shills. Companies
consider it essential to pay lip service to the "educational" content of their marketing programs. That helps explain why, after having suggested that students
place Gushers in their mouths and bite into them to make them gush, Lifetime
Learning proposes that teachers ask their young scholars "how does this process
differ from that which produces erupting geothermic phenomena?"

Count Your Chips and Gushers are golden oldies. However, Lifetime
Learning has not lost its touch. In 1995, it unleashed Tootsie Roll: The
Sweet Taste of Success on an unsuspecting world. Aimed at K–3 children,
one of the follow-up activities in the Tootsie Roll lesson suggests that teachers "have students interview family members about their memories of Tootsie Rolls and Tootsie Pops. When was the first time they tasted Tootsie Rolls?
What is their favorite Tootsie Pop flavor?"

The Tootsie Roll packet contains four activities, a teacher's guide, a color-
ful poster titled "A Never-Ending History of Fun with Tootsie Roll," a
coupon worth $.50 off the purchase price of Tootsie Roll products, and a
card the teacher can fill out to join Lifetime's "Educator Study Guild." By
filling out the card, the teacher not only helps ensure that he or she will never
be short of Lifetime materials but also provides the company with information about the number of students and teachers using its material—no doubt
to help the company set its advertising rates.

When the marketers promote their programs on the pages of *Advertising
Age,* there is little of the pretense of educational significance that accompa-
nies presentations to educators. No fiction about important educational content is necessary for the corporate clients the marketing firms are trying to at-

tract. Lifetime gets down to business when it talks directly to its potential clients. "THEY'RE READY TO SPEND AND WE REACH THEM!" screams one Lifetime Learning ad. "Kids are big spenders. But they don't spend much time listening to what marketers have to say," corporations are warned. "You need to capture their attention and Lifetime Learning Systems can show you how." The ad goes on:

> Kids spend 40 percent of each day in the classroom where traditional advertising can't reach them. Now, YOU CAN ENTER THE CLASSROOM through custom-made learning materials created with your specific marketing objectives in mind. Communicate with young spenders directly and, through them, their teachers and families as well. For more than a decade, Lifetime Learning Systems has helped over 300 corporations achieve their marketing goals, cost effectively, in the classroom. To find out how we can help increase your share of the youth market, call [. . .].

In another ad, Lifetime Learning is even more direct. Potential clients are asked to "IMAGINE millions of students discussing your product in class. IMAGINE their teachers presenting your organization's point of view. IMAGINE your corporate message reaching their parents through literature the students take home." The ad concludes with the invitation to "let Lifetime Learning Systems take your message into the classroom, where the young people you want to reach are forming attitudes that will last a lifetime."

There is no mention of encouraging school reform or improving teaching or addressing America's lack of competitiveness in these ads—with good reason. No one in his or her right mind can imagine that potato chips and fruit snacks are going to do anything to help reconstruct America's industrial base or improve the performance of America's schools. The people reading such ads know why these marketing programs are created, and they would laugh at such claims.

A Captive Market

Lifetime Learning isn't the only marketing firm trying to sell schoolchildren to advertisers. Consumers Union has identified over thirteen major marketing companies specializing in the school market.[19] Firms like Modern Talking Picture Service, Inc. (which became Modern Education Services in 1995), have national reach. Modern advertises that it can "get your product into the hands of the $81 billion teen market more ways than anyone . . . in a focused classroom setting. Through Modern's TeenPak sampling program, your product reaches a prime market—building brand loyalties when they count most."

In another ad, Modern tells advertisers they can "talk to the 'in crowd.'" The text under a photo of a teenage girl tells potential clients, "Her social life revolves around high school. Modern can make sure your sponsored video plays there. If she's in your target market, call us." In addition to sampling programs, services offered by Modern Talking Pictures include "sponsored A/V programs," "co-op teacher packages," and "teaching kits."

In one of its ads, another company, Media Management Services, Inc., wants potential advertisers to know it helps "companies of all sizes reach educators and students directly through innovative marketing campaigns, specially designed products, creative learning programs and classroom materials." According to Media Management, companies sign on with them for results. Their proclaimed results include: "High visibility. Early brand loyalty. New sources of business. Profitable secondary markets. A positive corporate image."

Since marketing firms have to keep their customers satisfied, their material is judged, first and foremost, by the extent to which it meets the objectives of their clients. The emphasis is not on providing the fullest and most accurate presentation of information to students. The fundamental difference between marketers and teachers distorts teaching as surely as a funhouse mirror distorts the image of anyone who looks into it. When teachers use products developed by marketing firms, instead of lessons taught to benefit students, the curriculum promotes the objectives of a third party whose interests may well conflict with those of the children, their families, and the country.

If all of the productions were as transparently self-serving and educationally barren as Lifetime Learning's Count Your Chips or Gushers Wonders of the World, some people might conclude (wrongly) that they are no big deal—just another example of the inability of American businesses to find more productive ways to spend their money. But it is harder to dismiss schools teaching children about nuclear power or the history, culture, and politics of foreign countries with materials paid for and approved by the nuclear power industry or a foreign government.

An exchange between a *Mother Jones* magazine investigator, playing the part of a potential client, and a Modern Talking Pictures representative demonstrates the seriousness of the problem:

> MOTHER JONES: This is the company's pet project. They're very concerned about putting out material that will help correct the antinuclear bias in most educational materials. So we don't want much tampering with the material. Is that a problem?

MODERN: I understand exactly what you're saying. We wouldn't want to write anything our client didn't want us to. It would have to be factual, of course.

MJ: Of course.

MODERN: But we try to be sensitive to our client's aims. . . . We wouldn't want to write anything that makes the sponsor unhappy.

MJ: Now, we're talking national—we want to get this into every school in the country. Can you handle that?

MODERN: We've done that for a lot of our corporate clients—Procter & Gamble, IBM. . . . We know how to get materials into the hands of educators.

MJ: I understand there's quite a demand for these kinds of materials now.

MODERN: Educators just eat them up.

MJ: . . . And by the way, we're looking at distribution in Third World countries: Mexico, South America, part of Africa—

MODERN: I'm sure we could help you.[20]

Whether the client goal is to sell junk food, tell a corporate "story," build support for nuclear power, or market a country and its foreign policy, educational marketers are ready to serve. Business is business for these marketers. Taiwan, Finland, and Saudi Arabia all have purchased the services of Learning Enrichment, Inc., of New York to produce materials for American classrooms. Not to be outdone, Lifetime Learning produces materials for Israel and Canada.

According to Peter Finn, who, as a reporter with the *Philadelphia Inquirer*, investigated efforts by foreign governments to influence U.S. public opinion by putting their stories into American classrooms, neither Lifetime Learning nor Learning Enrichment is registered as a foreign agent.[21] And both appear willing to conceal or obscure the identities of those who are paying them.

The letters addressed to teachers receiving the Count Your Chips and Gushers Wonders of the World packets from Lifetime Learning prominently identify the sponsor of the material. This is hardly surprising since the stuff is produced in order to increase the sponsor's name recognition and sell a product. In contrast, the letter that introduces the Israel: Land of the People packet makes no mention of the sponsoring agent. In the case of Saudi Arabia, Learning Enrichment's cover letter notes that its program "was developed by a team of editors, writers, and designers active in the American education publishing industry, and in consultation with classroom teachers. We also had the opportunity to work with the Information Office of the Royal

Embassy of Saudi Arabia, and benefitted from their expertise. We have collaborated to bring you and students the best in instructional materials about Saudi Arabia." Apparently, both Israel and Saudi Arabia do not want their sponsorship of these materials plainly stated.

It is hard to imagine how the public interest is served when American schoolchildren are taught about the world with curriculum produced by a firm hired by a foreign government to represent its own point of view—especially when the sponsorship of the material is concealed from both teacher and student.

If America's capacity to renew its democracy rests on an educated citizenry making well-informed public policy decisions, every American is poorly served when public schools turn their curricula into an educational flea market open to anyone who has the money to set up a table. Yet that is precisely what the relentless assault on funding for public education and repeated calls for "cooperation" with the business community are pushing schools to do.

In 1990, General Motors came up with enough money to mail a copy of its "I Need the EARTH and the EARTH Needs Me" environmental education video to every public, private, and parochial elementary school in the country. Produced in cooperation with the Environmental Protection Agency (yet another example of public-private cooperation), "I Need the EARTH and the EARTH Needs Me" is a slick presentation that offers glowing images of kids breathing, swimming, walking, and running in an idealized environment of pristine air, sparkling water, and picturesque landscapes. The emphasis in the video is on things like planting trees, conserving water while brushing teeth, recycling, and riding a bike on occasion. Judging by the video, mass transportation is virtually absent from GM's plan for a cleaner environment. However, car pools are recommended, as is recycling used motor oil.

GM's video urges all people to do their part, but doing their part does not include any sort of investigation into the politics and economics of pollution or any political activity that might help produce a cleaner environment. Perhaps GM believes that everyone is equally culpable—be it a fourth-grader who carelessly litters or a corporate executive who knowingly allows tons of toxins to be dumped into the air, water, and soil. The only difference seems to be that GM expects the child to be responsible. The corporate executive is never mentioned.

Instead of giving any hint of an ongoing battle over environmental policy, GM urges students to know that "we" (whoever that may be) are working to make things better. Students are assured that scientists are trying to make factories cleaner and to see to it that cars and trucks pollute less.

It would be hard to refute a single factual statement in the GM video and the accompanying teacher's guide. Nevertheless, since the picture painted is so incomplete, the video is misleading. Providing students with a comprehensive picture of environmental issues is probably less important to GM than how successful "I Need the EARTH . . . " has been in helping to paint a positive, environmentally responsible image of the corporation and framing environmental issues in a way compatible with GM's corporate policy. In other words, although it may not be good education, the video is good PR.

Decades of Battle

The struggle to ensure that public schools actually serve the public interest rather than the interests of companies like GM has been going on for years. In 1929, the National Education Association (NEA) published its *Report of the Committee on Propaganda in the Schools*.[22] The report's author, E. C. Broome, argued that corporate-sponsored materials should, in general, only be used if they are indispensable to the education of children. If widely adopted, this principle would virtually guarantee that most corporate-sponsored materials would be taken out of classrooms. Even the heartiest booster of school-business partnerships would have trouble making the case that a monstrosity like Gushers Wonders of the World is indispensable to the education of American children.

In the years following the NEA report, corporate attempts to place propaganda in the schools accelerated. In the early and mid-1950s, two professional organizations took notice and issued reports describing how to best use what they blandly referred to as "free materials."[23] By 1957, one researcher had found that 97 percent of the teachers he interviewed used sponsored materials. To his dismay, few of the teachers indicated that they used any ethical standard in deciding which materials to use, and virtually no teacher received any guidance on the matter from his or her school administrator.[24]

It was left to Sheila Harty to sound a clear and credible alarm in her 1979 report *Hucksters in the Classroom*. Harty found a shocking amount of self-serving corporate material was being used in the nation's schools.[25] She particularly focused on industry propaganda in four areas: nutrition, nuclear power, the environment, and economics. Since 1979, in the deregulatory, turn-a-quick-buck, what-business-says-goes, "public-private partnership" American political environment, this sort of corporate marketing in the schools has grown like mold spores in a warm petri dish. The continuing commercial onslaught led Consumers Union to call for schools to be made ad-free zones in its 1990 report *Selling America's Kids: Commercial Pressures on Kids of the 90's*.[26] The group's 1995 report, *Captive Kids*, details the extent to which school advertising is continuing.[27] *Marketing Madness* (also published in 1995), written by Michael Jacobson and Laurie Mazur of the Center for the Study of Commercialism, offers an encyclopedic assessment of commercialism in the United States—including the schools. It isn't a pretty picture.[28]

Despite some signs of increasing opposition among parents and teachers to corporate exploitation of the public schools, the onslaught continues apace. A number of efforts by concerned professionals have had little impact. In 1982, the Society of Consumer Affairs Professionals in Business (SOCAP) offered voluntary guidelines for business-sponsored consumer education materials. In 1989, the International Organization of Consumers Unions (IOCU) issued its Code of Good Practice and Guidelines for Controlling Business-Sponsored Educational Materials Used in Schools. In 1990, the Milwaukee Conference on Corporate Involvement in Schools developed guidelines for the use of sponsored materials that were subsequently adopted by several education associations and other organizations. And in 1996, the National Education Association began distributing what it calls "The Preserve Classroom Integrity Pledge," intended to check the use of corporate-sponsored junk.

Each of these sets of guidelines, as well as a list of organizations concerned with commercialism in schools, is included in the Appendix. To this point, however, most educators—never mind the general public—seem unaware of the existence of either professional guidelines or ethical standards intended to govern the use of corporate materials.

To complicate the debate, many educational organizations are themselves guilty of questionable practices. They often lend their names and credibility to programs and activities with corporate "partners." The same corporations that sell products in the schools frequently have booths at teachers' conventions and help underwrite the cost of professional conferences.

The American Federation of Teachers and the Association for Supervision and Curriculum Development both lent their names to the Chrysler Learning Connection, a program to encourage reading. The program is publicized in magazine inserts that feature prominent ads for Chrysler products side by side with the logos of the American Federation of Teachers and the Association for Supervision and Curriculum Development. The message is clear: Chrysler is a good corporate citizen that cares about children and their families. Two major educational organizations attest to it.

Besides the magazine ads, the program also includes a video and a poster, sent to every elementary school in the United States, featuring activities to help families encourage their children to read. The materials intended for the classroom don't promote Chrysler very hard, but the accompanying video-tape gives Robert Eaton, chairman of Chrysler, a chance to introduce himself to children and their families. The "educational" activities themselves might charitably be described as second rate. Certainly, they hardly exemplify the sort of high academic standard the cosponsoring educational organizations claim to support.

The American Library Association signed on with McDonald's and Scholastic to produce the highly commercial All-American Reading Challenge, a program described by the 1995 Consumers Union report *Captive Kids* as "basically an advertisement for McDonald's."[29]

Caught up in the commercial torrent, the professional organizations of educators risk losing whatever credibility they may have with the public as well as their ability to promote real education reform. Far fewer people would believe that the product evaluations in *Consumer Reports* are unbiased if, for example, the magazine takes ads from the companies whose products it rates. For the same reason, educational organizations risk the appearance—and the real possibility—of trimming their positions because they don't want to offend a corporate partner.

The Crowded Classroom

When he was secretary of education, Lamar Alexander never tired of saying that students have to learn a lot more these days than when he was in school. This is very true—but not necessarily in the way he meant it. Students and teachers today are being bombarded with videotapes, posters, calendars, offers to join clubs, catalogs, and announcements for performance troupes, along with countless offers to participate in promotions that promise schools they can sell their way to technological superiority.

Orville Redenbacher has offered to send schools money in exchange for popcorn labels (Redenbacher's, of course). If you send enough customers their way, Wal-Mart stores will provide IBM computer lessons. And Piggly Wiggly offers to donate 1 percent of the value of all eligible cash register receipts that students collect. Hershey's will cough up $.05 for every Hershey's candy wrapper kids and their families can gather together. Telephone Advertising Corporation will give schools a cut of the take if they are allowed to install telephone kiosks equipped with television monitors beaming out non-stop commercial messages.

It is almost impossible to capture the magnitude of the self-serving corporate invasion of the classroom since the mid-1980s. Red Lobster wants to help GM teach students about the environment. Wisconsin Gas can send in the "blue flame" to teach about energy conservation. Miller Brewing offers to tell children about the contributions of African Americans to our culture and how to combat alcohol abuse with education instead of legal controls. Wisconsin Industry Saving Our Environment is eager to get out the recycling message. The insurance industry tries to tell its story. Pizza Hut wants to help boys and girls learn to read, and so does Jello and Arby's and Crystal Light and Six Flags Corporation. Clearasil is MADD about drunken drivers. *USA Today* will help provide an "inside view" of newspaper publishing. Sparkle Crest stands ready to help in the battle for oral hygiene. And Ronald McDonald seems ready to stand for almost anything associated with something good.

There is more. Students can learn about nutrition using dittos from Chef Boyardee or about how to properly wrap food to preserve its freshness with information provided by Reynold's Wrap or about nuclear power using materials from the electric power company or about how to promote something called "total health" using handouts from NutraSweet. Girls can be taught about menstruation with materials supplied by Kimberly-Clark, and everyone can learn about the banking system from booklets developed by National Learning Productions and distributed by your local bank. Arrid deodorant offers to send an honor roll certificate to a teacher if students send in ten proofs of purchase. Star Broadcasting will pipe in music (complete with commercials) and share the profits with your school. Cover Concepts offers "free" textbook covers—covered with ads.

Life Savers candy wants children to know that number one of the eighty ways they can "share themselves" is to share Life Savers with a friend. Prego spaghetti sauce wants students to learn science by comparing the thickness of Prego sauce to that of Ragu. Revlon wants adolescent girls to know that the roots of self-esteem are in their hair and asks them to discuss the difference between a "good hair day" and a "bad hair day." Cheerios will trade you books for boxtops. Ground Round will help teachers motivate students by rewarding them for valued behavior with a coupon good for a free kiddie meal. Lysol issues a classroom "germ alert," complete with a can of its disinfectant spray and discount coupons. Students can learn gun safety from "Eddie," the National Rifle Association eagle, and hear that there are no endangered species from the Council for Wildlife Conservation (affiliated with the National Shooting Sports Foundation). Meanwhile, Mobil Oil wants

kids to think "critically" about critical issues like the North American Free
Trade Agreement (NAFTA). According to one of the Mobil lessons (produced by Learning Enrichment, Inc.), a critical thinker can come to only one
conclusion—NAFTA is a great idea. Even a cursory look at most of this stuff
would be enough to cause most people to wonder why in the world teachers
and principals continue to let it into their schools. It takes up valuable learning time and distracts, misinforms, and manipulates the students.

USA Today's "Inside View" is junk, although, since it is more obviously
self-serving than slick productions like GM's environmental video, it is probably less dangerous. Accompanied by an overblown sound track and lots of
hectic, quick-cut editing, this video celebrates the genius of *USA Today.*
"News and information as fresh as each morning's rising sun," trumpets the
narrator as images of the paper's high-tech prowess flash by. Anyone watching this production might be forgiven for coming away with the impression
that putting out a newspaper has little to do with editorial work or reporting,
values or ethics; news gathering in *USA Today's* world seems almost exclusively a technological activity. There are lots of satellites, computers, and
other gadgets but not many reporters on the scene. Unless you are interested
in a misleading and neutered version of the newspaper business, this video
isn't even worth using as a filler on a rainy day just before spring break (although some students may want to dance to the sound track).

If you mix free-market ideology, self-serving promotion of the banking industry, and a soupçon of sexism, you get Banking Is, a program produced by
National Learning Productions of Saint Albans, West Virginia. Designed to
be used by local banks to promote themselves, Banking Is includes an instructor's guide, a student study guide, and a booklet containing sample
checks for students to practice with, as well as an introductory videotape.
The instructor's guide starts off by recommending that "this program be in-
corporated into a required curriculum area to provide even exposure to all
students." It goes on to explain that "Banking Is [does not and cannot] discuss state laws and local customs. As a result, the participation of your sponsor's Student-Bank Counselor [is] imperative."

It would be hard to quarrel with some of the commonsense ideas about
personal financial management contained in this material. However, a teacher
can easily provide the same information without the industry propaganda.
Furthermore, the program contains some shameless distortions of the truth.
Students are told, for example, that "rushes on banks occurred many times.
. . . Since most of the bank's funds were out on loan to the people of the community and these debts could not be collected overnight, the banks would
fail." The fact that most of a bank's funds are on loan to people in the com-

munity will, no doubt, come as a shock to residents of many innercity neighborhoods. Then, too, Banking Is tells students that during World War II,

> our men went away to war and our women were left to manage households and work in defense plants. More people were getting paychecks and inexperienced people were needing financial advice. The banking industry came to the aid of the people. . . . Today your banker is willing and able to help you get your start in life. He is the best financial ally that you have. . . . It is your banker's business to know what is good for you and that responsibility is taken seriously. Your banker's advice is the best you will ever get on financial planning.

After having assured students that helpful bankers were there for the poor, ignorant women working in defense plants during the war and depicting bankers as better friends than the family cocker spaniel, Banking Is offers superficial political and economic analysis: "With all of its inflationary problems [how many teachers are going to point out the bias packed into that statement?], the American economy and free enterprise system are still strong symbols of a nation which is healthy and treats its citizens fairly. Most other countries have much more serious economic problems than we do." Perhaps that's literally correct. Unfortunately, the relevant countries for comparison are the Western industrial countries and Japan. Against that standard, this booklet's editorial voice distorts reality and discourages critical thinking.

Pizza and Other Educational Values

The decade-old BOOK IT! program from Pizza Hut seems to pop up in more and more elementary schools. With 22 million children enrolled annually,[30] it is probably the most popular of the "reading incentive" programs offered by corporations. BOOK IT! is designed to reward children with Pizza Hut pizza when they reach monthly reading goals set by their teachers. Each month that a child meets her or his reading goal, the teacher gives the child a "pizza award certificate." On their first visit to the local Pizza Hut to turn in their award certificates, the students are congratulated by the manager, given "outerspace buttons" and stars to put on them, and "one-topping personal pan pizzas." On each subsequent monthly visit (assuming the kids continue to meet their reading goals), they get one-topping personal pan pizzas and additional stars for their "outerspace" buttons.

Unlike Red Lobster, whose Earth to Kids' environmental program requires that children eat their "free kid's meal" rewards at the restaurant, Pizza Hut allows children to take their bounty and run, saving the adults who bring them from either having to sit and watch their offspring eat or order a Pizza Hut offering for themselves. BOOK IT! runs for five months. If all the children in the class meet their reading goals four out of the five months, the entire class (including the teacher) is given a pizza party. Students who meet their reading goals in all five months qualify for the "Readers Honor Roll," which is a record of their accomplishments signed by the teacher and the principal. In addition, each child gets an "earth" sticker to put on their BOOK IT! button.

Despite its popularity, BOOK IT! is a bad idea. Consider the reward. Even as children are being taught that a healthful diet is low in salt, fat, and sugar, they are offered a salty, high-fat meal that will probably be washed down with a sugary soft drink as a reward for reading. It's understandable that Pizza Hut wants to be associated with reading. It's less clear why schools are willing to undermine their curricula for the promise of a personal pan pizza.

The motivational method of the BOOK IT promotion is also questionable. The program is built on the sort of simplistic conception of human motivation favored by House Speaker Newt Gingrich, who suggests that the most effective way to encourage learning is to play up an external reward.[31] However, any teacher who cannot think of more effective ways to motivate students to read should be looking for employment elsewhere.

More serious still, BOOK IT! unethically uses schools to get Pizza Hut inside students' homes. Since the BOOK IT! program can create a classroom atmosphere in which a child who doesn't join in feels odd, it is very hard for a parent to demand that a son or daughter not participate. Parents who may want nothing to do with Pizza Hut are forced to either go along with the program or face struggles with their children. Moreover, children who do participate and meet their reading goals feel cheated if they are not then taken to Pizza Hut for the promised reward.

The experience of one Milwaukee mother illustrates the point. When her daughter's teacher used the BOOK IT! program, the mother tried to substitute a book for the normal reward of a Pizza Hut personal pan pizza. Her daughter would have none of it. It wasn't that the child was such a pizza fan, but she didn't want to be left out when the other children were talking about their Pizza Hut rewards. In the clash of values, Pizza Hut prevailed. The classroom atmosphere created by the BOOK IT! program had taught the woman's daughter that she had not really succeeded until she got her pizza.

A New Jersey father was similarly alarmed when his fourth-grade son came home with materials used in the New Jersey Stock Market Game, distributed by the New Jersey Council on Economic Education, the Securities Industry Association, and the Center for Economic Education at Trenton State College. In correspondence with the father, the national director of the game, Gloria Talamas, described it as a motivational teaching tool to introduce students to basic principles of economics, finance, and capital formation and to enhance mathematics and other classroom lessons.[32]

Familiar with the work of the Council on Compulsive Gambling of New Jersey, the father was afraid the game was inappropriate for children of his son's age. He questioned the game's educational effectiveness and worried that his child was being subtly taught to gamble. In a letter to his child's teacher, the father raised some serious questions: "Are nine-year-olds able to grasp the magnitude of investing $100,000 dollars? Are we exposing both sides (winners and losers) of the stock market to our children? Is there any indication that students in this class are more proficient at math? Are we teaching our children how many Fortune 500 companies market unsafe products?"[33]

As a result of this father's concern—and his persistence—the school subsequently agreed to work with the New Jersey Council on Compulsive Gambling to provide students who were taught the Stock Market Game with a supplemental program that would teach some of the dangers of playing the stock market.[34]

More and more parents are faced with the same problems as the mother in Milwaukee and the father in New Jersey because some business or other has attached itself to their child's school. Conflicts over sex education, religious values, and censorship regularly find their way into the media. However, the values issues raised by using corporate-sponsored materials in the schools rarely rise to the surface. Even Rush Limbaugh, who likes to position himself as an unflinching teller of uncomfortable truths, was backed off his criticisms of the BOOK IT! program.

During his May 25, 1995, radio show, Limbaugh learned that the BOOK IT! program he had (accurately) attacked as "bribes for books" was sponsored by Pizza Hut, a company for which he did commercials. In response, he proclaimed: "I'm demonstrating my independence. Just because I do a Pizza Hut commercial does not mean that I have been purchased hook, line and sinker."[35] But the next day, Limbaugh changed his tune: "Since the program ended yesterday I have been in, and my staff have been in, almost hourly contact with the officials at Pizza Hut. . . . Now, I've got my mind right, ladies and gentlemen. I've had it 'splained to me by a number of different people and I'm prepared here to do a mea culpa because I didn't understand what the whole thing was about yesterday."[36]

What it is about is power. The Limbaugh example illustrates that as comical as many corporate-sponsored materials may sometimes seem, they represent big money, and their sponsors are very serious. Big money translates into power and influence. Corporations don't exist either to serve the best interests of schoolchildren or to promote "family" values. Corporations are created to return profits to their owners. Despite the glorious, public-spirited rhetoric that is churned out by corporate promotion departments, the well-being of children and their families and the community will always be subordinated to that purpose.

Keep Drugs in Schools

The beer industry, for example, doesn't like to have the hazards of its product attacked in the classroom or the living room. It prefers to sponsor events for kids and their families or place its corporate logos discretely and tastefully on supplementary or promotional materials. The image it prefers presents beer as an integral part of good clean fun.

The Wisconsin Clearinghouse is a publisher of posters with antidrug messages, housed at the University of Wisconsin. Its posters are distributed to schools, churches, and drug prevention agencies. When the Clearinghouse sent out its fall 1995 catalog, it was immediately attacked by former Wisconsin governor Martin Schreiber. Schreiber, now a lobbyist and executive director of the Wisconsin State Brewers Association, was upset by a poster called "It's Only Beer." The poster featured a bottle of beer lying on its side and made to resemble a syringe. Under the beer bottle, the poster carried this message: "Beer contains alcohol. Alcohol is a drug. Alcohol is the number one drug problem in this country. Not marijuana. Not cocaine. Alcohol. Talk to your kids about alcohol."[37] Schreiber was outraged: "This is a burr under our saddle because it's a lie. . . . I've talked with communication and brewing industry experts, and they feel that this shock technique has a negative effect on young people."[38]

The poster was, in fact, accurate. However, if the Wisconsin Clearinghouse was an organization supported by corporate money, the poster would never have seen the light of day. As it was, Schreiber, whose consulting firm received $45,732 during the first six months of 1995 from various beer-brewing interests, tried mightily—and unsuccessfully—to force the Clearinghouse to pull its poster.[39] Nationally, the beer lobby was more successful. In 1994, it handed out $1.25 million in campaign contributions to 351 candidates and successfully helped to kill two measures intended to curtail alcohol drinking.[40]

The tobacco industry also has a problem: When used as directed, its products kill people. And the industry's influence is felt in the classroom. Consider the case of K-III Communications. K-III, the company that purchased Channel One from Whittle Communications, bought *Weekly Reader* in 1991. *Weekly Reader*, a magazine widely used in American schools, is read by 8 million children from preschool to sixth grade.

K-III Communications is a subsidiary of Kohlberg Kravis Roberts & Company. A leveraged buyout company, Kohlberg Kravis Roberts is a major shareholder in RJR Nabisco whose R. J. Reynolds division is the corporate parent of Old Joe, the cartoon dromedary that pitches Camel cigarettes.[41] Old Joe is a bad actor, but children love him. Introduced in 1988, the Old Joe ad campaign puts the cartoon camel on billboards, phone booths, baseball caps, and T-shirts. Often, he is pictured on a motorcycle or in a pool hall, surrounded by girl camels. Like Ronald McDonald, he also hangs out at promotional events. It didn't take long for observers to begin wondering who the intended target of the Old Joe cartoon campaign is. Research has suggested an answer. Between 1988 and 1991, Camel sales to children rose from $6 million to $476 million a year.[42]

Either Old Joe is an unguided marketing missile or he is doing exactly what he is supposed to do. Critics point out that people rarely start smoking after the age of eighteen and charge that with the more health-conscious adult market for their product shrinking, R. J. Reynolds is trying to build an early customer base.

Research published in the *Journal of the American Medical Association* revealed, among other things, that 91 percent of six-year-olds could match Old Joe with a cigarette (about the same number that could pair Mickey Mouse with the Disney Channel); that teenagers were more likely to respond favorably to Old Joe than adults; and that, although only 9 percent of adult smokers identified Camel as their brand, 33 percent of school-age smokers did.[43]

When Old Joe was featured on the cover of an issue of *Weekly Reader* with the headline "Are Camel Ads Attracting Kids to Smoking?" some people saw a double message and wondered about *Weekly Reader*'s motives. They had reason to be concerned. In 1995, *Education Week* reported that researchers evaluating tobacco-related articles in *Weekly Reader* and another weekly children's magazine between 1989 and 1994 found 68 percent of the *Weekly Reader* stories included the tobacco industry's views as compared to 32 percent in the other magazine. More significantly, the researchers found that after *Weekly Reader* was purchased by K-III, the number of articles on tobacco-related topics that contained an antismoking message declined dramatically. Before K-III owned *Weekly Reader*, 65 percent of its tobacco-related stories contained an antismoking message; after K-III took over, only 24 percent of the stories did.[44] Evidence like that makes it hard to accept corporate claims that businesses only want to promote the public interest by sponsoring materials used by children in schools.

A Pattern of Abuse

One or two examples of dishonest, self-serving, dangerous, or downright bizarre corporate material might be ignored as aberrations. But it's no laughing matter when, by their sheer volume, sponsored materials threaten to turn the school curriculum into a booming, buzzing confusion; when the energy and focus of a school is constantly being diverted from the education of children to the promotion of commercial interests; when the trust parents have that what their children are being taught in school is important information, honestly presented, is routinely violated; and when children are encouraged to associate a particular product with school success.

As is so often the case, the children who have the least are also often exploited the most by school marketing schemes. Schools attended by poor and working-class children are the most likely to be inadequately equipped and have outdated curriculum materials. Children in those schools are most likely to be assigned to overcrowded classrooms and taught by teachers with the least experience in large school systems, where it is easier to get around any prohibitions about advertising in the schools. The teachers, desperate for curriculum materials and with little time to assess the value of the "free" handouts they receive, have virtually no critical information available to help them. They may have principals who encourage them to use the junk, reasoning that what marketers send them is better than nothing.

Advertisers exploit the teachers' desperation and their altruism very effectively. Marketers know many teachers would be willing to wear a sandwich board and walk up and down Main Street hawking bathroom disinfectant if it meant their students could get a computer. So it is that children who already have less money spent on them than the affluent offspring of business executives are harmed again by having more of their time and attention diverted by advertising scams that push them further and further behind academically.

At a time when poor children have been killed for their shoes, they are forced to watch advertising messages for high-priced sneakers. At a time when American children are increasingly overweight and at risk of coronary disease, they have been taught how the heart functions from a poster advertising junk food and then served high-fat meals by the fast food concessionaires that run their school cafeterias. At a time when too many children abuse alcohol, they are taught history by a brewery. At a time when many children are literally made sick by the air they breathe, they are told that some of our nation's biggest polluters are their friends. And at a time when young people hunger for real connections and genuine relationships, they are fed illusions by people for whom they are little more than units of consumption.

The Critics Take a Powder

In the face of this assault on our children and on the public interest, the silence of political and corporate leaders is deafening. The chorus of well-placed heavy hitters pitching market-based education reform would do well to take a close look at how the market is already working in America's schools. It isn't a pretty sight.

Three prominent critics of public education illustrate the problem. Former Bush administration secretary of education Lamar Alexander rarely misses an opportunity to push private school vouchers and criticize the performance of public schools. Without a hint of embarrassment, Alexander was willing to make big money investing in Whittle Communications, then the corporate parent of Channel One. Not surprisingly, Alexander has had little if anything to say about advertising or special interest propaganda in schools and the negative effect such materials might have on the quality of a school's educational program.

Chester Finn, a former official in the Reagan administration's Department of Education, a founder of the Excellence in Education Network (now a project of the conservative Hudson Institute), and coauthor of *What Our Seventeen-Year-Olds Know* (a book complaining about how little American teenagers know about the basic facts of Western civilization), spends a good deal of his time traveling around the country complaining about the "dumbing down" of the American school curriculum. He doesn't seem to have much to say about grotesque nonsense like the Gushers Wonders of the World program or similar trash corporations send flooding into America's schools. Indeed, Finn was on the original design team for Chris Whittle's Edison Project, a plan to develop a chain of for-profit schools that at one point considered ways to utilize commercials aimed at students to help pay for its operation.

Former Reagan administration secretary of education William Bennett, author of *The Book of Virtues*, has been on a variety of "values" crusades, such as his effort to get consumers to reject advertisers who support "sleazy" daytime talk shows on television. A harsh critic of what he regards as inadequate public school curricula, teaching methods, and performance, Bennett also seems to have nothing to say about the sleazy materials put in schools by corporations. And he has not expressed outrage at how such materials may encourage student cynicism about the value of schools, not to mention the values of the adults who control them. All three of these men command media pulpits. Apparently, however, the bully pulpit isn't so bully when it comes to criticizing the corporate pals that help finance your ambitions.

Business leaders who have no difficulty roaring about the need for school reform (such as Louis V. Gerstner Jr., the CEO of IBM) are suddenly mute when it comes to the corporate exploitation of schoolchildren. Members of the Business Roundtable and the U.S. Chamber of Commerce may have a lot to say about what they think is wrong with American schools, but they, too, seem to have nothing to say about marketing products to children in classrooms.

Seizing the Moment

In the absence of any real political or business leadership and with the leadership of professional organizations slumbering, the corporate feeding frenzy in our schools has become a self-perpetuating phenomenon. Executives who might not otherwise be interested in marketing in the schools now have to ask themselves if they are at a competitive disadvantage if they don't. For many, the thought of losing market share probably proves too frightening, so they leap in and join the fray. With little hope of assistance from political and business leaders, the job of turning back the tide is left to members of the educators' professional associations (which are themselves often linked to corporations in some unlikely partnership), individual teachers, principals and superintendents, local boards of education, parent groups, consumer organizations, and concerned citizens.

Fortunately, even without leadership from government or from the boardroom, effective action is possible. The public schools do, after all, still belong to the people. Citizens can write their representatives and senators and demand that school-based advertising no longer be tax deductible. They can attend school board meetings, ask for a list of all sponsored materials and programs used in their district, and request an accounting of how much staff time is devoted to these programs and how much school time children spend involved with them.

School boards can be pushed to develop explicit guidelines governing the use of sponsored materials—guidelines that, at a minimum, require that those materials be subject to the same evaluation procedures as the regular school curriculum. Parents can tell their child's school principal that they do not want their child being taught or evaluated for work done using corporate-sponsored materials or for participating in corporate promotions. They can demand that their child be provided alternative educational experiences during the time taken up by corporate-sponsored materials or promotions. Citizens can write to their state superintendents of public instruction and their state representatives and senators and tell them they want schools to lose state aid for any time devoted to advertising. Finally, consumers can begin to make life uncomfortable for companies that advertise in schools. They can tell advertisers that they will not purchase products marketed in schools and that they will encourage others to follow suit. Consumers can strike at the public relations payoff that leads many firms into the classroom.

The exploitation of our schools by corporate hucksters willing to put their short-term profit ahead of the public's long-term well-being makes the already difficult task of school improvement harder. As corporate America's market-based reform band plays, commercialism is engulfing our schools and children, advertising messages are blanketing our classrooms, more and more time is devoted to trivial, distracting, dishonest, and harmful activities, and ever larger numbers of our children receive an education that falls far short of any defensible standard of excellence or equity.

3

High-Tech Hucksters Go to School

In 1959, Saatchi & Saatchi, the New York advertising agency, had a problem. They had just created the first television ad aimed exclusively at children but there was nowhere to show it. Unwilling to see the Trix rabbit go homeless, Saatchi & Saatchi invented Saturday morning children's television so their ad would have programming to interrupt. Thirty years later, Chris Whittle, a yuppie marketing marvel from Tennessee, proposed interrupting the school day with a "newscast" designed to be interrupted by commercials. Whittle called his creation Channel One and planned to bring it to life with millions of high-voltage advertising dollars. The "vast wasteland" of American commercial television was going to school.

As a result of all of the publicity generated by the Channel One proposal, people all across the country were curious about the man behind the plan—Chris Whittle. Although well known in Tennessee and well connected politically, Whittle was relatively unknown outside the marketing industry until the launching of Channel One. What the rest of the world quickly found out was that Whittle was a controversial go-getter with a gift of gab who fancied himself a "visionary." As his spokesman, former *Fortune* managing editor William Rukeyser, told it, "Chris likes to say, when they catch up with us, all they'll find is our warm campfires, because we'll be over the next hill"[1]—

quite a romantic image. However, more than a few marketing insiders re-garded Whittle's ideas for so-called place-based advertising (in doctors' of-fices, schools, and so forth) with considerable skepticism.

Whittle seemed to bask in the image of the good-hearted commercial buc-caneer willing to boldly go where no marketer had gone before. During his college days, he and a friend, Philip Moffitt, created *Knoxville in a Nutshell,* a campus guide for college freshmen that was later adapted for other schools and marketed on a hundred campuses.[2] He secured his reputation as a whiz kid after he and Moffitt decamped to New York, took over an ailing *Esquire* magazine, and made a lot of money by successfully returning it to profitabil-ity in the early 1980s. When Whittle and Moffitt split in 1986, Moffitt got *Esquire* and Whittle took over their company, 13–30 Corporation. He re-named it Whittle Communications.

Prior to launching Channel One, the biggest moneymakers at Whittle Communications were "wall media." Essentially, wall media consisted of large posters that combined fluffy editorial content (often featuring a popu-lar personality or sports figure), attractive graphics—and advertisements. The posters were designed to grace the walls of doctors' and dentists' offices. There was also a version for schools called "Connections."[3]

"Connections" posters were mounted in metal cases with locked glass cov-ers supplied by Whittle. They were placed in conspicuous, high-traffic areas of schools. Periodically, a Whittle Communications representative turned up, unlocked the case, and put in a new poster. Since they were not con-nected to the school curriculum except by chance, the posters took up generic topics that their designers thought would attract the interest of ado-lescents. No matter what the editorial content, however, the posters always featured large ads across the bottom. Sometimes this made for strange pair-ings. For example, one particularly infamous "Connections" poster called "The Beat of Life" featured a graphic illustrating how the human heart func-tioned along with ads for junk food across the bottom. The Center for the Study of Commercialism awarded Whittle its Lemon Award for this egre-gious act of advertising.

Connections Plugs In

With several profitable print marketing vehicles under his belt, Whittle was ready to go electric. Channel One was born. Designed to reach a clearly tar-geted audience (adolescents) in an uncluttered ad environment from which they could not escape (classrooms), using a high-tech come-on (a satellite feed to participating schools and the free use of television monitors) and the rhetoric of curriculum improvement, Channel One flashed across the marketing world's midnight sky like a meteor. The January 16, 1989, *Advertising Age* announced the project with the British tabloid–style headline "New Whittle Shocker."[4]

Most people outside the marketing industry probably think advertising follows the creation of a newspaper, magazine, or broadcast vehicle that attracts an audience. But this is not necessarily true. Whittle's genius was his ability to find clever ways to turn the standard formulation on its head. He invented products or vehicles whose sole purpose was to serve as launchpads for advertisements keyed to a well-defined audience—the desire to advertise created his products. In the words of one observer, "For Whittle, editorial content is something you wrap around advertising to make it presentable."[5]

The idea for Channel One came out of a marketing focus group session organized to discuss single-sponsor wall posters for high schools.[6] The Channel One concept was simplicity itself: Produce a twelve-minute program with ten minutes of "current events" and two minutes of commercials aimed directly at teenagers in their classrooms, then put the show up on a satellite and provide schools that signed on with a satellite dish to pull it in, a control console to tape it, and wiring to send it singing into the color television monitors Whittle placed in each classroom.

Any school that had a combination of grades within the 6–12 range could have Channel One "free." All it had to do was sign a three-year contract that guaranteed the program would be shown at least 90 percent of the days the school was in session, that nearly all (85 to 90 percent) of the students would watch, and that the program would be shown in its entirety. Editing out the ads was not allowed.

Whittle pitched Channel One as a way of providing high-tech equipment and up-to-date "current events" information to schools that might not have the money to buy either the equipment or the most current curriculum materials. He also hummed along with a popular conservative tune composed by Reagan administration education insiders William Bennett, Diane Ravitch, and Chester Finn. The song might have been called "They Sure Are Dumb These Days." The lyrics told the sad story of adolescent America, ignorant of even the most rudimentary political, geographic, and economic facts because of the thundering incompetence and misguided values of the "education establishment."

Chris Whittle, marketing executive extraodinaire, cannily positioned his brainchild as an agent of adolescent enlightenment. Give Channel One twelve minutes, Whittle promised, and it would bring students the world. It would shine light where previously ignorance had reigned supreme. In the words of one of the full-page ads Whittle put in the *New York Times* in 1989: "Considering the fact that teenagers in this country have actually identified Jesse Jackson as a baseball player and Chernobyl as Cher's full name, even critics of Channel One acknowledge the dire need for exactly such a program."[7]

Formally announced in January 1989, Channel One advanced quickly behind a barrage of similar high-powered advertising. After a five-week, twenty-five-program test in six schools in March 1989, Whittle proclaimed the program a success and attacked its growing number of critics in yet another full-page *New York Times* ad:

> Students who watched Channel One scored significantly higher on identical tests than comparable students at high schools without Channel One.
>
> To put it simply Channel One works.
>
> We have no doubt, of course, that some diehard critics of the commercials that allow us to fund Channel One and provide the hundreds of millions of dollars' worth of equipment necessary to air it will still rail against the program.
>
> But what's becoming more and more apparent is that these critics are willing to condemn a generation of students to its current distressing level of awareness for the sake of an abstract principle.
>
> And one that was abandoned a long time ago, at that.
>
> From classrooms to libraries, educational materials are already sponsored by a substantial amount of advertising. So to oppose Channel One on that basis simply isn't logical.[8]

Launched in March 1990 in 400 middle and high schools, Channel One was reaching 2.2 million students in 3,300 schools by September. By the end of 1990, 5,000 schools had signed on. A year later, Channel One could be seen in more than 9,000 schools.[9]

Principles, Even Abstract Ones, Die Hard

Despite its rapid growth, the project continued to be dogged by controversy everywhere it went. The idea of forcing children to watch commercials on television in school didn't sit well with education groups, parents, school boards, and countless newspaper and magazine editorial writers. The reaction from around the country was overwhelmingly negative. The *Christian Science Monitor* argued that schools should, "zap the commercials."[10] A Gallup poll commissioned by *Advertising Age* found that adults gave the idea of including ads in a news show for schoolchildren "a failing grade."[11] The

School Library Journal called Channel One "Whittle's ed-tech Trojan horse."[12] *Consumer Report* asked, "Is the classroom for blackboards or billboards?"[13] The *Boston Globe* considered the program "a classroom intrusion."[14] And a commentator in the *Rantoul (Ill.) Press* reminded local school board members considering Channel One that

> advertisements appeal to consumers' emotions, not intellect. Allowing them in the classroom will nurture the same non-thought process local educators exhibited when Whittle representatives cooed and barked their product.
> To the degree truth sells their product, advertisers will be truthful.
> Our schools exist for a rather different purpose—to impart truth regardless of its monetary value.[15]

Channel One was labeled "educational junk food"[16] and attacked as "academic acid rain."[17] Speaking for thousands of school administrators, the president of the National Association of Secondary School Principals dismissed Channel One's educational potential out of hand: "There's no need to test bad ideas in the classroom. We know selling junk food in the cafeteria is bad nutrition, and we know it's bad education to bring commercials into the classroom."[18]

In short order, the National Parent-Teacher Association (PTA), the National Association of Elementary School Principals, the National Association of Public Television Stations, the National Education Association, the National Association of Secondary School Principals, the United Church of Christ Office of Communication, the American Association of School Administrators, Action for Children's Television, the American Federation of Teachers, and state superintendents of schools from Alaska to Rhode Island publicly declared that Channel One had no place in classrooms.

Although Channel One had hit a raw nerve, Whittle knew that the educators attacking him also had a public relations problem, for they had allowed advertising and corporate propaganda into the schools for years. As a result, they were vulnerable to the charge that their howls of moral indignation over Channel One were disingenuous. In 1988, for example, the Wisconsin superintendent of public instruction allowed his name to be affixed to a Hardee's restaurant coupon good for a free "cool twist cone" or "big cookie treat" handed out to students who participated in the Families in Education Activities program. And all too many teachers didn't seem to have any qualms about using other corporate-sponsored materials such as videotapes, lesson plans, and incentive programs.

Despite the complicity of schools in a multitude of advertising scams, what set Channel One apart in the minds of most educators was the fact that it used the coercive power of the state to *force* children to watch its commercials. Historically, denying a person of his or her liberty has only been justified by a legitimate appeal to the highest and most compelling public interest. In the United States, very few claims pass that test; typically, they involve issues relevant to society's protection (conviction of a crime); the protection of society and the individual (involuntary commitment to a mental institution); or the preservation of democracy (compulsory school attendance).

No one could plausibly argue that watching commercials is of overriding importance to the public interest. In fact, if anything, commercials represent the opposite of the public interest. They are created to promote the special interests of advertisers and the marketing firms that do their bidding. Therefore, when a school signed up for Channel One, it was, in effect, denying children their liberty in order to promote the special interests of advertisers and violating a public trust by allowing children to be exploited by Whittle for his own enrichment.

Sanitizing the Shill

Attempting to buy Channel One legitimacy and a claim to higher public purpose while at the same time exploiting any divisions among educators and parents over the issue of advertising in schools, Whittle named a star-studded board of twelve worthies to give advice about the direction of the project. The panel was headed by former Reagan administration secretary of education Terrel H. Bell, godfather of the *Nation at Risk* report, and included: Albert Shanker, president of the American Federation of Teachers (who said he would serve as a "watchdog"), billionaire political gadfly H. Ross Perot; Alex Haley, author of *Roots*; Kenneth Rossano, chair of the U.S. Chamber of Commerce; Frederick W. Smith, chair of Federal Express; and the former governor of Tennessee, future Bush administration secretary of education, and Whittle investor Lamar Alexander. According to Whittle, the advisory panel would "demonstrate that many leaders in the field of education agree with our point of view."[19]

Whittle was more than willing to exploit any angle, use any argument, and spend as much money as necessary to get Channel One into the schools. When it was banned from North Carolina's public schools by the state board of education in 1990, Whittle ignored the ban and signed a contract with the Thomasville, North Carolina, board of education anyway. The state board sued and, in a case that went to the state supreme court, Whittle argued, in part, that the advertising in Channel One was not different in nature or form from advertising already in schools. For its part, the state board countered that the Whittle contract requirement that effectively forced children to view the commercials was what set Channel One ads apart.[20]

In April 1991, the North Carolina Supreme Court decided in Whittle's favor, pegging its decision on the issue of local control. The court ruled that the decision about whether to use Channel One should be left in the hands of local school boards.[21] The success of the local control argument illuminated an interesting paradox. Presumably, local control over the education of children in a school district was intended to assure that the community, through its duly elected school board, would oversee the content and organization of the school's curriculum as well as establish the overall policies and procedures for running the district. In practice, this most often meant that the curriculum was developed by the school's professional staff with the advice and consent of the school board.

By choosing to sign up for Channel One, however, a school board was deciding to abdicate its authority over a twelve-minute portion of the school day. Channel One is produced in a distant location, takes up topics that are not reviewed or approved in advance, and presents them in a way that is not selected for their appropriateness to the rest of a school's instructional activities. In this respect, it is the negation of local control. School boards that approve Channel One are agreeing *not* to control their school programs. Instead, those boards, which embody local political authority, cede their decisionmaking responsibility to a corporation whose decisions are dictated by the prospects for profit in a commercial market, not by the needs of the local communities.

Nevertheless, the local control argument worked for Whittle. He used it over and over again to counter attempts to impose statewide bans on Channel One. In 1992, the Texas State Board of Education handed Whittle perhaps his biggest victory when it accepted the local control argument and refused to ban the program. Instead of a ban, the board opted for nonbinding guidelines that allowed local school districts to decide whether to sign up for Channel One. The effect of the board's action was to protect Whittle's position in Texas, which, with 1,061 schools signed up, represented Channel One's biggest market.[22]

The Texas Board of Education's decision was immediately attacked by the state PTA, which had worked hard for an outright ban. It accused the board of education of selling schoolchildren to the highest bidder. Texas PTA president Shirley Igo complained that as a result of the decision, students "will continue to be the captive audience and primary target of a blatantly commercial program, whose content is objectionable and far below the standards the board and local districts demand of educational materials."[23] The spokesman for Texas commissioner of education Lionel "Skip" Meno countered that "the commissioner felt like this [the board's nonbinding guidelines] would give districts the opportunity to manage their own affairs in a responsible manner without having undue state regulation."[24]

The guidelines recommended by the Texas Board of Education, though not binding on school districts, hardly represented an endorsement of Channel One. Among other things, local districts were asked not to show the program during academic class periods. The logic of the Texas board's guidelines might charitably be called odd. If Channel One's primary purpose was indeed educational, it made no sense to ban it from academic class periods in schools using it.

Tax Assessors Get an Education

The guidelines adopted by the Texas Board of Education seemed little more that an attempt to give the appearance of action in response to public pressure to ban Channel One. The Texas education commissioner's inappropriately close relationship to Whittle was revealed in 1994 when a parent, Karen Miller, asked the Texas Education Agency to provide her with a list of all the schools in the state using Channel One. The agency refused. It called the list a "proprietary trade secret," which, it contended, made the list exempt from disclosure under the terms of the Texas Open Records Act.[25]

The agency claimed it had gotten the list after signing a nondisclosure agreement with Whittle and, thus, was required to keep the information secret. The Texas Education Agency's action raised the issue of whether a citizen's legal rights can be circumvented by an agreement between a private entity and a public body—as well as questions about whom the agency was working for and whose interests it represented.

Faced with the prospect of an attorney general's opinion that would have compelled disclosure of the information, Channel One declined to enforce its agreement with the Texas Education Agency, and the information was provided to Karen Miller. She immediately handed it over to her county tax assessor's office—the Harris County Appraisal District. As a result, it was discovered that Channel One was failing to pay the Texas business personal property tax on the equipment it had installed. After overcoming considerable resistance from Channel One, the assessor established the value of the equipment in the spring of 1995. In Harris County (which accounted for about 10 percent of the Texas students watching Channel One), Channel One was required to pay $2 million in back taxes, interest, and penalties.

The tax assessor's calculations shed some light on the actual value of the equipment Whittle installed. The numbers were considerably smaller than the $50,000 figure most often mentioned in press accounts of the technological investment Whittle was making in schools. The Harris County Appraisal District set the replacement cost of Channel One's "head-end" equipment (satellite dish, antenna, VCR console, and so on) at $3,498, the cost of the TV monitors at $250, and the cost of installation at $175 per monitor.[26] Using the district's figures and assuming one television monitor for every twenty-three students as called for in Channel One contracts, the total amount Whittle Communications paid for the purchase and installation of all of the hardware necessary for an eight-hundred-student school totaled $18,373.[27] Meanwhile, advertisers were paying Whittle close to $200,000 every time a thirty-second commercial was broadcast on his program. Channel One was taking schools for a ride—but it wasn't on a high-tech information superhighway.

Shut Out of New York

Channel One grew rapidly in the early 1990s, but its growth was uneven. Most of Whittle's successes were in the South and Midwest. Channel One was locked out of New York and California. On June 16, 1989, despite the editorial backing of the *New York Times*,[28] Channel One was denied access to New York's public schools by the New York Board of Regents.

The regents, accepting the recommendation of Education Commissioner Thomas Sobol, agreed that an arrangement with Channel One probably represented an unconstitutional gift or loan of a public school building to a private individual, that many other sources of current affairs programming were available to schools, and that the development of a technology infrastructure in the public schools was a public responsibility.[29] The attitude of the New York Board of Regents was so hostile toward Channel One that, in response, *Advertising Age* ran an editorial entitled "The Channel One Lynch Mob" suggesting that "the ad industry has a major teaching job to do on those who determine educational policy because the Whittle plan, if nothing else, has exposed to the advertising community the animosity these policy makers have toward a basic ingredient in the free-enterprise system."[30]

Given the advertising glut already in America's classrooms—and the ad copy on the paper's own pages bought by marketing firms touting their access to schools—the *Advertising Age* editors' expression of concern about the hostility and mistrust of educators was comical. It was true, however, that

Channel One had in the minds of many crossed over the boundary of acceptable practice. Despite frenzied lobbying by Whittle, the New York regents rebuffed Channel One twice more. In February 1990, they adopted a regulation banning schools from entering into a contract that compelled children to view televised commercials. On June 25, 1993, they reaffirmed their regulation and once again supported Commissioner Sobol's argument that "we must provide safe haven for children free of commercial taint."[31]

Apparently anticipating that his creation was near death at the hands of the regents, Whittle was ready with a legislative strategy to resuscitate it. On February 16, 1993, the chair of the New York Assembly Education Committee, Angelo Del Torro, introduced Assembly Bill 3688-A. An identical bill, 3671-A, was introduced in the state senate by the Education Committee chair, Charles D. Cook, on March 17, 1993. The Del Torro–Cook bills obviously had nothing to do with educational concerns. They were about advertising dollars and the political influence those dollars can buy. This striking example of special interest legislation would have overruled the regents' ban and grant local school boards the authority to decide whether to allow "supplementary electronic instructional materials containing commercial advertising" in their schools. If the Del Torro–Cook bills became law, the only supplementary electronic instructional materials *not* subject to regents' approval would have been those that contained advertising.

The Del Torro–Cook bills languished in committee in 1993. However, in New York, bills not voted on in the first year of a two-year legislative session are not dead until the end of the legislative session on the second year. This meant that both bills were still viable at the start of the 1994 legislative session.

Whittle spent big money to keep Channel One on life support in New York. According to J. Robert Daggett, former executive assistant to the New York commissioner of education, Whittle hired the New York law firm of Bower and Gardner to plead his case with the legislature. Bower and Gardner is one of the largest and most powerful lobbying operations in New York. One of the senior partners is Stanley Fink, the long-time Democratic speaker of the assembly who retired after the 1990 legislative session. The two people doing most of the arm-twisting in Albany were Kenneth Shapiro, former chief counsel to Fink when he was speaker, and Peter Piscitelli, a long-time lobbyist who formerly represented the city of New York and the New York School Board, among other clients. Each of these men was well connected to both Republicans and Democrats, and each was considered among the most effective and influential lobbyists in Albany. And they didn't come cheap. Whittle had to plunk down $75,000 in 1993 just to start their meters running.[32] In 1994, Channel One changed lobbyists and plunked down $25,000 to hire Wilson, Elser & Moskowitz.[33]

Open Warfare in California

The hostility greeting Channel One in New York was practically a ticker tape parade compared to what Whittle faced in California. California's state super-intendent of public instruction, Bill Honig, called Channel One perhaps "the worst idea in the history of American education" and declared open war on the project. He launched an ad campaign of his own in June 1990 and pledged to withhold state aid for the amount of time students watched the commercials on Channel One from any school that showed it. Honig's anti–Channel One ads pointed out that if the program was allowed in schools, students would be forced to watch six hours (or about one school day a year) of commercials for candy, cosmetics, and high-priced sneakers. The ads urged readers to write letters of protest to advertisers on Channel One.[34]

Channel One was promoted as a "free" offer of technology and much-needed educational programming to cash-poor schools. Honig demanded a closer look at the "free" offer to see how much it really cost. In a May 25, 1989, memo to Joe Symkowick, chief counsel of the Legal and Audits Branch of the California Department of Education, Jim Wilson, the director of fiscal policy planning and analysis for the California Department of Edu-cation, put the cost of two minutes of Channel One's commercials in Cali-fornia's public school classrooms (grades 7–12) at $48,146,224 in state aid over a three-year contract period—even after deducting the expense to Whit-tle of the "free" technology Channel One would loan to participating schools (assuming the inflated $50,000 value).[35]

In other words, if every eligible public school in California were to sign on to Channel One, state taxpayers would pay about $16 million in state aid to schools each year to require children to watch two minutes of commercials every day. Far from being free, Channel One would provide Whittle with a direct subsidy from state taxpayers. In addition, since Channel One retained ownership of the equipment it installed in participating schools, it also re-tained the tax depreciation rights that went with it—to the tune of 40 per-cent over its taxable lifetime. Suddenly, Chris Whittle's market solution to the alleged current events gap among American adolescents looked like just another corporate rip-off of taxpayers' dollars, with the exploitation of their children thrown into the bargain.

The ad campaign produced by California's superintendent of schools was designed to accomplish two objectives: first, to push the legislature to pass legislation barring Channel One, and second, to scare off potential advertis-ers by threatening them with overwhelming adverse publicity. In 1989, the danger that potential advertisers would be scared off by the intense negative reactions to Channel One appeared very real. Before and immediately after the trial run of the program in March, there was open speculation—and considerable skepticism—about Whittle's ability to sign up the 5,000 schools he said would be necessary to make the project viable or to attract enough advertising support even if he did.[36]

As was so often the case in Whittle's career, the headlines told the story: in the *Wall Street Journal* on March 2, 1989, "Criticism of TV Show with Ads for Schools Is Scaring Sponsors";[37] in *Advertising Age* on March 13, 1989, "Whittle Sticks by 'Channel One' Rollout";[38] in the *Wall Street Journal* on May 1, 1989, "Future of Whittle's Channel One Unclear";[39] in the *Wall Street Journal* on August 8, 1989, "How Chris Whittle Faltered on the Issue of TV Ads in Schools";[40] in *Advertising Age* on September 18, 1989, "Whittle: 'Channel One' Is a Hit";[41] and in the *New York Times* on September 18, 1989, "Channel One Gets Sponsors."[42] In the end, enough schools were willing to sign on and the prospect of an "uncluttered" ad environment filled with millions of free-spending teens proved irresistible to enough advertisers to launch Channel One successfully.

Armed with plenty of advertising revenue, plus the $185 million Time had spent to purchase a half interest in his company in 1988 and more money later ponied up by Phillips Electronics and Associated Newspaper Holdings to buy into the company, Whittle was more than willing to spend big bucks to buy credibility and influence in his quest to pry open classroom doors for Channel One.

In 1992, when the California Department of Education sued to prevent the East Side Union High School District in San Jose from televising the twelve-minute program, Whittle paid for the legal muscle to defend the district. Elias Chamorro, principal of the high school in question, also was paid a $1,200 annual stipend and travel expenses by Whittle to sit on the Channel One advisory board.[43] When questioned about the propriety of paying a public school official, Jim Ritts, Channel One president for network affairs, indicated he saw no conflict of interest. In Ritts's view, "If you were trying to buy influence, it would certainly take a great deal more money."[44]

Perhaps Ritts was remembering the eighteen-month period in 1990–1991 when Whittle had indeed spent a great deal of money ($640,000) lobbying the California legislature in a successful effort to block legislation that would have banned Channel One. A *Los Angeles Times* article reported:

> "They covered all the bases," a veteran legislative staff member said. "They have Merksamer for the Republicans [Steven A. Merksamer was chief of staff to former Republican governor George Deukmejian]; Rose and Kindel for the Democrats, and Denny Carpenter for the old-boy network. . . . And they've got Bobbie Metzger to orchestrate the whole thing," Metzger, one of Sacramento's

most successful political consultants and public relations specialists, is a former aide to former Assembly Speaker Willie Brown [since elected mayor of San Francisco] and has strong ties to both parties. "I've never seen this magnitude of lobbying on an education issue," said State Sen. Art Torres.[45]

According to the *Wall Street Journal*, Whittle had spent more than $1 million on lobbying in California by August 1993.[46] Apparently, it was money well spent. Whittle was able to defeat three attempts to rein in Channel One legislatively. In 1993, the third try failed after some questionable parliamentary wheeling and dealing. The *Sacramento Bee* called the successful effort to derail the bill a "legislative mugging" and blistered the politicians involved: "Whether the votes were switched or avoided out of loyalty to the speaker, loyalty to the lobbyists, or midnight conversion is hard to say. But the result is the continuation of the piecemeal sale of the California public school day and the force feeding of ads to young students. For that the Assembly and its 'education' committee should be ashamed. With friends like this, the state's education system needs no enemies."[47]

California's superintendent of schools, Bill Honig, fared better in court. On September 9, 1992, California Superior Court Judge Jeremy Fogel ruled that Channel One could be shown in state schools. However, teachers had to have the right not to show it, and students whose teachers did show it had to have alternative activities provided by the school district. Parents were also to be informed that their children did not have to watch the program.[48] The judge agreed that it would be a violation of state law to coerce students into watching either the commercial or noncommercial parts of the program.

The regulations the California Superior Court's ruling imposed on districts that wanted to use Channel One effectively removed the coercion in Channel One's structure. In so doing, the regulations raised new problems for school districts desiring to use Channel One. Any California school that wanted to use it was now required to call attention to the fact and risk opposition from parents armed with the right to take their children out of class when it was shown and the right to demand that the school provide alternative educational activities.

The effective exclusion of his program from the California and New York markets undermined Whittle's ability to maintain the rapid pace of Channel One's growth. Since Channel One was the only remaining big moneymaker for Whittle Communications in the early 1990s, its earning plateau took its toll. Strapped for cash because of money hemorrhaging from the company's other units—including the grandiose Edison Project plan for a chain of for-profit schools—Whittle Communications reported a $20 million loss for the year ending June 30, 1993.[49]

Advertisers Sold Power over Students

In the California court case, Whittle had argued that the advertising in Channel One had merely an "incidental" effect on students. Presumably, this meant that in the scheme of things, the advertising on Channel One was of small importance compared to the impact of the news content of the program on students. This was a curious claim for a couple of reasons. The news in Channel One, just like the editorial content of the "Connections" wall posters, favored MTV-type, quick-cut features that covered "soft" subjects rapidly and superficially. It was often criticized for being influenced by the interests of advertisers.

Advertisers would have good reason to be shocked upon hearing that the thirty-second ads for which they were paying somewhere between $190,000 and $200,000 were only *incidental* to the program. For one thing, that was not what the advertisers had been told. Channel One's pitch promised them access to the largest teen audience in history in an environment in which *"the usual distractions of telephones, stereos, remote controls, etc. are nonexistent—* making the impact and attention delivered by the news and commercials on Channel One far superior to that of any other media reaching teens."[50]

Channel One was, according to Whittle Communications, "more than television; [it was] a direct pipeline" to the teen market. It promised a powerful "point of entry to the American consumer market" and the opportunity to "establish brand loyalties and perceptions that will last a lifetime."

Case studies used by Whittle to demonstrate Channel One's effectiveness included the Kodak "Choice Moments" campaign that, according to Whittle, helped Kodak change its stodgy corporate image to one of a company with a "hip and cool" aura that made products that "teens like." Another company, Little Caesar's, signed on with Channel One to build volume. Channel One provided a rich opportunity for Little Caesar's because, in Whittle's words, "teenagers represent an enormous target for a pizza chain. They are twice as likely to order a pizza. They are brand loyal." After a four-week campaign on Channel One, Whittle claimed that the number of teens reporting Little Caesar's on two key measures, "last pizza purchased" and "intent for the next purchase," increased dramatically.

Channel One's "It's Like This" campaign performed even more wondrous works for a leading soft drink, according to Whittle. It helped Pepsi convince teens that Pepsi "cares more than other soft drink companies," "really listen[s] to teens," "cares what teens think," and "gives teens a voice." What this feast of rhetorical empty calories might actually mean—other than that Pepsi was somehow promoted as "good"—is anyone's guess.

Sprint signed up with Channel One to bump up consumer awareness. As a result of events such as "The Sprint Poll," Channel One claimed to have increased the "unaided brand awareness" and "unaided advertising awareness" of Sprint. Not only that, teens viewing Channel One also saw Sprint as an "up and coming company" they would use.

The Hidden Persuaders

The average person may or may not be repelled by the duplicity of Whittle telling educators and judges one story (Channel One's primary purpose is to increase students' current events knowledge) and advertisers another (Channel One is a "pipeline" to the teen market). However, that is standard practice among marketers who put advertising in schools. To a certain extent, marketers are able to get away with their two-faced lines because of the widespread public belief that people are not really influenced by commercials anyway. When adults are asked if ads affect them, 75 to 80 percent regularly say no in surveys done by market research firms. In schools, teens wearing high-priced designer clothes commonly say they buy them because the clothes are "good" or because they "just like them," not because they were influenced by commercials.[51]

American children see so many TV ads—200,000 by one estimate before they even reach first grade—that many educators and other adults seem to think that they are simply part of the "real" world and do no harm.[52] Educators who defend using Channel One despite its commercials tend to argue that the ads represent an unfortunate but acceptable trade-off to gain the use of the TV equipment and have access to the "newscast." Apparently, these educators believe that since no immediate, direct, or visible harm is done by ads, then there is no harm at all.

In his book *The Pitch*, Hugh Rank, a communications professor at Governor's State University in Illinois, identifies a number of "hidden" harms of advertising.[53] Rank argues that although many harms are delayed, indirect, and invisible in the short term, they are nonetheless potent. He makes a comparison to the effects of DDT, lead, and asbestos poisoning.

The products (e.g., junk food and high-priced designer clothes) and points of view (e.g., the importance of plastics and the need for chemicals in agriculture) that are pushed on kids in school by corporations contribute to negative environmental and economic effects that are lasting and difficult to trace back to a single cause. Nevertheless, the impact of the ads is very real. According to Rank, they help promote unbridled materialism, which obliterates all values other than those of the commercial marketplace. In contemporary American culture, commercialism has already helped make the term *citizen* virtually synonymous with the term *consumer* and the possession of objects synonymous with happiness.

Ads help create and exacerbate economic problems. For example, as anyone familiar with credit card commercials knows, they promote indebtedness by stimulating both the desire for possessions and the urge to satisfy that desire immediately. Between 1993 and 1995 alone, credit card debt increased 47 percent in the United States.[54] Growing numbers of children are now working to purchase or pay off debts for expensive clothes, electronics, and other items that ads have taught them are essential to their well-being. The number of hours they work to acquire possessions takes time away from their studies and from family and community activities that would benefit them and society in the short and long term. Ads also have helped create and sustain a disposable culture that is choking on its own waste, and they promote a theory of economic growth that, if followed to its logical conclusion, could very well result in irreversible and catastrophic environmental degradation.

Opponents of commercialism are drawn from a broad constituency. Channel One is opposed, for example, by both the Ralph Nader–inspired Center for the Study of Commercialism and the Christian parents' organization Citizens for Excellence in Education, which launched a national boycott of PepsiCo in 1992 because of its ads on the program.[55]

A Knoxville, Tennessee, parent, Steven Wallace, sued the city's board of education on the grounds that Channel One provided no educational content and that forcing his son to watch the program violated his religious beliefs. Students at North High in Fargo, North Dakota, walked out of classes rather than watch Channel One.[56] Teachers in Albuquerque, New Mexico, fought Channel One in part because they felt the ads it broadcast were sexist.[57] And four teachers in Flat Rock, Michigan, were threatened with dismissal when they refused to interrupt their lessons to make room for Channel One.[58]

The conservative Eagle Education Fund's Colorado newspaper approvingly reported a review of Channel One conducted by a Wilson Bryan Key. Key, described as having been a professor of communications studies at five major universities, acted at the behest of the Colorado Pro-Family Coalition's board of directors. After viewing Channel One, Key concluded that the programming was, "junk, a waste of time" and that "recess would be more beneficial." Key was unable to determine if Channel One used subliminal techniques.[59]

After finding out that his name was being used by Channel One in its promotional materials, American Federation of Teachers president Albert

Shanker resigned from Channel One's "council of advisors." The National Education Association vowed to fight Channel One and to put pressure on advertisers.[60]

In a 1993 study of two pairs of Michigan high schools, Bradley Greenberg and Jeffrey Brand found that students who watched Channel One were more likely than other students to agree with the statements "money is everything," "a nice car is more important than school," "designer labels make a difference," and "wealthy people are happier than the poor." In other words, the impact of Channel One was to reinforce materialistic values.[61]

With rhetoric reminiscent of the Right whenever it tries to sell whatever is good for business as education reform, Whittle tried to portray opposition to Channel One as being led by self-interested groups afraid of change and progress. However, the opposition was much too varied and widespread for the charge to ring true. Too many people coming from too many directions immediately understood that when schools signed up for Channel One, they were not making a harmless decision nor were they making a "neutral" decision. Such schools were instead abdicating their responsibility to carefully consider what should be presented to students as important knowledge and appropriate educational experiences. Schools using Channel One became agents of special interests. In that role, they helped promote commercial values that encouraged their students to behave in ways that the rest of a school's curriculum often attempted to repudiate (for example, eating junk food, spending more money than they could afford, and using "disposable," unnecessary, or unhealthy products).

Behind the Educational Facade

As Channel One's original three-year contracts came up for renewal, districts all over the country turned down the chance to sign on again. As one parent in Texas commented, "Channel One will be road kill on the information superhighway. It takes from our students and our schools far more than it gives."[62]

Whittle was clever enough to play on the common misperception that ads are harmless, to emphasize their "incidental" effect on students who watched Channel One, and to portray them as a necessary evil. He also rarely missed a chance to cast himself as a visionary who had come up with an idea to help underfunded schools purchase up-to-date technology and instructional materials. Few marketing executives were willing to go to the lengths that Chris Whittle went to in portraying his motives as high-minded and his ideas as important. In fact, what irritated many of his marketing peers was what they saw as his insufferable pretension. According to one news report: "He vested his 42 'properties,' as they are called around Knoxville headquarters, with an intellectual mantle that seemed laughably out of proportion to what they were: Service magazines and posters that were mostly given away free to small audiences and paid for by one or a few advertisers."[63]

In 1990, to deflect the attacks of critics who accused him of offering a worthless "current events" program in order to sneak televised commercials into schools, Whittle financed a three-year study of the effect that viewing Channel One had on the "current events" knowledge of students. He refused, however, to allow the researchers to assess the impact of the ads shown on the program. Whittle's study was conducted under the auspices of the Institute for Social Research at the University of Michigan by Jerome Johnston of the University of Michigan and Evelyn Brzezinski of Interwest Applied Research. In 1990–1991, by Whittle's researchers' own accounting, Channel One contained only about 4 minutes of "hard news" per program (or 9.5 hours per school year). Given so little news content, it was hard to imagine that the program would have much effect at all on student learning. It didn't.[64]

By the time the findings of the third and final Whittle-funded evaluation were released in 1994, the time devoted to "hard news" on Channel One had increased to 6.5 minutes per program. The researchers reported that teachers liked Channel One, that principals liked Channel One, and that students liked Channel One. Did students watching Channel One learn more? Not really. The report concluded with eminently sensible advice: "To achieve maximum benefits for students, teachers must be prepared to help students assemble the somewhat fragmented knowledge that we know as 'the news' into a coherent picture of world events."[65]

Whether a remotely controlled news program with commercials that interrupted every school day for 12 minutes to deliver 6.5 minutes of random "current events" was the best way for teachers to help students understand the world around them was apparently beyond the scope of the research Whittle sponsored. So was the question of whether Channel One was a better choice than the 15-minute *Newsroom* program on Cable News Network (CNN), provided free with a daily guide for teachers—and without commercials—to over 23,500 schools nationwide, almost twice as many as Channel One.[66]

When all is said and done, if the point is to use television instead of a newspaper, magazine, or book, then perhaps a video created by a teacher to organize a lesson around a significant news event would be the best choice of all. Such a video is guaranteed to be well integrated into the overall instructional plan and tailored to the particular needs and interests of the students in the class.

The research commissioned by Whittle was not the only research done on the effects of Channel One. To serve Whittle's own interest in the impact of Channel One ads on student viewers, McCullom and Speilman, a New York market research firm, was commissioned by Whittle to call the homes of selected students who had Channel One shown in their classrooms; researchers asked for each student by name and conduct a detailed, forty-five-minute interview on the student's buying habits and his or her reactions to the products advertised on Channel One. When news of the research leaked out as a result of parental complaints, Whittle refused to discuss the study publicly, claiming it was proprietary information belonging to his clients. He would say, however, that Channel One "works." By that, he meant that students who watched Channel One had greater brand awareness of products advertised on the program than students in non–Channel One schools.[67]

On the more salient question of educational value, the Southeastern Educational Improvement Laboratory surveyed 3,000 high school students and 140 teachers in North Carolina and Mississippi in 1991. It found that neither Channel One nor CNN's *Newsroom* had a significant effect on what students retained unless teachers reinforced the broadcasts—which they rarely did. Perhaps the most alarming finding in this study was that students thought that the products advertised on Channel One were good for them because the ads were shown in the classroom.[68]

Class in the Classroom

The degree to which Channel One exploited particular students was documented in a 1992 *San Jose Mercury-News* investigative report. *Mercury-News* reporters found that Channel One had targeted poor schools in California—especially schools with large Latino populations—as part of a strategy to wedge its way into the California market. This was the familiar pattern of businesses trying to pass off their profit-making ventures as school reform and social revolution by becoming sudden converts to the empowerment of the most desperate among us. According to the *Mercury-News* report, Whittle "was able to turn a simple debate over the ethics of beaming commercials into classrooms into a power struggle over the right of ethnic communities to decide what is best for their children."[69]

Whittle's basic political tactic also was familiar: spread around a lot of money. He spent heavily to transport Latino teachers, administrators, parents, and students to legislative hearings; to pay the legal costs of the predominantly Latino high school challenging the state superintendent's right to ban Channel One; and to underwrite a meeting of the Hispanic caucus of the California School Boards Association, among other things. The only problem was that anyone who looked closely realized Channel One wasn't a remotely Latino issue. California state senator Art Torres asked and answered the key questions: "Was [Channel One] bilingual? Do they have Hispanics in the program? Is it a Hispanic company? No."[70] But Senator Torres should have realized the essence of good marketing is in the illusion, not necessarily the reality.

The *San Jose Mercury-News* reporters were not the only ones who noticed how often Channel One kept popping up in schools attended by poor children. The first major act of UNPLUG, a youth-led organization founded in 1993 to fight commercialism in education and promote genuine local control of the schools, was to release a study conducted by University of Massachusetts communications professor Michael Morgan. Using a 17,000-school sample—nearly half the schools in the United States with any combination of grades in the 6–12 range—Morgan found that schools using Channel One were not from a cross section of America. Schools using Channel One were overwhelmingly those that served children living in poverty. They also tended to have much higher numbers of African American students. Schools with the greatest concentration of low-income students were more than twice as likely to have Channel One as schools serving more affluent students. Of all schools spending less than $10 per year per student on texts, 67.5 percent used Channel One, and only 1 in 5 schools spending $75 or more on texts allowed the program. Only 1 in 10 schools at the upper end of per-pupil spending ($6,000) had Channel One, but 6 in 10 schools at the lower end ($2,599) did. And the greater the percentage of African American students in a school, the more likely it was that the school had Channel One.[71]

The UNPLUG study suggested the students least likely to be able to afford the products advertised on Channel One were the students most likely to see the ads. It seemed a perverse situation that could only add to the cynicism, frustration, and bitterness of children living in poverty. Instead of being provided safe and wholesome schools, adequate curriculum materials, and real opportunities to improve themselves, they were being exploited to increase the profits of others.

Not everyone would take such a negative view, of course. Terry Moe, for example, the coauthor of *Politics, Markets and America's Schools*, a bible of sorts to conservative private school voucher advocates, found Channel One to be a boon to the poor. Writing in the *San Francisco Business Times*, Moe noted, "It is difficult to be innovative when you are poor because many innovations cost money. Sometimes a lot of money." But Moe also had discovered that poverty has a silver lining. "Fiscal scarcity can be a driving force for change, prompting people to search out new, unorthodox ideas for improvement." It was Moe's happy, if undocumented, conclusion that "everyone benefits from a system that encourages people like Whittle to come up with ideas like Channel One."[72]

Moe's analysis was divorced from any consideration of the economic and social costs that Channel One imposes on school districts, and Moe himself was apparently untroubled that the alleged benefits are being imposed on only our poorest children. Consequently, his analysis was as empty of content and as remote from the real world as the Pepsi commercials on Channel One. His main purpose seems to have been to paint a smiling face on the market, which, presumably, had suddenly become interested in caring for schoolchildren.

The Expensive Education of Mr. Whittle

Whether or not the market will provide for schoolchildren, it did take care of Chris Whittle. By 1994, his media empire was in tatters. He was forced to close two major electronic "place-based" advertising vehicles launched after Channel One: "Special Reports," intended to soothe patients waiting in doctors' offices with a steady flow of commercials, and the much-touted "Medical News Network," aimed at doctors themselves. Both proved to be money-losing fiascoes. Meanwhile, the Edison Project, Whittle's grand plan to blanket America with for-profit schools, had failed to attract a single new investor after its widely heralded debut and was rapidly running out of cash.

That made matters worse when Whittle's single large source of revenue, Channel One, hit a fiscal wall. As news of Whittle's financial plight, his extravagant personal and corporate style, and his ineptitude as a manager spread, Phillips Electronics, one of his major corporate partners, shoved him out of the CEO position and installed their own man, Don F. Johnstone. Unable to overcome the strategic and financial liabilities he inherited from Whittle, Johnstone presided over the liquidation of the company.

On October 3, 1994, the *Wall Street Journal* reported that Channel One had been sold to K-III Communications Corporation for approximately $250 million, an amount that excluded Whittle's unpaid tax liabilities. The rest of what was left of Whittle Communications was to be sold off over the next two years, and the partnership dissolved.[73] Whittle himself, reportedly almost broke with assets and debts of about $35 million each, began to sell off personal property even as he desperately tried to salvage his most ambitious educational scheme, the Edison Project. The two major outside in-

vestors in Whittle Communications wrote off virtually their entire investments—Time Warner to the tune of $185 million and Phillips Electronics,
$175 million.[74]

K-III Communications is controlled by Kohlberg Kravis Roberts & Company—a leveraged buyout firm that is also a large investor in RJR Nabisco, a
major cigarette manufacturer. K-III's acquisition of Channel One did not
bode well for American schoolchildren. A company known for its relentless
concern for maximizing profits,[75] K-III was attacked shortly after taking over
Weekly Reader (the newspaper for elementary school students) for slanting
tobacco-related stories away from a "don't smoke" message.

In 1995, K-III took up where Whittle had left off by mounting a well-or-
chestrated, heavily financed campaign to convince the New York legislature
to overturn the New York Board of Regents's ban on Channel One. Bills introduced in the assembly by State Representative Steven Sanders (A 2496-B)
and in the senate by Senator Charles D. Cook (S 2271) sought to give local
school districts the right to sign up for Channel One. Once again, Channel
One's owners attempted to divert the issue from exploitation of schoolchildren to "local control."

As in 1993, Kenneth Shapiro, the well-connected former chief counsel to a
long-time speaker of the assembly, was working the legislative corridors for
Channel One.[76] He was backed up by none other than Henry Kravis, one of
the owners of Kohlberg Kravis Roberts & Company. Kravis, who personally
contributed $25,000 to the campaign of New York governor George Pataki,[77]
was evidently hoping that the political winds in Albany would blow in Channel One's direction this time. In a year of widespread cuts in education funding, Channel One supporters were rewarming their old come-ons about getting "something for nothing" and the "importance of providing high-tech" to
prepare students for the world of tomorrow. Assembly Education Committee
chair Sanders, a Manhattan Democrat, claimed, "At a point in time when
there are dwindling resources for state and local education, this is an opportunity to get quality education and apparatus into schoolrooms."[78]

Opposing the legislation was a broadly based coalition that included parents, teachers, administrators, consumer activists, public broadcasting stations, the New York Education Department, and the New York Board of Regents. Rhoda Karpatkin, president of Consumers Union, summed up the
position of the opponents: "K-III has tried to confuse the issue by arguing
that the Board of Regents' decision to ban Channel One obstructs the free
choice of local school districts. They neglect to mention that the Regents'
ban protects kids across the state from being forced to endure a relentless series of marketing appeals throughout the entire school year. The issue is not
local control—it's whether advertising belongs in the classroom."[79]

The Sanders-Cook legislation died in committee in 1995.[80] However, it could, like Freddie Krueger, return at any time to haunt the dreams of New York students.

The Low Life of High Tech

As the struggle over Channel One continued in New York and elsewhere, an important issue remained largely outside the debate. The question of whether using the technology offered by Whittle was really a good idea, even without the commercial programming, was rarely raised. Virtually everyone accepted as a given that the television equipment Whittle offered as the bait to entice schools to sign up for Channel One somehow represented an opportunity for schools to improve their instructional program and step out of the technological underclass.

In fact, there is little evidence to suggest that children learn better or even as well from a television presentation as they do from a lesson organized and presented by their own teacher. Television technology also carries some serious negative effects. For example, the steady increase in the number of hours Americans spend watching television roughly parallels the decline in American civic engagement. As Harvard government professor Robert Putnam contends, "Each hour spent viewing television is associated with less social trust and less group membership, while each hour reading a newspaper is associated with more."[81] A quick visit to a few schools and classrooms would convince most people that what children need more of is sustained educational relationships with competent adults, not more television programs or even computer monitors.

Although clichés about the "computer literacy" needed to navigate the "information superhighway" are used with great authority by corporate executives, politicians, and educators, there is no commonly agreed upon definition of either term. No one knows what "computer literate" students would know or be able to do, much less whether it would be desirable for them to do it. And no one can describe what a school in the fast lane of the "information superhighway" looks like or how its revolutionary new design can be reasonably thought to increase student knowledge.

Douglas Noble, an educational researcher who tracks corporate attempts to "revolutionize" American education via technology, takes a jaundiced view of the relentless fads that have swept the corporate high-tech innovation industry since the 1960s. Noble points out that advice from the now defunct U.S. Office of Technology and Assessment about how schools can best make the bold leap into a bright, new technological future has changed almost yearly over the last decade or so. In 1983, teachers were told to teach their students how to program computers in BASIC. In 1984, they were told to use LOGO in order to help their students think as well as program. In 1986, they heard that programs of individualized instruction would lead to the world of tomorrow. In 1988, the word was, teach word processing. In 1990, curriculum-specific computer tools such as history databases were all the rage. In 1992, students were to create products of their own using hypertext multimedia programming. In 1994, the Internet was the promised land.[82]

The résumés of the corporate "visionaries" who keep promising to lead the schools out of the technological wilderness don't offer much inspiration. A look at the track records of these individuals suggests that educators and parents should search elsewhere for their prophets. Former CEOs John Akers of IBM, John Scully of Apple, and Kay Whitmore of Kodak were all influential in helping shape federal education policy during the Bush administration, and their companies were held up as models for schools to learn from as they "restructured." Yet, according to Noble, all three were dumped after their mismanagement brought their firms to the brink of disaster.[83] The thought of defrocked hustler Chris Whittle as a model for school administrators is pathetic.

Channel One offers neither a bold new technology nor any reasonable possibility of increasing student learning. It is simply one of the latest and most grotesque attempts by corporate America to create and exploit an educational market for information superhighway technologies that are driven far more by the needs of the advertising and entertainment industries than by the best interests of America's schools and the children they serve.

Nevertheless, technology has become a kind of Holy Grail for corporate executives and educators alike. It is sought with a childlike faith in its magical ability to heal whatever maladies may afflict the seeker. For the executives, technology offers the enticing possibilities of profits from selling hardware and software to schools and large-scale reductions in the public school workforce similar to the technology-driven savaging of private sector jobs in the 1980s. For educators, technology offers a chance to openly embrace change and demonstrate they are not the enemies of progress, as they are so often painted by corporate critics.

With so little required in the way of concrete performance, the profiteers behind the two main efforts to develop for-profit schools in the 1990s—Education Alternatives, Inc., and the Edison Project—had only to promise to use computers and technology in the classroom to be hailed as educational revolutionaries.

Schools for Profit:
Follow the
Yellow Brick Road

When Michael Milken, the junk bond king, was let out of prison, he said that he wanted to be involved in education because he considered it one of the biggest moneymakers for American business.[1] He isn't alone in that opinion.

Minneapolis handed over the superintendency of its public school system to Public Strategies, a private consulting firm, in 1993. In 1994, Education Alternatives, Inc., of Bloomington, Minnesota, won a contract to run the entire Hartford, Connecticut, school system. In 1995, Alternative Public Schools of Nashville, Tennessee, took over one of three elementary schools in Wilkensburg, Pennsylvania; it was the first time the company had run a school anywhere. Since 1990, these companies and the highly publicized Edison Project founded by Chris Whittle have captured headlines by attempting to make money running public schools. Other companies, such as Sylvan Learning Systems and Huntington Learning Centers, contract with individuals and school districts to provide more limited educational services.[2]

Advocates of these attempts at privatization in public education (often called "public-private partnerships") claim they are the wave of the future, supported by a broad, bipartisan political consensus. The Goals 2000: Educate America Act initiated under Republican President George Bush, passed by a Democratic-controlled Congress, and signed into law by Democratic President Bill Clinton in March 1994 seems to give credence to the bipartisan claim. The law contains a provision allowing states to use federal money to experiment with privatization.[3]

Much more open to question are supporters' descriptions of public-private partnerships as a bold new public policy initiative that will transform failed public school systems by infusing them with competition and private sector know-how. Disciples either do not know or, for good reason, would rather forget that privatization was widely tried in public education in the late 1960s and early 1970s. It was called "performance contracting."

The Nixon administration loved performance contracting. Then, as now, a good deal of the performance contracting focused on schools attended by poor children. And then, as now, it was argued that the knowledge and efficiency of private companies competing for contracts would be the engine used to bring educational achievement to schools where it had previously been elusive.

The *Baltimore Sun's* William Salganik remembers the wave of enthusiasm for performance contracting quite well:

> More than 100 schools around the country tried performance contracts during the 1970–71 school year. Companies large and small rushed in—as large as Westinghouse, as small as a new company formed by football star Fran Tarkenton. The cover story in *The American School Board Journal* in October 1971 was "Almost Everything You Need to Know About Performance Contracting."
>
> Soon, everything you needed to know about performance contracting consisted of this: First, a federal evaluation found that performance contracts worked no better than traditional programs. Second, there was evidence of contractors cheating. In addition to general shoddy work in a number of schools by some bottom-line-oriented contractors, skeptical members of the teacher's union in Providence, Rhode Island, found a contractor teaching parts of the standardized test that was to be used to evaluate progress and determine payment.[4]

Salganik has his facts straight. After conducting a review of three years' experience with performance contracting, Gerald H. Wohlferd concluded that commercial firms were no better at teaching children than public schools, that private firms required as much or more money to do the job, and that some companies used questionable methods to make a profit.[5]

The Office of Economic Opportunity (OEO) and the Rand Corporation studied the performance of performance contracting and found little evidence to support the enthusiastic claims of its proponents.[6] A 1972 *New York Times* article might have been used as an obituary for the idea:

> The OEO pronounced a reluctant but blunt judgment of failure today on performance contracting—the use in public schools of private concerns, teaching machines and incentive payments in an effort to conquer slow-learning poor children.
>
> Thomas K. Glennan Jr., OEO Director of Research, commented: "There is great value . . . in learning which basket we should not be putting our eggs in. . . . Better to stop now, rather than wait until hopes and spending have become enormously inflated."[7]

As quickly as it had appeared, performance contracting in education disappeared as a serious educational policy alternative. But it was destined to return with enthusiastic fans who are willing and eager to suspend disbelief.

Same Old Tune, Same Old Criticism

The 1980s produced a bumper crop of failed ideas packaged and sold as a "revolution." Among the "revolutionary" ideas pursued with enthusiasm, first by President Ronald Reagan and then by President George Bush, was contracting out—in other words, performance contracting. There was, it seemed, almost nothing that the government did that the private sector could not do more cheaply and better according to the free-market ideologues at the helm of the federal bureaucracy. Before long, private contractors instead of civil servants were performing a wide range of governmental tasks.

The results of that "revolutionary" effort, however, were far from stellar. On December 2, 1992, a front-page *New York Times* article described the findings of a study prepared for Richard Darman, the outgoing Bush administration director of the Office of Management and Budget (OMB). The OMB study found that "after years of effort to transfer Government work to private companies, the White House acknowledged today that contractors were squandering vast sums."

The *Times* story described the report as one of

> the most incisive critiques ever published by the Government of a central tenet of the Reagan-Bush era: the idea that private companies can do the Federal Government's work better and for less money. . . . Although opponents have argued that many Government responsibilities are inherently unsuitable for

private enterprise, President Ronald Reagan and President Bush pushed hard to increase Government contracts to private companies.

The Government spent $210 billion in the 1992 fiscal year on contracts for goods and services, or roughly one-sixth of all Government spending. . . . The White House investigators said they were unsure just how much money was being wasted. . . . But they wrote that there was unsettling evidence that the problem was endemic across all the civilian agencies. In almost every instance where auditors have looked closely at contracts, they have found problems.[8]

A little more than a year after the OMB report was released, the *New York Times* reported that profiteers running private schools were looting federal coffers by taking educational grant money and enriching themselves instead of educating their students. The *Times* noted that

in the most dramatic cases in recent years, directors of for-profit trade schools and colleges have looted the budgets of these loosely regulated Federal student aid programs to buy themselves Mercedes-Benzes, travel the world, subsidize a drug habit, invest in religious causes or pay themselves million dollar salaries. The profiteers especially harm poor students who are enticed to . . . enroll at for-profit, fly-by-night trade schools using Federal loans, get no useful training, cannot find jobs and wind up defaulting on the loans, ruining their credit rating and their hopes of escaping poverty. And it is the taxpayer who foots the bill for those defaulted, federally guaranteed loans.[9]

Privatization schemes are inevitably advanced in a deregulatory public policy environment, at least in part promoted as cost-saving measures. But their proponents tend to omit the essential element for realizing cost savings from such schemes—rigorous oversight. That isn't as surprising as it sounds. Rigorous oversight is expensive. When the costs of oversight are added to the cost of a private contract, it is likely to mean that not only will there will be no net savings, there also may well be increased costs. That's why proponents of privatization prefer to speak loudly (if not clearly) about how private sector "expertise" will ensure quality and how "competition" will ensure efficiency and low cost without the need for "interference" from government regulators.

The Mythical Crisis

Given the blind enthusiasm of top government officials for private enterprise in the Reaganite political climate of the 1980s, it was only a matter of time before privatization in public education was once again a serious topic of discussion. There was also another important element pushing education toward privatization—what David Berliner describes as the myths about public education. He argues that myths "may . . . be misleading the majority of the citizenry and undermining the American people's confidence in one of their most cherished institutions."[10]

Berliner is on to something. For example, it now has become the conventional wisdom that a decline in the mean scores on the Scholastic Aptitude Test (SAT) since 1965 proves there has been a decline in American educational standards. However, Berliner notes the decline occurred between 1965 and 1975, and scores between 1975 and 1990 were quite stable. Further, the decline that alarmed so many people actually amounted to about five fewer items answered correctly on the SAT. As Berliner writes:

> Far from being ashamed of this loss, educators should celebrate it. Why? Because it is explainable by the fact that much greater numbers of students in the bottom 60 percent of their graduating classes have been taking the SAT since the 1960s. As educational opportunities and higher education became available to rural Americans and to members of traditionally underrepresented minorities, more of these students started taking the SAT. Since they were frequently from impoverished communities and from schools that offered a less rigorous academic curriculum and fewer advanced courses than wealthier schools, it is not surprising that they tended to score lower than advantaged, suburban, middle-class, white students. This is why the mean number of items correct is less than it was.[11]

Berliner thinks educators should be "filled with pride that we have played a major role in the achievement of two of America's most prized goals of the 1960s—a higher high school graduation rate, particularly for minority children, and increased access to higher education. We accomplished both goals with a loss of only a few correct answers on the SAT."[12]

Not only does the much lamented decline in the SAT tests evaporate when examined closely, but the folks who design the test, the College Entrance Exam Board, also specifically warn it is not designed nor can its results be used to draw the general conclusions public school critics repeatedly cite.[13] The SAT is taken by different kids every year, the kids who take the test do so voluntarily, and the test measures only individual performance at a specific point in time. Therefore, the test-makers say, it cannot be used to form conclusions about school performance over time. However, critics of school performance have never allowed such facts to cloud a good polemic.

Berliner also contests two other "myths"—that the public education system is a bloated bureaucracy and that Americans spend more on their schools than citizens in any other country and have little to show for it. With 14.5 employees for every administrator, Berliner notes, education is leaner than, for example, the transportation industry (9.3 to 1), the food products industry (8.4 to 1), the utilities industry (6.6 to 1), the construction industry (6.3 to 1), and the communications industry (4.7 to 1). Central office professionals plus principals, assistant principals, and supervisors in the public schools make up a mere 4.5 percent of the total employee population of the schools.[14]

Although Americans may pay more for *higher* education than any other nation, he says, they certainly do not spend more on K–12 education. In 1988 dollars, the United States ranked ninth among sixteen industrialized nations in per-pupil spending in grades K–12. To match the *average* percentage of per-capita income spent by the other industrial nations, the United States would have to spend $20 billion more per year than it does on K–12 education. Add to that the fact that no other industrial country distributes spending on K–12 education so unequally and it becomes clear the myth that the United States outspends and underperforms in K–12 education has no basis.[15] In Berliner's view, "We are among the most cost-efficient nations in the world, with an amazingly high level of productivity for the comparatively low level of investment that our society makes in K–12 education."[16]

Berliner's arguments about the cost of public education are bolstered by a 1995 Economic Policy Institute Report.[17] And his interpretation of school performance indicators is supported by a detailed analysis of education statistics undertaken by Sandia National Laboratories in 1991. The Sandia report's authors reviewed every commonly used measure of the performance of America's schools—including dropout rates, standardized test scores, educational funding, international comparisons, and future workforce requirements. They admitted they were surprised that, instead of finding disastrous declines in school performance, they found steady or slightly improving trends.[18]

Referring to the mismatch between the calls for radical education reform and the evidence used to support them, Clark Kerr, president emeritus of the University of California, comments: "Seldom in the course of policymaking in the U.S. have so many firm convictions held by so many been based on so little convincing proof."[19]

The Master Myth

Ideological zeal and a steady drumbeat of erroneous criticism helped prepare the ground for the most recent privatization initiatives. However, that may not have been enough to get them serious consideration without widespread acceptance of a master myth—the myth that money doesn't matter.

This myth is typically used to rationalize gross inequalities in the amount spent to educate children who happen to live in different school districts and to defeat attempts to increase educational spending. It has also helped produce the popular belief that the problems faced by poor (especially urban) school districts are not the result of a lack of funds but primarily the result of the schools' inability to use the available money effectively. Some people have grown fond of arguing that poor schools should not get any more money until they perform better. This is a little like a doctor telling a patient that no medication will be forthcoming until the patient's condition improves.

In large part, the data used to underpin the assertion that money doesn't matter come from a series of articles by Eric A. Hanushek, published between 1981 and 1991,[20] and from a book he coauthored in 1995, entitled *Making Schools Work.*[21] Hanushek claims his data show "there is no strong or systematic relationship between school expenditures and student performance.[22] However, University of Chicago researchers have reanalyzed those data, using more powerful statistical methods, and they conclude, "The question of whether more resources are needed to produce real improvement in our nation's schools can no longer be ignored. Relying on the data most often used to deny that resources are related to achievement, we find that money *does* matter after all."[23]

If public schools are not a disastrous failure, if money does indeed matter, and if privatization has a history of failure, then what can possibly account for privatization's continuing attractiveness to policymakers?

There are several possible explanations. Perhaps increasing numbers of the governing elite are now willing to write off large numbers of schoolchildren. Perhaps some people are willing to believe that it really is possible to get something for nothing and others merely think that education reform will be cheaper and easier if corporate America profits along the way. Perhaps white suburbanites don't want to invest more money in the education of poor, black children in cities. Perhaps some urban school administrators feel trapped by their circumstances and are willing to try anything championed by those who hold the real power in their communities.

Enter the Traveling Salesmen

Even with all these reasons, however, it is unlikely that privatization would have become one of the most widely discussed education reforms of the

1990s without the brilliant marketing efforts of Chris Whittle's Edison Project and John Golle's Education Alternatives, Inc. At the dawn of the 1990s, it was EAI and Edison that caught the public's attention with their well-publicized claims to be able to improve student achievement, keep costs down, introduce high-tech teaching reforms, transform public education—and turn a profit at the same time.

Initially, Chris Whittle didn't seek to run public schools. He just wanted access to classrooms to sell the products and services of his clients. The ideas of running schools themselves came later.

The story begins in eastern Tennessee in the late 1980s. In 1988, Whittle told the educators assembled at the Eastern Tennessee Education Association annual convention that "at least a fourth of the nation's advertising budget, as much as $100 billion annually, could be diverted into advertising in our classrooms." He predicted, "If educators send a signal to the business community that they will accept advertising sponsorship of teaching tools . . . American teachers will soon have the best equipped, most modern classrooms in the world."

In the most conveniently forgotten portion of that visionary speech predicting the commercial takeover of public education, Whittle acknowledged that "in an ideal world this should not happen." But, he added, "we don't live in an ideal world."[24]

As a native of Tennessee's McMinn County and a graduate of the University of Tennessee, Whittle was speaking to a hometown crowd about the ideas he was soon to put into practice in Channel One. Whittle's comments to the Tennessee teachers must have been persuasive. At the 1989 meeting of the National Education Association Representative Assembly, the Tennessee delegation tried to head off a resolution opposing Channel One because it would require students to watch commercials. A Channel One supporter in the Tennessee delegation, Linda Wilson, argued in reference to the equipment associated with the program, "We are fools if we don't take some of that money."[25]

The Tennessee delegation failed in its effort to derail the NEA resolution opposing Channel One. However, by fall 1990, Whittle had succeeded in inducing schools all over the country to sign up for his "news" program—commercials and all. Over and over again, school district administrators said the lure of "free" technology was the factor that most influenced their decision to support Channel One. Whittle showed how easy it was to convince many people to accept an explicit connection between school improvements (regardless of how dubious) and private profit as a legitimate educational policy option.

First Take Twelve Minutes, Then the Whole School

With Channel One still in development, Whittle came back before the Eastern Tennessee Education Association to talk about how a vision of a "new American school" had emerged from his efforts to create Channel One. Not surprisingly, technology was central to Whittle's vision. The *Tennessee Education Association News* reported: "Mr. Whittle envisions a high-tech school of the future where each student will have a computerized learning station, without textbooks or classrooms, and each teacher will have an office, 'just like real people—with phones.' . . . He said the 'new American school' should operate year-round and with longer hours for day-care services, should enroll children at a much younger age, and should reduce the pupil-teacher ratio to about a third of what it is now."

According to the *News*, Whittle also predicted: "The new system will not cost more than the current system." When asked to name people who might be able to bring such a vision to life, the first person Whittle mentioned was former Tennessee governor and president of the University of Tennessee Lamar Alexander.[26] That Alexander's name came so readily to Whittle's mind was only natural given the close personal association between the two men and Alexander's status as an investor in Whittle Communications.

On March 7, 1990, in comments at the Tennessee Business Roundtable education conference meeting, John Naisbitt, author of *Megatrends*, predicted a trend toward privatizing "health care, postal service—and yes, education." According to Naisbitt, "We have to introduce some kind of competition where we have teachers and schools competing to get kids. Those that can't attract students will go out of business."[27]

Lamar Alexander and Chris Whittle were also on hand to speak to conference attendees. Alexander called for "radical changes" and "brand-new elementary and secondary schools." Whittle claimed, "We don't need more cash. We need more creativity." It would, he said, take "'a modern-day Edison' and seed money from the federal government to redesign the American school. . . . [Whittle] estimated that it would take $1 billion and four years to develop a prototype suitable for replication in the 50 states."[28]

Within a year of his comments at the Tennessee Business Roundtable, Alexander had been sworn in as secretary of education—despite serious reservations expressed during his Senate confirmation hearing about, among other things, his financial involvement with Whittle Communications. As secretary of education, Alexander promoted a plan to establish "break-the-mold" schools in each congressional district in order to promote educational reform nationwide and help achieve the Bush administration's America 2000 agenda. He also proposed the creation of the New American Schools Development Corporation, which would be financed by large corporations and foundations to channel money to schools whose innovative proposals it deemed worthy. A major feature of Alexander's reform agenda was vigorous support for private school vouchers to transfer public funds to private educational ventures.

Within this friendly political environment, Whittle formed Whittle Schools and Laboratories as a private, for-profit company to serve as the corporate home for a research and development effort he called the Edison Project. Although the Edison Project initially featured a virtually identical cast of characters, it was legally separate from Channel One's corporate parent, Whittle Communications.

Whittle announced his plans to the world on May 15, 1991.[29] He envisioned a nationwide chain of innovative, for-profit schools built from the ground up and charging no more for tuition than the amount spent to educate children in public schools. The timetable he established was remarkably specific and grandiose: The Edison Project team would be recruited through the remainder of 1991, and it would create the blueprint for the new American school in 1992 and 1993. From 1994 to 1996, it would raise capital, develop the necessary technology, and construct schools for the first 200 campuses. In the fall of 1996, the first 200 schools would open, serving 150,000 students (probably ages 1 through 6). In 1997, it would begin adding one age unit per year and marketing the entire system and its technology. It would start opening additional campuses in 1998, achieving an enrollment of 2,000,000 by 2010, at which time the system would be copied nationwide, either in full or in part.[30]

The $60 million Whittle estimated would be necessary for the Edison Project team to create a blueprint for the "new American school" was to come from Whittle Communications earnings, existing partners, and new partners. The total of $2.5 to $3 billion required to create a new, nationwide school system was to come from new partners and banks.[31]

To some observers, the remarkable similarity between the agendas of Chris Whittle and Lamar Alexander was suspicious. Adding to the suspicions were reports that, while he was governor of Tennessee, Alexander was paid $125,000 in consulting fees by Whittle; that Alexander had purchased $10,000 worth of Whittle stock that he transferred to his wife when he became president of the University of Tennessee, which Whittle bought back for $330,000 a year later; and that Alexander, while president of the University of Tennessee, had served on the Channel One advisory board.[32] Whatever else might be said, there was little doubt that the Alexander-Whittle relationship was a public-private partnership that apparently benefited both parties.

In spring 1991, with George Bush riding high in the polls and Alexander securely ensconced as secretary of education, Whittle set about pitching his almost comically grandiose vision of the Edison Project to potential investors and recruiting a design team. Whittle claimed that just as Thomas Edison did not invent a better candle, he, Chris Whittle, was not going to invent a better school but something radically different and superior.

Whittle unveiled the Edison Project team to the public at a February 27, 1992, news conference. Design team members included conservative economist and school critic John Chubb (the voucher connection) and conservative education ideologue Chester Finn (proof of *serious* curricular intentions). Dominique Browning, former managing editor of *Newsweek*, who had no discernible educational credentials, also was named to the team. Browning characterized the gang this way: "Some people here know a lot about education; some people know a lot about technology; and some of us don't know anything about anything and we need to catch up."[33] But when someone is trying to sell himself publicly as the new Edison, knowing how to play the media doesn't qualify as not knowing anything about anything.

Whittle's biggest catch was Benno Schmidt, whose surprise resignation as president of Yale University on May 25, 1992, to join Edison as its CEO was front-page news in the *New York Times*.[34] As the *Wall Street Journal* explained, Schmidt lent the Edison project considerable credibility.[35] Nevertheless, Schmidt was not without baggage, as the lead-in to Richard Bernstein's June 14, 1992, *New York Times Magazine* story made plain: "It's been a tough year on campus. The University's top leaders have quit, the faculty has revolted and many of the hallowed halls are falling apart."[36] According to the story, Schmidt's accomplishments at Yale were, at best, arguable. Nevertheless, at least one famous Yale alum, former President Bush, was overjoyed not only about Schmidt's service to Yale but about his future with Edison as well: "'Benno,' said the crackly voice, speaking through the static from Air Force One, 'I just want you to know that I think what you're doing is truly wonderful. We desperately need innovation in this country. We're very proud of what you have done at Yale, but this is more fundamental.'"[37]

Schmidt reportedly left Yale behind for a salary between $800,000 to $1,000,000, plus equity in the company.[38] He opined in a *Vanity Fair* article, "Education in this country needs radical revolution, not reform in the usual way."[39] If the reports of his salary were accurate, Schmidt was perhaps the highest-paid "revolutionary" in world history.

High-pressure lobbying by political and education insiders is a standard feature when the Edison Project comes to town. In Texas, for example, Edison hired former Texas education commissioner William Kirby to twist arms for the project.[40] However, no local insider could match the clout of Edison's president, Benno Schmidt.

Basking in the warm glow that having friends in high places can produce, Whittle played his Schmidt card for maximum advantage during autumn 1992. Articles about the project and its leaders sprouted like mushrooms on a moist forest floor. *Vanity Fair*'s August 1992 issue featured an article entitled "Chris and Benno's Excellent Adventure."[41] In its September 17, 1992, "Tempo" section, the *Chicago Tribune* featured a story about Whittle ("Preppy Pitchman") that asserted, "If anyone can sell an education revolution, it's Chris Whittle."[42] The September 18–20, 1992, issue of *USA Weekend* featured Whittle on its cover and headlined a story about him and the Edison Project with "Will He Save Our Schools?"[43] Everything Chris Whittle touched, if you believed the media hype, turned to gold. Then George Bush was defeated.

Although Whittle repeatedly denied that the Edison Project would have to rely on government-funded vouchers to be financially viable, it had been apparent to many observers that the project could only succeed if Lamar Alexander's advocacy of private school vouchers succeeded. With Alexander out as secretary of education, their skepticism was quickly borne out.

In a *New Republic* essay, "Dim Bulb," Sara Mosle examined the economics of the Edison Project and concluded: "The problem with Whittle's schools isn't that they will succeed, but that they can't—at least not as he has described them.[44] . . . Whittle's own team can't say how he will do it. . . . Asked how the schools can possibly succeed, design-team members are reduced to reciting vague articles of faith. Peters implores: 'You'll have to trust us.' Chubb proposes, 'Wait and see.' And Browning suggests that observers adopt a 'willing suspension of disbelief.'"[45]

Suspending disbelief would have required real faith and determination on the part of potential investors, especially once they became familiar with the growing costs associated with the scheme. In 1989, Whittle estimated it would be necessary to come up with $1 billion for a prototype system. By 1991, he was seeking between $2.5 and $3 billion to establish a nationwide system of 200 schools by 1996. Most investors who came to Whittle's revival meeting and peeked into the tent were not converted. Apparently, they agreed with Hudson Institute research fellow Denis P. Doyle's observation that "the likelihood of [turning a profit] is about zero."[46]

Dark Days for Edison

When the bad news started to come, it came quickly and relentlessly. On May 5, 1993, the *Wall Street Journal* reported that Whittle was reducing the amount of money he was seeking from private investors from $2.5 billion to $750 million. The article also noted that although Whittle had promised to spend $60 million researching his ideal school system, he had thus far spent only $20 million.[47]

On July 30, 1993, the *New York Times* reported that Time Warner (owner of 37.5 percent of Whittle Communications) had expressed a willingness to sell its stake in Whittle Communications "along with other assets that are not producing income." The *Times* story also quoted venture capitalist Alan Patricof, who explained Edison's problems raising money this way: "No one company can put up enough money [for Edison]. It will have years of losses and no corporation wants to absorb those kinds of losses through their income statement."[48]

An August 2, 1993, *Wall Street Journal* article revealed that Whittle had failed to raise the $750 million he sought. The story went on to say that Time Warner, which had earlier contributed to Edison, had refused to put up any more money. The article also cited "people familiar with the situation" who said that only $170 million of the $750 million Whittle had sought was to be earmarked for Edison (not the entire $750 originally reported). The remaining $580 million was apparently to have been used to buy out Time Warner's stake in Whittle Communications.[49]

On August 3, 1993, the *Wall Street Journal* reported that Associated Newspaper Holdings (a British conglomerate that publishes tabloid newspapers and owned almost 25 percent of Whittle Communications) and Phillips Electronics NV (a multinational Dutch electronics firm that owned another 25 percent) would provide $40 million to keep Edison afloat as a school-development project. The report said, however, that it was unclear whether this was a new commitment of money.[50]

An August 8, 1993, *Wall Street Journal* story explained that although Phillips Electronics and Associated Newspaper Holdings would provide the money they had promised, there would be no more when that was gone.[51] Thus, apart from money out of his own pocket and the initial funds pledged by his partners, Whittle was unable, after two years of intense effort, to attract support from a single additional investor.[52]

According to the *U.S. News and World Report*, the money Edison had on hand would last only through 1994, after which it would be necessary to raise at least another $120 million.[53] Edison officials were still talking big—they planned to run one hundred public schools by the fall of 1995 and open twenty private schools in the fall of 1996.[54] However, with numerous accounts of financial difficulties at Whittle Communications (including a *Wall Street Journal* report that the partnership had lost $20 million for the year ending June 30, 1993), it was not clear where Edison could go to find the additional money it needed.[55] It was clear, however, that despite brave talk by Whittle and Schmidt, the Edison bulb was dimming.

The amounts of money associated with the Edison Project changed and changed again after Whittle first floated the idea. So did the descriptions of the scope and purpose of the project. Since Whittle held information about the financial health of Whittle Communications close to his vest and revealed only the information that suited his purpose or that, for whatever reason, got out, it was almost impossible to measure his claims against his ability to deliver.

One thing was sure, though: There continued to be enough troubling signs that all was not well with the Edison Project or Whittle Communications to make most investors wary. Perhaps because of the cash squeeze, Whittle Communications was twice caught broadcasting two and one-half minutes of commercials on Channel One in early 1993, instead of the two minutes allowed by its contract.[56] As the problems became more difficult to conceal, the *Wall Street Journal* reminded readers that "despite years of introducing much-publicized media products, Whittle has never met its founder's grand projections."[57]

Within a year of Lamar Alexander's departure from Washington in January 1993, the Edison Project's grandiose plan to build a nationwide chain of schools by 1996 had completely collapsed. In the words of an August 16, 1993, *Newsweek* story, "Mr. Vision" had met "Mr. Reality."[58]

Down but not out, Schmidt and Whittle charted a new course for the Edison Project. A friendly editorial in the *New York Times* confirmed that Whittle's success at casting himself as a serious educational reformer was standing him in good stead in his hour of need. The *Times* editorial board reasoned that the Edison Project's failure to attract investors "doesn't condemn the concept of for-profit schools. It just confirms that education reform is a lot harder than it looks. . . . [The Edison Project is] expected to take advantage of the growing trend toward public-private partnerships in education and manage a select number of failing public schools."[59] Perhaps exhausted by their labors, the *Times* editors did not explain why the creators of a losing proposition like the Edison Project should be trusted with the management of a school. Nor was there any mention of where profits were to be found in failing schools.

Benno Schmidt lost no time in putting a positive spin on Edison's failure to interest outside investors. The August 16, 1993, issue of *Newsweek* reported that he wondered "why reporters 'use the words "scaled back"' [to refer to the Edison Project]." According to the *Newsweek* story, "The way Schmidt tells it, Edison was overwhelmed by educators calling for help and is only responding to what 'the market is telling us.'"[60] It was not clear which market Schmidt was referring to in his remark. In the next two and a half years, neither the financial nor the education market responded with enthusiasm, overwhelming or otherwise, to the news that Edison was now going to devote itself to running public schools.

Following Schmidt's curious declaration of overwhelming support from somewhere, Whittle Communications (which had been Chris Whittle's source of cash) and the Edison Project (which had yet to earn a penny) lurched from one crisis to the next, brought on by mismanagement, investor skepticism, and resistance to the basic concept of letting a for-profit firm run public schools.

Whittle succeeded in concealing the details of his financial troubles for a while because Whittle Communications and Edison were both closely held corporations and therefore not subject to the same financial disclosure requirements that govern publicly traded companies. However, some unpleasant facts could not be suppressed. *Wall Street Journal* headlines chronicled the bad news: "Whittle Plans to Largely End Print Business";[61] "Whittle Is Facing Big Battle to Retain Drug Advertisers for Medical Network";[62] "Some Big Advertisers Fail to Show for Whittle's Classroom News";[63] "Whittle Prepares to Close Network for Doctors' Offices";[64] "Whittle to Shut Its Book Unit for Lack of Ads."[65]

According to the Associated Press, Whittle had laid off 250 workers and "restructured" three core businesses between 1992 and 1994: Channel One, the Medical News Network, and the Edison Project.[66] The problem for Whittle was that the Medical News Network and the Edison Project were costing money, not generating revenue. Indeed, shortly after the announcement of Whittle's restructuring, the Medical News Network was shut down. Meanwhile, investors continued to spurn the Edison Project. Among the companies reported to have turned down the Edison pitch were Paramount Communications, Viacom International, Walt Disney, Cox Newspapers, and Tele-Communications, Inc.[67]

After three years of trying, Whittle had been able to convince only two of his partners in Whittle Communications—Associated Newspaper Holdings and Phillips Electronics—to throw in any money, and they now made it clear that no more money would be forthcoming.

By 1994, the days of rapid growth for Whittle's single profit-making venture, Channel One, were over. Channel One was adding few schools to those already under contract, and a number of advertisers were reconsidering their commitment to a project whose advertising rates they considered too steep.

By February 1994, things had gotten bad enough at Whittle Communications that Phillips Electronics forced the company to install a new CEO, Don Johnstone, in an effort to bring some management discipline to the troubled firm. Johnstone claimed to have cut $40 million in costs after two months on the job.[68] However, even his efforts were unable to salvage a company that was hemorrhaging money on ill-considered projects, bloated salaries, and mismanagement.

In spring 1994, it appeared that unless Channel One were allowed into the New York market, even the viability of Whittle Communications itself might be at risk. Channel One had been banned from New York by action of the New York State Board of Regents in February 1990. The regents reaffirmed their ban in June 1993. By May 1994, Whittle was engaged in a furious and ultimately unsuccessful lobbying battle to try and overcome the ban legislatively.

By July 1994, financial collapse seemed at hand. "Whittle's Bridges Falling Down," blared the headline of a July 18, 1994, *Advertising Age* story. It began: "Triggered by the default last month on $100 million bridge loan, Christopher Whittle's media empire is headed for imminent break up. . . . 'He's cashing out. He's selling half the cow,' one knowledgeable Wall Street source said. 'This raises the issue: How credible can he be in the future? A year ago he was trying to raise half a billion for the Edison Project and failed.'"[69] Chris and Benno's "excellent adventure" wasn't looking like much fun anymore.

On August 10, 1994, the *New York Times* confirmed the sale of Channel One to K-III Communications, a media conglomerate controlled by the leveraged buyout firm of Kohlberg Kravis Roberts.[70] Because Channel One had been the moneymaker for Whittle Communications, the sale left the company with only a handful of assets to be sold off piecemeal, including a distribution system for sampler products on college campuses and a women's basketball team.

The deal also left Chris Whittle with a few ill-defined responsibilities at K-III and not much else to do except devote himself to the Edison Project. Time Warner CEO Reginald K. Brack Jr. also would have time to devote to other pursuits. Brack, who had engineered Time Warner's $185 million investment in Whittle Communications, had to write off the entire amount as a loss. Shortly afterward, he lost his job.[71]

If things had been bad at Whittle Communications, they weren't much better at Edison. Company officials, apparently trying to avoid the taint of Chris Whittle's financial woes and his reputation as a rotten manager, were rumored to be trying to push him out. They began to describe him as having a "minority" ownership position, with little or no say in the day-to-day management of the company.[72]

However, even as writers for three major national magazines were describing his rise and fall in excruciating detail ("Grand Illusion," *New Yorker*, October 1994;[73] "The Whittle of Oz," *Vanity Fair*, November 1994;[74] and "An Acerbic Encounter with Chris Whittle," *GQ*, December 1994[75]), Whittle remained characteristically upbeat. He told the *Boston Globe* that the idea of the Edison Project being scaled back was a "misperception in the media." He said that although running 100 schools in 1996 was the original plan (it's impossible to know which "original" plan Whittle was referring to), "in truth, we're opening a year early. We'll have 15 to 20 sites in the fall of 1995. We're opening fewer sites but earlier." He went on to claim that the company had "letters of intent" from 24 school districts.[76]

Although Whittle was putting on a brave face for the *Boston Globe*, Edison management was still struggling to find financing. Having nearly exhausted the $40 to $60 million seed money from Whittle Communications partners Time Warner, Associated Newspaper Holdings, Phillips Electronics, and Whittle himself on extravagant salaries, marketing, and "development," Edison faced the prospect of not having enough funds to open a single school unless it could find additional financial backing.

By this point, Edison management was saying it needed another $25 to $50 million by the end of 1994 if it were to open any schools at all. And even some early supporters were turning hostile. As William Raspberry, a columnist for the *Washington Post* who had earlier written kindly about the Edison Project, put it: "Unless I'm missing something, J. Walter Thompson Whittle is promoting, and Willy Loman Whittle promising delivery of a product that Thomas Edison Whittle hasn't gotten around to inventing yet."[77] Meanwhile, Whittle kept a stiff upper lip, telling the *Christian Science Monitor* on December 28, 1994, "As we speak, we are putting the finishing touches on the financing, which we call the launch financing, which actually is the money that opens the schools."[78]

When the Edison Project finally announced it had found additional funding in February 1995, that funding turned out to be pretty small potatoes. It was enough to open the doors of a few schools—but just barely. The package totaled $30 million over a three-year period, with $12 million coming from the Sprout Group (a venture capital group owned by Lufkin & Jenrette Securities), $3 million from a group of investors led by Edison president Benno Schmidt, and $15 million from Whittle himself.[79] The new Edison Project board was headed jointly by Whittle and the Sprout Group.

The Edison Project, launched with the proclamation that it was going to raise $2.5 billion to start a nationwide chain of private schools, had, after almost four years of trying, been able to find exactly one outside investor to put in a total $12 million over a three-year period. The new plan was to run a total of four schools (in Boston, Massachusetts; Mount Clemens, Michigan; Wichita, Kansas; and Sherman, Texas) in the fall of 1995. Perhaps more embarrassing than the small number of schools was the fact that, far from offering a "revolutionary" high-tech educational program with innovative software and hardware galore to market to eager schools throughout the nation, Whittle's schools fell back on a grab bag of "best practices" that had been available in public schools for some time.

By the time Edison had found enough cash to open a handful of schools, Whittle had lost his communications empire. And in a development heavy with irony, given the rhetoric of privatization, even his former headquarters building in Knoxville, Tennessee, had been sold—to the federal government. The building, a neocolonial edifice he spent $55 million constructing in 1991, was purchased by the U.S. General Services Administration. The selling price was $20.4 million, out of which Whittle had to pay the city of Knoxville $7.1 million to pay off bonds issued by the city to help finance the building originally.[80] This was hardly an illustration of the kind of performance that was likely to save many schools.

The Edison Project's financial difficulties should be a cause for alarm among policymakers and those responsible for administering public school funds. The complications caused by joining a public school district with a private firm whose source of revenue is tax money but whose internal financial operations are concealed behind a "proprietary" curtain is an invitation to abuse. Since Edison, unlike a public school district, is not financially transparent, it is virtually impossible to uncover conflicts of interest, to assess the financial health of the company and its ability to discharge its obligations, or even to make sense of its claims of profit or loss in a particular district.

While Edison was being buffeted by the financial markets, it was not faring much better in many communities where the firm made its pitch. Once again, the headlines told the story: "Firms Face a Hard Sell in Seeking to Run Schools for MPS," *Milwaukee Journal*, August 11, 1993;[81] "'Edisonscam:' Exposing the Edison Project," *Milwaukee Courier*, May 21, 1994;[82] "Edison Project Draws Criticism," *Lubbock (Tex.) Avalanche-Journal*, August 25, 1994;[83] "Free-Market School Plan Hits Brick Wall; State Districts Get

Too Little Money for Edison," *Denver Post*, November 6, 1994;[84] "No Agreement Near Between Edison, AISD," *Austin American-Statesman*, November 11, 1994;[85] "Future Bleak for Project; Company's Cost Too High, Worthington School District Says," *Columbus (Ohio) Dispatch*, November, 29, 1994;[86] "Battle Lines Drawn on Edison Project," *Sherman* (Tex.) *Democrat*, February 24, 1995.[87]

Of the four schools Edison eventually began running in the fall of 1995, only one, Renaissance Charter School in Boston, showed any real promise of making money for the company—and then only because of some very sweet deals cut by Massachusetts governor William Weld. Weld, running for the U.S. Senate in 1996,[88] built a national reputation as an education reformer. He is an aggressive advocate of privatization and loves charter schools. In Boston, the two concepts came together in the Renaissance Charter School. When it opened in 1995, Renaissance was the largest charter school in the country—and one of the relatively few whose educational program would be run by a for-profit firm.

In large measure, the school was made possible because Weld arranged a $12 million state loan to renovate the former University of Massachusetts building it occupies and a lease deal that gave the facility to Edison at an estimated $1.5 million below the property's market value. This is not to mention the money taken from the Boston Public Schools for each child who attends Renaissance. By one estimate, the school will be the beneficiary of $52.4 million over the five-year term of its charter school contract.[89]

There's no question that Renaissance was a heck of a deal for Edison, but it's hardly an example of the free market at work. It's a good, old-fashioned government subsidy and therefore not much of a model for how the performance of public schools can be improved and their costs reduced by having them run by private firms. In fact, quite the opposite seems true, according to an examination of Renaissance in late 1995 by the *Boston Globe*, which found a number of educational shortcomings despite the school receiving about $1,000 more per pupil in tax funds than the average Boston public school. Although the student population was 52 percent black and 18 percent Hispanic, the teaching staff included only 2 black instructors. Only 1 special needs teacher had been budgeted to serve the estimated 10 percent of the 630 students who required special education. "These people don't know Boston and some of them don't know our kids," said a black attorney on the school's parent advisory council.

Students had yet to receive the much-touted laptop computers, and teachers failed to perceive much that was innovative or fresh and exciting about the highly structured Edison educational program. "The curriculum is good and demanding, but there's not a lot of room for creativity," said a first-grade teacher. "It seems like it's always reading time, math time, always a time."[90]

EAI—Founded on Fantasy

Before Edison's flashy entry into the for-profit school management sweepstakes, public attention had been dominated by Education Alternatives, Inc., based in Bloomington, Minnesota. EAI was launched in 1986 by John Golle, a former salesman for Xerox. Golle bought a unit of Control Data Corporation as part of his attempt to establish a network of computer-intensive private schools using a copyrighted program called Tesseract (named after a fantasy world in the children's book *A Wrinkle in Time*).[91]

Golle set up two private schools (in Eagan, Minnesota, in 1987 and Paradise Valley, Arizona, in 1988) before abandoning the idea of a chain of private schools in order to develop EAI. The idea behind EAI was to offer Golle's Tesseract program and an assortment of management services to public schools. EAI first drew national attention when it signed a five-year contract to run South Pointe Elementary School in Dade County, Florida, in June 1990. The signing of the South Pointe contract raised interest in the company among school districts around the country. That interest, in turn, helped the company generate almost $6 million on the stock market when Golle took EAI public in April 1991.[92]

Two months later, EAI signed a five-year contract worth $250,000 to implement its Tesseract program in two elementary schools in the Salt Lake City area. Although the schools were apparently satisfied with Tesseract, the district found the program too expensive, and the contract was canceled after a year and a half.[93] In March 1992, EAI landed a four-month contract with the Duluth, Minnesota, school board to act as superintendent. After a brief and unhappy relationship, the company's contract was not renewed.

EAI (and privatization of public schools) was thrust into the national educational debate when the company landed a five-year contract to run nine Baltimore public schools in July 1992. Until EAI signed the Baltimore contract, it had piled up $8.8 million in losses, surviving on its ability to convince investors that big profits were just around the corner.[94] The Baltimore contract made it seem as if the promised land was on the horizon—at least for a moment.

Wasting no time to declare EAI a success (and demonstrate the political significance of privatization), then-Secretary of Education Lamar Alexander promptly turned up at one of the schools, Harlem Middle School, in autumn 1992 to present EAI with a "Breaking-the-Mold" award and declare himself pleased at "the wonderful changes that have been made in Baltimore."[95]

Alexander wasn't EAI's only important political supporter. The governor of Maryland (and former mayor of Baltimore) William Schaefer; Robert Embry, president of the Maryland Board of Education, past president of the Baltimore Board of School Commissioners, and head of the influential Abell Foundation; Baltimore mayor Kurt L. Schmoke, a close supporter of President Clinton; and Walter Amprey, the new superintendent of the Baltimore public schools, all helped ease the company's entry into the Baltimore market.[96]

EAI's support and political clout did not end at the state borders. In the very first issue of *The Education Investor* in August 1993, editor John McLaughlin declared EAI a "trailblazing success story."[97] John Walton (of the Wal-Mart Waltons), a major EAI shareholder, helped arrange for Hillary Rodham Clinton to visit an EAI school, with suitable photo opportunities, in April 1994.[98]

It might seem odd at first that a for-profit company would try to build its fortune running schools attended by some of the most impoverished children in the country. However, a closer look suggests the logic that lies behind EAI's contract to run innercity schools. Privatization is rarely discussed in affluent communities. It only seems to come up for debate in poorer districts, where an effective conservative policy and media apparatus have equated "public" with "bad," where the most basic requirements of physical plant maintenance have frequently been ignored, and where a lack of high-achieving students is considered evidence of professional incompetence. Faced with such tremendous problems and so little support, it is understandable that some urban school superintendents would be attracted to take what Washington, D.C., superintendent Franklin Smith has called "the outside option."[99]

The successful dissemination of the ideas that the problems of urban schools are intractable and that spending more money won't make any difference has led many to accept that there is nothing to lose by "shaking things up" and trying privatization. Unfortunately, a careful assessment of EAI's performance between 1992 and 1995 suggests that privatization did, if anything, make matters worse.

Anyone who has spent time studying public education realizes that reform is a long-term process that requires sustained effort and commitment. Most scholars of public education would probably agree with the point made in a March 1994 *Education Investor* commentary: "Anyone who thinks private sector involvement is a quick fix to chronic problems in American education is wrong. Whether from the perspective of a school superintendent, a board member, the leader of an education company, or a member of the media, touting private management or privately provided services as a cure-all is foolish and unrealistic."[100]

It is clearly important to assess whether firms such as EAI and Edison, the largest and best financed of the for-profit companies offering to manage schools, have the resources and the commitment to support a sustained effort to reform the schools they manage. Judging from their record, the prospects for privatization improving the quality of education in the United States are not good.

Privatization Works Its Wonders

Consider EAI's first major venture—its five-year, $1.2 million contract to implement the Tesseract program at South Pointe Elementary School in Dade County, Florida. Amid backstage rumbling that EAI was not reducing class size as promised and questions about the company's handling of money raised privately, the school district refused to relinquish management of the school. As Superintendent Octavio Visiedo put it, "I have plenty of competent administrators and excellent teachers."[101]

By most accounts, EAI's South Pointe was a good school. However, for a number of reasons, South Pointe was never a good vantage from which to view EAI's prospects. The school was built to order for the Tesseract program; EAI was given a number of waivers concerning labor and purchasing regulations, among other things—and EAI did not manage the school. EAI also pledged to raise $2.42 million from private sources to supplement the money that the district paid.[102] Whatever else it may be, this was no "better results for the same money" proposition. And despite all of the media and corporate hype, Dade County officials steadfastly rejected repeated EAI offers to expand its role in the district.

Anyone interested in EAI's long-term prospects should have noticed that, as of January 1994, the company had raised just half of the $2.4 million it had promised Dade County in 1990.[103] In May 1995, when Dade officials announced that EAI's contract would not be renewed, the company was still $1 million short of its pledge. It also should be noted that after EAI had run the Tesseract program for five years under conditions designed to its specifications, test scores at South Pointe Elementary School were no better than at a comparable school in the district.[104]

The financial record of EAI is, charitably speaking, mixed. EAI made its first public stock offering in 1991 and raised $5.7 million. A second offering in 1992 brought in an additional $1.9 million. And a third offering in 1993 raised $31.2 million.[105] EAI stock offered at about $4 in 1991 was sold at the 1993 offering for $22.50. This was quite a respectable performance—on the surface. Actually, however, EAI's profits were not nearly as good as its stock price seemed to suggest. The company lost approximately $8.8 million from its founding through the end of the 1992 fiscal year. It was EAI's five-year, $135 million contract to run eight elementary schools and one middle school in Baltimore in June of that year, along with generally celebratory press coverage and the support of some enthusiastic stock analysts, that drove EAI's share price up. EAI did manage to earn its first profit in fiscal year 1993, but the company's principal sources of income were revenues from the stock offerings and interest earned on that money.[106]

After being awarded the Baltimore contract, EAI's stock value fluctuated considerably in response to news of success or failure in obtaining additional contracts. It reached a high of 48 3/4 in November 1993, before turning sharply downward after prospects for expanding in Baltimore or signing up new school districts dimmed. According to a February 28, 1994, *Business Week* story:

> You would think that after plunging from 48 to 26 in just three months the stock of Education Alternatives . . . , would be able to shake off the bears. Not quite. The shorts believe the stock will fall some more. . . . Howard M. Schilit, an accounting professor at American University and author of the recent book, *Financial Shenanigans: How to Detect Accounting Gimmicks and Fraud in Financial Reports*, [says] "I won't be surprised if auditors find the company has been recording revenues inappropriately." . . . Stan Trilling of Paine Webber says the company's rich p-e "is a myth, because it had an operating loss in the first six months of this fiscal year."[107]

Apparently, at least two EAI stockholders agreed. They filed a lawsuit in January 1994 and contended that "EAI has issued statements and used accounting methods that paint an overly positive picture of its current and future financial position. . . . The suit claims that stock prices were pushed to artificially high levels by the accounting methods that exaggerated the company's size and by Mr. Golle's [Chair and CEO of EAI] predictions of company growth that had 'no reasonable basis.'"[108]

EAI management dismissed the complaints about the company's accounting practices and the investor lawsuit as so much ill-founded carping. A *Washington Post* story, "Dick and Jane Sell Short," even raised the possibility that the greed of "short sellers" (stock market speculators who, in effect, bet that a stock's price will fall) were planting negative rumors about EAI to enrich themselves. The article concluded: "While state-sponsored education may have its problems, one of them is not a group of speculators who stand to make a profit if the program is a flop."[109]

Although the suit was subsequently dropped,[110] both Golle and former St. Paul, Minnesota, superintendent of schools David Bennett, who was president of EAI from April 1991 until his resignation in July 1995, had contributed to the suspicion that EAI was an overhyped proposition, a bubble that was ready to burst.

In autumn 1993 when EAI stock was riding high, they each exercised stock options that brought them huge profits. Bennett realized a profit of $460,000 by exercising options on 14,860 shares of common stock for $5.69 each and selling them for between $36.50 and $36.75 each on September 23, 1993. Bennett's sale of stock represented his entire interest in EAI at the time.[111] Golle reaped a profit of $1,758,500 when he exercised options for 50,000 shares of common stock at $3.08 each and sold them for $38.25 each between September 29, 1993, and October 8, 1993. When Golle completed his sale, he still retained 377,102 shares of common stock.[112]

Anyone with knowledge of the record of educational performance contracting during the Nixon administration would have predicted that, before long, EAI officers would be suspected of fraud and abuse, that the EAI program would cost more than the company said it would, and that the performance of the schools EAI managed would not improve and might get worse. That is exactly what happened.

In 1994, the company had to repay Baltimore $338,500 it had received as a result of using inflated enrollment figures for the schools it managed after the city challenged both the competence and the integrity of EAI's management. According to the *Baltimore Sun*:

> Hours before the meeting Tuesday [January 25, 1994] at a U.S. Senate subcommittee hearing on school privatization, Mr. Golle angrily responded to a question from Sen. Arlen Specter (R-Penn.) about press accounts that EAI owed the city money.
>
> "It's just not true," Mr. Golle said. "It is a contrived story that is without merit, and we resent it."
>
> Soon after Mr. Golle spoke, [Baltimore superintendent] Dr. Amprey and other school system officials said EAI indeed owed $338,500 based on overstated enrollment figures.[113]

Aside from questions of impropriety in its accounting methods, EAI was vulnerable to charges that it did not represent a cost-efficient alternative to the Baltimore Public Schools. Judson Porter, director of finance and procurement for the Baltimore schools, reported that in the first year of the contract, the district paid EAI $23.3 million (after deducting overhead costs) but that it would have cost the district only $20.6 million to run the nine EAI schools itself.[114]

The additional $2.7 million spent on the EAI schools could only have come from three places: Either the taxpayers paid more, the Baltimore school administration provided less money for other students in the system, or an outside source of funds was found. If EAI schools cost more money, many asked, why not eliminate EAI and its profits and invest all public money directly into the schools?

Just as troubling as the extra cost of EAI schools was the company's failure to deliver on one of its most basic educational premises—that less money should be spent on support activities and more money should be spent on classroom instruction. Instead, during its first year in Baltimore (1992–1993), the company actually diverted money away from classroom instruction to support services. EAI spent $750,000 on lawyers, travel, and consultants and took $2 million home to Bloomington for "overhead."[115] Once again, the personal behavior of John Golle only served to heighten hostility over the company's failure to live up to its promises. Many found the entrepreneur's construction of two new houses in exclusive neighborhoods in Minnesota and Arizona and his stable of nine cars offensive since the money to support his lifestyle came from running nine schools attended by some of the most desperately poor children in the United States.[116]

Not concerned with the morality of the matter, the business press complained that his clothes, jewelry, and car were "'flashy' to the point of hindering his sales efforts."[117] Some described the situation as a "culture clash" between the values of the private sector and the values of public education. This charge was true enough. By education standards, Golle might be "flashy," but he was hardly out of line in the free-spending culture imported from corporate America. The Edison Project's Benno Schmidt was reported to be hauling in somewhere around $1 million a year, and a collection of Edison vice presidents were drawing annual salaries rumored to be in the $300,000 range.

And despite the rhetoric about the schools they ran remaining public schools, Edison and EAI executives bragged about no longer having their salaries subject to public scrutiny. As Edison senior vice president Deborah McGriff (former superintendent of the Detroit public schools) put it: "I won't tell you what [my salary] is now, because I'm not a public employee and I don't have to."[118] Edison's Manuel Rivera (former superintendent of the Rochester, New York, public schools) stated: "This is the nice thing about working for a private company. . . . You don't have to disclose every-thing."[119] Or as EAI's Phillip Geiger (former superintendent of the Piscat-away, New Jersey, public schools) said: "Let's put it this way. . . . It's not more than I'm worth, but it approaches it."[120]

Corporate education merely reflected the self-enriching practices that were common among top managers in other U.S. corporations. By 1991, Ameri-can CEOs were pulling in 50 to 100 times the pay of the average worker (compared to Japanese CEOs, who earned only 16 times as much as the av-erage worker).[121] CEOs such as IBM's Louis V. Gerstner Jr. who had harsh words for the cost of the public education system didn't seem to mind acting like regal potentates in their own little corners of the world. Gerstner, in the midst of a massive round of layoffs at IBM, hired a personal chef for $87,000 and a $30,000 signing bonus.[122] To many, the lifestyle and income of John Golle suggested that bringing the expertise of the private sector to public ed-ucation meant enriching a few top executives while failing to deliver the promised results either for poor children or for taxpayers.

The twists and turns in EAI's fortunes could be read in Baltimore's news-paper headlines. For the first year, they were generally rosy: May 17, 1991—"Contract Plan for City Schools Given Support";[123] June 10, 1991—"Minn. Firm to Run Nine City Public Schools";[124] June 11, 1992—"Schools Plan Greeted with Optimism";[125] June 17, 1993—"Amprey Wants to Widen Firm's Role in Schools."[126] At the end of EAI's first year, the *Baltimore Sun* editorialized:

> Tesseract has come through its first academic year with generally positive marks. Schools are cleaner, computers costing millions of dollars are in place and, most important there are signs—only signs—that the grades of the 4,800 Tesseract students are on the upturn. . . .
>
> We want this experiment to succeed. So do city officials. So does EAI. If Dr. Amprey decides to expand the program this summer, hard questions first must be asked—and answered. A thorough evaluation of Tesseract is essential. The signals, though, are positive, and we remain optimistic about this exciting but high stakes endeavor.[127]

During the 1993–1994 school year, the headlines turned somewhat gloomier for EAI: December 4, 1993—"Probe of EAI Sought; Enrollment Figures Might Be Inflated, Councilman Says";[128] March 4, 1994—"Give All Schools As Much Funding As Those EAI Runs, [Baltimore city council pres-ident] Clarke Urges";[129] March 31, 1994—"Teachers Union Asks for Federal EAI Investigation";[130] May 5, 1994—"Amprey Says He Wants EAI to Run All Schools."[131]

By the end of its first two years in Baltimore, EAI had turned a warm endorsement by the teachers' union into open hostility. The company faced charges of mismanagement, overcharging, and failing to deliver on its promises, and it had stirred a rebellion inside the Baltimore school administration, forcing the superintendent to defend the company against charges leveled by his own staff.[132]

EAI and Baltimore superintendent Walter Amprey continued to claim that the project was a success story. They asserted that allegations by its critics were either ill informed, based on misunderstandings, or the result of special interest (read teachers' union) hostility to the idea of privatization.

Trouble in the Classroom

The American Federation of Teachers local had indeed turned from an enthusiastic supporter of bringing EAI to Baltimore into a harsh critic of the company's performance. In 1994, both the Maryland State Teachers Association, an affiliate of the National Education Association (which, unlike the AFT, opposed private management of public schools), and the American Federation of Teachers issued reports documenting the company's shortcomings.

Observations in three EAI Tesseract schools in Baltimore in January 1994 by Olivia Reusing raised questions about the actual educational program being delivered. Reusing, whose research was commissioned by the Maryland State Teachers Association, found

> no methodology to distinguish the teaching in Tesseract schools from the unflattering portraits of typical classroom routine described so well by Goodlad (1984) and Sizer (1984) in which teacher talk predominates and students take a passive and receptive rather than an active and expressive role. I did not see any teacher or intern acting as a guide for students who were actively directing their own learning or engaged in problem-solving. On the other hand, teaching practices and the school environment at Sam Coleridge Elementary School [a non-EAI Baltimore public school] more closely reflected Tesseract goals than the privatized schools themselves.[133]

Reusing's research was followed in May 1994 by an AFT research report that, among other things, undermined the company's claim that Tesseract schools featured smaller classes. EAI had promised to reduce class sizes in the schools it ran. However, it was always a little unclear just what the company meant by "reduced class size." At times, EAI spoke about increasing the number of adults in the classroom. Research on the benefits of reducing class size, however, makes the assumption that "pupil-teacher ratio" refers to the number of students per teacher, not per adult. By confusing the meaning of reducing class size, EAI claimed it had achieved its goal by replacing experienced teacher aides earning about $12 an hour and benefits with college-graduate "interns" (without teaching certification) earning about $7 an hour and no benefits. It was unclear how children's learning was to be enhanced by this plan. The AFT report attacked EAI on this point, arguing: "Seasoned paraprofessionals, who come from school neighborhoods . . . were replaced by inadequately trained, low-wage interns with very high turnover rates. This created instability in classrooms, as students lost relationships with familiar, trusted adults, and teachers were diverted from teaching to train as many as four new interns a year."[134]

The union noted that its local, the Baltimore Teachers Union, had not opposed EAI initially and was not opposed to "private management of public schools in principle, as long as public schools remain under public control and the laws governing the public interest are upheld."[135] But the report went on to document declines in student achievement; increases in pupil-teacher ratio; inappropriate removal of children from special education programs; diversion of money from classroom instruction to overhead, improvement of physical plant, and profit; irregularities in the administration of funds for low-income students; and failure to fulfill EAI's promise to fully implement its Tesseract instructional program. The complaint about class sizes echoed one of the biggest complaints from teachers in EAI's showcase school, South Pointe Elementary. Some teachers there said they taught 39 students in a class instead of the 24 EAI had promised.[136]

A second AFT research report, "EAI's Mismanagement of Federal Education Programs," released in December 1994, outlined deficiencies in EAI compliance with federal regulations on providing services for low-income children under Chapter 1 and for children with exceptional educational needs.[137] Despite confirmation of these criticisms from other sources, including a finding by the Maryland Department of Education that EAI failed to provide exceptional education services required by federal law in three of its schools,[138] both EAI and the Baltimore school superintendent repeatedly dismissed the teachers' union allegations as self-serving propaganda.

However, when the lid blew off for EAI on June 4, 1994, it was not as the result of any attack by teachers. The *Minneapolis Star Tribune* published a front-page exposé of the company's educational and financial performance that suggested that many of EAI's claims of success were self-serving propaganda used to land contracts, lure investors, and boost stock prices. *Star Tribune* reporters Joe Rigert and Carol Command found that EAI not only spent more money than the public schools and failed to deliver on its promises but also falsified test results. During EAI's two years in Baltimore, the reporters said, it had operated with extraordinary advantages by illegally deviating from special education rules, by not being required to pay for all of the exceptional education teachers the school district's own staff thought were required, and by having rules waived by the Maryland School superintendent.[139]

Less than a week after the *Star Tribune* story broke, Baltimore superintendent Amprey, facing growing opposition, dropped his effort to expand EAI to more schools in the city.[140] Although Amprey continued to defend EAI, he could not stop the revelations and the bad news pouring in on all sides.

EAI wasn't the only one in trouble. There was a strong suggestion of a conflict of interest involving Superintendent Amprey's trips to Hartford, Connecticut, and Napa Valley, California, to promote EAI to school districts in those areas.[141] The headlines were relentless: June 17, 1994—"EAI Fails to Improve Test Scores";[142] July 18, 1994—"Md. Cites 3 Schools for Special Ed Violations";[143] October 18, 1994—"EAI Schools Test Scores Fall Short; Reading and Math Gain in City but Drop in Classrooms Run by Company";[144] October 19, 1994—"Pressure Grows to Terminate EAI Experiment"; [145] October 26, 1994—"EAI Schools Fail to Match Citywide Attendance Gains";[146] and October 27, 1994—"Amprey Trips Paid for by EAI."[147]

On October 19, 1994, the *Baltimore Sun* took Amprey to task in an editorial. The editors were outraged that selected EAI test results touted at a June 1994 press conference were found to be both false and misleading. When test results for all of the Baltimore schools were released in fall 1994, it was revealed that EAI students were not outperforming other Baltimore schoolchildren as Amprey had claimed. In fact, they were doing less well academically. The editorial noted that at the time of the June press conference, EAI was negotiating to run the Hartford public school system. The newspaper called for an independent investigation because "Superintendent Amprey has sacrificed his credibility by becoming 'too publicly identified as an EAI cheerleader.'"[148] By the end of October, the chair of the Baltimore city council education committee, Carl Stokes, was openly calling for either a sharply revised EAI contract or outright termination.[149]

As EAI's prospects in Baltimore grew ever more tenuous. EAI's executives continued to claim the company was succeeding. In September 1994, EAI president David Bennett wrote in an education journal: "By pooling the talent and resources of seasoned educators and the private sector, Education Alternatives, Inc. is reinvigorating school systems in several cities."[150]

Born-Again Savior

Bennett's description hardly matched the civil war going on in Baltimore over EAI's performance. Perhaps he was looking ahead to Hartford, Connecticut, where his company was about to land a contract to run the entire school system and counting on the news to draw favorable comments on the business pages.

If so, he wasn't disappointed. EAI signed a contract to take over the management of the Hartford public school system on October 3, 1994.[151] And sure enough, on October 14, 1994, a *USA Today* business section story was headlined "Education Alternatives Makes Grade." It went on to note: "Despite the stock's volatility, the company [EAI] has terrific growth potential, analysts say. 'A lot of experts think 10 percent to 20 percent of public schools will be run by public-private partnerships in the next five to 10 years,' says Kevin Harris of Summit Capital." The story also reported that districts taken over by the state were rated as a natural market for the for-profit firms.[152]

When EAI signed the Hartford contract, the public-private deal was heralded (again) as a model for the nation. All the arguments that were used in support of EAI in Baltimore were dusted off—and then some. Denis Doyle, then a senior fellow at the conservative Hudson Institute, claimed Hartford was "a near perfect setting for the experiment in private management." Ted Kolderie, a senior associate at the Center for Policy Studies who strongly supports market-based reforms, viewed the arrangement as "perfectly reasonable."[153] Apparently, Doyle and Kolderie had been out of the country or asleep during EAI's involvement with Baltimore.

Nobody disagreed that Hartford was a troubled school system. Despite high per-pupil costs, Hartford students were failing to achieve as well as other Connecticut students. To many, this was the result of the city's intense poverty and racial isolation. In fact, as EAI was negotiating to run the Hartford school system, the Connecticut Civil Liberties Union was in court (*Sheff v. O'Neill*) trying to win a judgment that would create a metropolitan school plan designed to overcome the enormous disparity in the educational opportunities available to children in Hartford and those living in surrounding suburbs. There was little argument about Hartford's problems. The question was whether EAI represented a solution.

EAI began making its presence felt in Hartford as soon as the ink was dry on its contract. As in Baltimore, it arrived with support from the powers that be. Hartford mayor Michael Peters, city council majority leader John O'-Connell, and a 6-to-3 majority of the school board all seemed to be of the "nothing to lose" school of thought. As in Baltimore, EAI promised a massive infusion of outside capital for technology and school improvements. In Hartford's case, the promise was for about $20 million during the five-year term of the contract. As in Baltimore, EAI promised to raise the achievement level of Hartford's students without raising costs in the 32-school, 25,000-student district.[154] It didn't take long for the bloom to come off the rose.

EAI was both attacked and praised for its role in negotiating a no-raise teachers' contract in early 1995.[155] However, grumbling spread as EAI settled in and it appeared to many that the company was dragging its feet in bringing in the technology it had promised in the winter of 1995. When the company proposed its 1995–1996 school budget, city officials blew up.

EAI's budget called for eliminating 300 teaching positions. It was opposed by Superintendent Eddie Davis and widely attacked for the effect it would have on class size and other instructional services.[156] School principals appealed to the board of education. One claimed that the EAI budget would leave his school with no counselors, no vice principals, and no nurses.[157] To some, it appeared that EAI was planning to raise the money for its promised technology through internal budget cuts rather than investments brought in from outside. There was also the dark suspicion that since EAI's contract with Hartford allowed it to keep half of any budget savings it uncovered, the company was moving quickly to make a financial killing.

The mood grew even darker in Hartford as news of EAI's billing practices spread. The company proposed to charge the city $1.2 million for first-class air travel, two pricey downtown condominiums, interest on money the company spent managing the schools, legal fees, financial services, office rent, and photocopying charges. The fees included $200 per hour for telephone consultations and meetings with a public relations firm and for interviews with the press. And then there was the $238,333 EAI claimed it already had spent on school improvements. That was just the beginning. The company estimated its costs would reach $2.8 million by the end of the school year.[158] In the words of one *Hartford Courant* headline, the debate on EAI was tearing (the) city's soul.[159]

Just as in Baltimore, EAI was proving it was indeed possible to make a bad situation worse. By the end of May, the school board and city council had rejected EAI's budget proposal, and the school board had virtually eliminated EAI's role in managing Hartford's schools. Only through the intervention of Hartford's mayor and city council leaders—worried that liabilities if they canceled EAI's contract might jeopardize a recently passed tax cut—was a role for EAI resurrected.[160] In mid-1995, the job EAI finally settled for was to run only 6 of the city's 32 schools and carry out a vague set of districtwide responsibilities that promised to ensure continued confusion and conflict.

For the quarter ending June 30, 1995, EAI reported a loss and wrote off $5.5 million in debt it said it had incurred in Hartford.[161] The city of Hartford had thus far approved payment of $343,079.[162] In November 1995, the pro-EAI majority of the school board, formerly seven members on the nine-member board, was reduced to five in local elections.

While EAI was being bloodied in Hartford, it was getting run out of Baltimore. Asked in a *Baltimore Sun* interview if he thought the city's mayor would pull the plug on EAI, John Golle responded with characteristic bluster: "No way, no way, no way, no way. The have-nots all of a sudden have something that the haves don't have. Good, clean, safe schools loaded with technology. Just try to take it away from the have-nots, just try. I dare you, you just try."[163] Of course, taking from the have-nots to gouge out his profits was exactly what Golle had been doing for three years in Baltimore.

On June 5, 1995, the *Baltimore Sun* reported the additional $18 million that EAI had required to run its schools had been taken from other Baltimore public schools. That money would have been enough to purchase 9,000 computers or add a teacher to the staff of every Baltimore school. The school district's own analysis showed that if the entire school system were funded at the same level as EAI, another $100 million would have to be added to the city's education budget.[164] This was hardly a model that poor, urban school districts would ever want to adapt.

On June 6, 1995, Baltimore mayor Kurt Schmoke said he would decide whether to keep EAI based on the results of an independent analysis of the company's performance conducted by the Center for Educational Research at the University of Maryland–Baltimore County. At the very least, the mayor said, he planned to renegotiate the contract.[165] In August 1995, the University of Maryland report was released. It showed no difference in overall educational effectiveness; in the general condition of buildings and grounds; in parent rating of factors such as cleanliness, homework, student enthusiasm, school pride, or safety; in the impact of technology on learning; or in student academic achievement (except that EAI students were doing worse in reading than students at other city schools). Besides failing to outperform the other Baltimore public schools as touted, the EAI-run schools cost 11.1 percent more to operate.[166]

Despite EAI's poor showing, it appeared for a time that Baltimore might keep EAI on—if the company was willing to renegotiate its contract. However, when the city faced a revenue shortfall in autumn 1995 and demanded EAI accept $7 million less per year, the company balked. On November 22, 1995, Baltimore city officials announced they were canceling the EAI contract. On word of the cancellation, NASDAQ briefly suspended trading on

EAI stock. By the end of day, when trading had resumed, EAI shareholders found the stock value stood at 4 3/8.[167] On November 30, 1995, the Baltimore Board of School Commissioners officially terminated the EAI contract. The once mighty for-profit EAI empire had been reduced to six schools in Hartford, a community far more hostile than Baltimore had ever been.

Reaping Education's Nonexistent Financial Bounty

By the beginning of 1996, the Edison Project was a shadow of what it once claimed it would be. Instead of preparing to open a for-profit chain of two hundred private schools, the company was reduced to running four elementary schools, and it had barely enough capital to do that. EAI had looked for contracts from one end of the country to another (in Pinckney, Michigan; the District of Columbia; San Diego, California; Portsmouth, Virginia; Indianapolis, Indiana; Hawaii; and New Jersey[168]), and it had been rebuffed everywhere. At the stockholders meeting following the termination of its Baltimore contract, EAI's management said the company's future was in the suburbs.[169] However, since the company was carrying more chains than Jacob Marley's ghost, it was hard to imagine that many districts would want to invite EAI in. In late January 1996, Hartford followed Baltimore's example and canceled its contract with EAI. The company had been paid only $343,000 of the $11 million it had billed the school district.[170] As of February 1996, EAI's single contract was for $100,000 to help the Wappingers Central School District, in a suburb north of New York City, develop a district budget.[171]

Some people might like to portray the experiences of the Edison Project and EAI as unique to those companies or as failures resulting from the distinct personalities of Chris Whittle and John Golle. Even more commonly, they are described as the result of "politics" or the power of "special interests." The evidence does not support such an interpretation. The problem is with the idea of privatization itself. As the *Hartford Business Journal* wrote in a prescient May 1994 editorial: "State and local governments have been running these systems around the world for years. They end up running them because there's no money in it, just like there's no money in running a police department, fire department and so on. You can't turn an inherently unprofitable business into a profitable one just by turning it over to the private sector."[172]

EAI tried to convince the public and investors it had found a way around this fundamental problem. Instead, what it demonstrated was that to make a profit, the company would have to either take money from school system employees (a model private sector management favors), take it away from other schoolchildren in the system, raise it from outside sources, or use all three approaches.

EAI made money in Baltimore primarily because its much publicized claim to do a better job and spend the same amount of money as the school district already was spending was, from the beginning, a shell game. EAI defined "the same amount" to mean "average per-pupil expenditure." Anyone even slightly familiar with school finance knows two things: Elementary schools are cheaper to run than middle and high schools (EAI focused on elementary schools in Baltimore), and the money a school actually receives excludes such centrally budgeted items as fringe benefits, transportation, and other districtwide overhead expenses.

In 1995, for example, the "average" cost per pupil in the Milwaukee Public Schools was $6,143. The average for *elementary* schools was $4,969. After excluding centrally budgeted items, elementary schools actually received, on average, $2,958 per pupil.[173] By contracting for the Baltimore districtwide per-pupil average (including secondary schools), EAI guaranteed its profitability and assured that children in all the Baltimore schools it didn't run would receive less. The EAI "model" could never have been adopted for the entire district because there would be no remaining students to provide the company with its profit.

EAI and Edison also make a good deal of their corporate partnerships to provide noneducational services. In 1991, EAI formed what it called the Alliance for Schools That Work with KPMG Peat Marwick and Johnson Controls World Services, Inc. In essence, this means that EAI functioned as a general contractor with overall responsibility for the management of the contract as well as providing all educational services under the contract. It subcontracted with KPMG Peat Marwick for financial services and with Johnson Controls for noninstructional services such as building maintenance.[174] Edison has a similar agreement with Bovis Management Systems, Inc., to provide noneducational services.[175]

From the first days of EAI's involvement with the Baltimore public schools, considerable attention was focused on the capital investments made by EAI in Baltimore to clean up, repair, and modernize the school buildings it operated. However, comparatively little money can be saved by installing new windows and more efficient heating and cooling systems. The only way to cut costs substantially is to reduce labor costs. One way to reduce labor costs is to increase the number of students each teacher teaches. However, both EAI and Edison claimed they would reduce class size. If class size is not reduced, the only way to reduce labor costs is to lower the salary and benefits of support staff such as secretaries, food service workers, and custodians. That is exactly what EAI appears to have done in Baltimore.

Johnson Controls does not reveal what it paid the custodians it employed to clean and maintain EAI schools in Baltimore because it considers the information proprietary. It is rumored that custodians at EAI schools were paid substantially less than their counterparts at other Baltimore public schools. EAI also replaced teachers' aides who earned about $12 per hour and fringe benefits with "interns" whom it pays $7 per hour and no benefits.

Such reductions in salary and benefits offer real cost reductions. However, they carry a high social and educational price tag. At a time when the hue and cry is for work not welfare and when there is considerable concern about the condition of family life in impoverished urban neighborhoods, it is bad social policy to reduce the wages and benefits of school support workers. In many instances, those jobs represent an important source of income for the very families that provide stability in their central city communities and decent home environments for their children. People of color often dominate job classifications such as teacher's aide, custodian, and secretary.[176] It doesn't make much sense to reform schools by pushing the parents of children who attend those schools into poverty. It is hard to resist the conclusion that by signing a contract with EAI or Edison, a school district is, in effect, assuring a transfer of wealth from minority workers in the community to white investors somewhere else—a sort of domestic colonialism.

School superintendent Franklin Smith got the message loud and clear when he proposed hiring EAI to manage as many as 15 of the public schools in Washington, D.C., in December 1993. A March 4, 1994, *Washington Post* story was headlined "School Privatization Shelved: With D.C. Board Split and Opposition Growing, Smith Retreats." The story revealed that "to some parents, Smith seemed to be opening a path for whites to regain control over a school system now dominated by African American educators like Smith himself. . . . 'We are struggling for self-determination in Washington, D.C.' said Thelmiah Lee . . . whose son attends Roosevelt High School. . . . 'With 89.9 percent of the school student body African American, why would we bring in rich, white folks . . . to run our schools?'"[177]

Neither the EAI nor the Edison educational programs contain any startling departures from good educational practice. There is no breakthrough. It is surprising that it took the Edison design team almost two years and millions of dollars to produce a series of documents ("An Invitation to Public School Partnership," "Partnership School Technology," "Partnership School

Design," and "Student Standards for the Primary Academy") that, when stripped of their attractive graphics and idiosyncratic language, describe practices that have been accepted for years.

EAI and Edison both like cooperative learning and *love* technology and learning contracts, and they seem to have rediscovered developmental psychology, student-centered teaching, and the middle school model of education. The pedagogy is enlightened. However, the educational programs of either the Edison Project or EAI do not require for-profit schools. Indeed, the AFT analysis of the EAI experience in Baltimore illustrates how the need for profit undermines the educational programs of for-profit firms.

The market has, at least for now, rendered its judgment. EAI and Edison look like losers to investors. Given their high cost, their history of failure, and the great potential for fraud and abuse, it may seem surprising that for-profit privatization schemes are still being considered seriously by a number of administrators and policymakers. But there are several reasons why privatization plans are likely to continue to be considered by urban school districts for at least the next few years. Poor, urban districts have been put in a box by the chronic underfunding of their schools and the dramatic increase in the number of children in their classrooms who are desperately poor and who have exceptional educational needs.

Because many of the variables that might help these children succeed seem outside the school district's control, it is, no doubt, tempting to hand the burden of being "accountable" to someone else. Despite all their talk about accountability, neither EAI nor Edison are prepared for accountability that translates into "no results, no money."

In a written response to questions from the Milwaukee Public Schools, Edison presented its compensation philosophy:

> Edison does not believe that its compensation should vary with student performance. . . . We see several problems with a pay-for-performance system. . . . Education is a complicated business and we have many, many objectives. . . . Educational progress is notoriously difficult to quantify. We are committed to providing objective measures of student progress in every field of the curriculum. And we are confident that progress will be made. But we would be dishonest to say we can precisely forecast progress in every area quantitatively. . . . The partnership will not be improved, nor students helped, if the partnership schools are denied funds because a particular quantitative benchmark is missed. . . . We ask that MPS look at the big picture when judging the quality of the partnership.[178]

There are, without a doubt, plenty of public school superintendents and principals who would be very grateful for the opportunity to be held accountable the way Edison proposes to be held accountable. Edison is making the same arguments that public school educators have made for years—with a notable lack of sympathy from the same policymakers and politicians who now support privatization.

It is not hard to imagine some urban superintendents' thinking EAI and Edison are no-risk propositions. If they fail, the school system will, for once, escape the blame. If they succeed, the superintendent lays claim to the title of "visionary." But as attractive as this scenario may seem to overworked super-intendents, it represents a false hope. There is a good deal at risk when a school district signs a contract with a private "partner." The district risks a potential scandal if the contract is not properly administered, and most dis-tricts do not have the experience or the resources necessary to properly mon-itor such complex contracts. The district also risks making things worse for most children in the district. Edison and EAI each have the potential to re-duce the amount of money available to educate other students in the district in order to meet their own contractual payments. This can diminish the edu-cational quality of the district overall. In addition, the district risks polarizing the community in the struggle to bring in a for-profit contractor for particu-lar schools and thus undermine the chances of districtwide reform.

Another lure of the for-profits is their offer to make capital improvements that school districts often cannot afford to make themselves. EAI received an extraordinary amount of good publicity for cleaning up and painting the nine schools it manages in Baltimore. It also installed new windows and made other improvements. By all accounts, the schools *looked* better. An-other attractive item in the Edison school design is the promise of a com-puter in every student's home. Although the educational program that the computer will support is only vaguely described, many people react to the promise of a computer in every home as if they had just won the lottery. It is a clever marketing tool.

What sometimes gets lost in the discussion of capital investments and high-tech hardware, however, is the simple fact that none of these improve-ments are gifts. The school district will have to repay EAI and Edison for these improvements in the form of profits. A school district has only three obvious alternatives to raise the additional money that must be paid to the operator of the privatized schools: It must reduce the amount of money available to other schools, find an outside source of revenue, or raise taxes. The only other possibility is to reduce the money spent on instruction and instructional support in the privatized schools. In Baltimore, two things hap-pened. The amount of money available to non-EAI schools was reduced, and EAI took money away from instructional support in its schools in order to make a profit.

Even the much touted capital investments by for-profit firms are problematic. They are, in some respects, like backdoor bond issues for poor, urban school districts. A real bond issue, however, amortizes capital debt over a long term at favorable interest rates. When a school district pays to fix up schools with one of these private, backdoor bond issues, it finances capital improvements out of operating costs. That is like buying them with a charge card. The district then ends up paying higher debt service payments (in the form of profits to the contracting firm) and having less money for the education of its students.

Despite the lack of good results, privatization is likely to continue its forward momentum for some time. The education "industry" now has its own newsletter, "The Education Industry Report," that provides "news and commentary on the emerging education industry."[179] It includes an index of the performance of education stocks. The education "industry" also has its cheerleaders among stock analysts, most notably Michael Moe of Lehman Brothers. All of this continues to give the industry legitimacy and attract investor interest. In February 1996, for example, Lehman Brothers sponsored a get-together for potential investors in for-profit education companies. EAI and the Edison Project were among the firms pitching themselves, and word was that, despite their track records, their presentations sparked considerable interest. Privatization also continues to have ardent education cheerleaders, such as Denis Doyle, now a visiting fellow at the Heritage Foundation, who coauthored a paean to privatization published in the March issue of *Education Week* that managed to characterize Chris Whittle as a model entrepreneur.[180] And niche firms such as Sylvan Learning Systems that offer well-defined and carefully limited services are likely to continue to grow as school districts seek to save money by "outsourcing" parts of their programs.

There are a couple of obvious markets for private management: if the practice of states taking over "failed" school districts spreads or if more local school districts gain the authority to close schools they believe are underperforming. Charter school laws and private school voucher legislation provide openings for the for-profit operators. None of those approaches has any clear connection to improving the quality of education. They could, however, provide new opportunities for converting tax dollars to private profit.

Within education, privatization may continue to provide a comforting illusion of change without the sacrifices that would be necessary to bring about real improvement. It helps perpetuate the myth that the fundamental problems of schools are caused by bureaucratic structures, incompetence, and the self-interested greed of unions, instead of crushing poverty, racism, and a lack of jobs created by government and corporate economic policy.

EAI and Edison are merely extending those policies when they sacrifice the lowest-paid workers in the school district so that wealthy investors will consider school reform a profitable investment. Real school reform, especially in our nation's poverty-ravaged urban centers, would require sacrifice not by the poorest but by the most privileged members of our society. Real school reform requires a vision of justice—something the highest-paid visionaries at the Edison Project or EAI can never provide.

5

Private School Vouchers: A False Choice

In the early 1870s, demoralized by their crushing defeat in the Franco-Prussian War and the social turmoil that followed, many French citizens angrily attacked the public school system as the source of their woes. They embraced simplistic political declarations, claiming that it was "the Prussian teacher [who] has won the war. In Germany, where the teacher is supervised or directed by either a priest or a pastor, . . . where the school teaches obedience instead of revolution, that is where you should look for the secret of victory."[1]

Just over a hundred years later, the authors of *A Nation at Risk*, aflame with their own crisis rhetoric, declared that America was headed for a disastrous defeat in a global economic war. And once again, as in nineteenth-century France, public schools were blamed. In both nineteenth-century France and contemporary America, the evidence linking each nation's plight to the alleged failure of the schools is at best arguable. And in both eras, fans of the teaching of religious obedience have seized upon the perceived crisis to try to divert public taxes into the firm hands of priest and pastor.

In 1872, a French parliamentary commission recommended a religious school voucher plan remarkably similar to those currently being championed

117

in the United States, with government vouchers to be spent on private or religious education. However, in nineteenth-century France, hostility to the idea of providing public money to support church schools was so widespread that the plan was never taken up by the French Assembly.

In the United States, the constitutional prohibition against church-state entanglements, public opposition to the use of tax funds for religious schools, and a lack of other alternatives to public schools kept voucher schemes on the fringes of the mainstream debate over educational reform until the 1980s, when they were revived by a resurgent conservative movement.

In the 1950s, the idea of using vouchers for private schools was supported by economist Milton Friedman's high-flown conservative rhetoric about unfettered markets ensuring political liberty and material progress. But the concept was, in fact, an openly racist response to court-ordered desegregation.

The earliest voucher plans in the United States were in the South. In 1956, the Virginia legislature passed a "tuition-grant" program and in 1960 a "scholarship" plan that provided students with tax dollars they could use to pay the tuition at any qualified nonsectarian school in their district. The express purpose of the Virginia laws (and other "freedom of choice" plans like them passed by southern legislatures) was to help maintain segregated school systems in the wake of the 1954 U.S. Supreme Court's *Brown* v. *Board of Education* decision.[2]

That history is relevant today. The long-term damage from vouchers and other political mechanisms used by southern whites to avoid desegregation is still with us. As white parents rushed to set up private academies and thereby avoid sending their children to desegregated public schools, the political base of support for public education shrank. White parents sending their children to private schools repeatedly voted against increasing taxes to educate black children going to public schools.

By 1984, press reports told of a "new" racism in the "new South." In Sumter County, Georgia, for example—where former president Jimmy Carter went to school—tax support for the public schools was cut by two-thirds between 1970 (when the district was desegregated) and 1984 as whites fled to private academies.[3]

This is the political dynamic the contemporary private school voucher movement threatens to nurture on a national scale. If voucher advocates succeed, public schools are very likely to lose their broadly based, bipartisan political support. What will be left is a public school system cast adrift politically that could quickly become an intensely segregated, chronically underfunded repository of the most disabled, the poorest, and the most difficult to educate children.

Despite the danger they pose, there is little question that over the past forty years, private school vouchers have moved from the darkest edge of racial politics in the 1950s and 1960s into legitimate political discussions in the 1990s. This transformation was possible, in part, because vouchers have consistently found support among Catholics eager to use tax dollars to save their schools, free-market zealots, and people of all political persuasions who were dissatisfied with various shortcomings of what David Tyack, a historian of public education, has labeled "the one best system."[4] Like the glowing embers in a hearth, the voucher movement was ready to burst into flame when the political wind changed in the late 1980s and early 1990s, and some very well-heeled neoconservative supporters piled on the logs.

We've Been There

In the late 1960s, the voucher idea caught on with the administration of President Lyndon Johnson. At that time, vouchers had a vocal constituency not just from the Right or the business community but also among "deschoolers" influenced by the writing of Ivan Illich,[5] progressive and black nationalist "free schoolers,"[6] social critics of the public education bureaucracy such as Paul Goodman,[7] and liberal academics like Christopher Jencks.[8] The chance to craft so-called regulated voucher plans ensuring that the poorest recipients got the largest vouchers appealed to many on the Left.

President Johnson's Office of Economic Opportunity developed a voucher proposal that was subsequently embraced by President Richard Nixon's administration. There was so little grassroots enthusiasm for the idea, however, that Minneapolis, Rochester, Kansas City, Milwaukee, Gary, and Seattle all rejected the opportunity to participate in an experimental program. The only community that agreed to try the OEO plan was Alum Rock, California, where it was implemented within the public school system with disappointing results and subsequently abandoned.[9]

Nixon did more than simply carry a Johnson administration proposal to its logical conclusion. He also attempted to satisfy both his conservative business constituency and religious (primarily Catholic) supporters of private school vouchers, who saw them primarily as a way of saving their own troubled schools. By the late 1960s, the editors of *Barron's National Business and Financial Weekly*, aping Milton Friedman, were describing public schools as a "harmful monopoly" that should be broken up.[10]

In 1971, the Panel on Non-Public Education of Nixon's Presidential Commission on School Finance openly expressed a desire to publicly fund religious schools. However, "parochiaid" and any other plan to send public money to religious schools not only faced widespread public opposition, it also risked being ruled unconstitutional. In 1971, the Supreme Court erected a difficult hurdle for advocates of tax dollars going to religious schools. In its 8-to-0 ruling in *Lemon* v. *Kurtzman*, the Court held that to be constitutional, the plan had to meet three standards: Its purpose could not be secular, its main effect could neither advance nor inhibit religion, and it could not excessively entangle the state with religion.[11]

Although "parochiaid" died for lack of sufficient political support and the real threat that it would be ruled unconstitutional by the Supreme Court, the idea of private school vouchers remained very much alive. Indeed, the "parochiaid" debate rehearsed many of the current arguments over private school vouchers.[12]

In 1983, 1985, and 1986, the Reagan administration tried unsuccessfully to move voucher legislation through Congress. The 1985 effort is worth noting because it sought to reestablish the link between vouchers and "empowering" the poor that had attracted progressives in the 1960s and 1970s by turning the federal government's Chapter 1 program (which provides increased resources to school districts serving large numbers of poor children) into an individual voucher program.[13]

The Other Choice—Public School Choice

With his free-market arguments for private school voucher proposals going nowhere, Reagan tacked into the political wind and began to talk about *public school choice*. It was a savvy tactical shift that immediately raised the visibility of and support for "choice." Choice was suddenly transformed into a strategy to reform rather than dismantle the public school system. Furthermore, it was associated with educational excellence and, perhaps more important given its history, racial equity through its link to the popular magnet school concept.

Magnet schools were used by many school districts to promote school integration by offering a diverse array of innovative curriculum options and thereby attract voluntary transfers to integrated schools.[14] In making the shift, Reagan seemed to separate choice from its racist and religious roots—a wise move. Over the next eight years, beginning in Minnesota in 1988, public school choice laws (also called open enrollment) were enacted in fourteen states.[15] These laws allowed students to choose to attend any public school in the state that had room for them.

George Bush, the self-styled "education president," stayed close to the Reagan position for the first two years of his presidency. However, by the end of 1990, his policy was clearly shifting away from reforming public schools toward using vouchers to abandon them. Between 1990 and 1992, he sent Vice President Dan Quayle to Oregon to speak on behalf of a voucher ballot initiative there; he expressed strong (and well-publicized) support for Wisconsin's 1989 private school voucher law; he included "parental choice" in his 1991 America 2000 reform initiative; and in 1992, he announced he was sending a voucher plan he dubbed a G.I. Bill for Children to Congress as part of his budget.[16]

Bush and his secretary of education, Lamar Alexander, missed few opportunities to argue that vouchers would empower parents and unleash the market to reform what they said was a failed school system. Perhaps to shore up his support among the right wing of the Republican party, George Bush returned the voucher idea to its roots in free-market ideology and state support for private and religious schools. It was left to Bush's Democratic challenger, Bill Clinton, to take over the Reagan administration's "public school choice" position during the 1992 presidential campaign.

Words do matter. It was a breakthrough of sorts when supporters knowledgeable about advertising and public relations began to intentionally blur the distinction between public school choice and private school voucher plans. By the early 1990s, voucher supporters were never so foolish—or so overt—as to call their plans "parochiaid." Private school voucher plans were now sold under the religiously neutral and positively charged brand name of "school choice."

Voucher supporters, many of whom had not previously been strong advocates for the impoverished, frequently focused on plans for poor children to increase the idea's political attractiveness. To sidestep constitutional obstacles against funneling public funds to private schools, the transaction was defined as aid to poor parents who would, in turn, "choose" the private school their child would attend. This process of rhetorical money-laundering all came together in Wisconsin's 1989 "parental choice" law.

The Milwaukee Voucher Experiment— Success Without Results

The Wisconsin law originally set a ceiling of about a thousand low-income students (up to a maximum of 1 percent of the children attending the Milwaukee Public Schools) who could attend—at state expense—private, nonsectarian schools within the city that were willing to participate in the program. Each child attending a private school in the program would be supported by a voucher worth approximately $2,500.

To protect the private school status of participating schools, the Wisconsin law did not require that they meet the same educational standards that Milwaukee's public schools had to meet. It did not require that the teachers at the choice schools be certified. It did not require that the curriculum of the schools be reviewed or accredited by any outside agency.

Choice schools had to meet only one of four educational requirements: (1) At least 70 percent of the pupils in the program had to advance one grade level each year; (2) the average attendance rate had to be at least 90 percent; (3) at least 80 percent of the students had to demonstrate significant academic progress, or (4) at least 70 percent of their families had to meet parent involvement criteria established by the private school. Choice schools did not have to accept children with exceptional educational needs, and they did not have to meet the financial disclosure or other record-keeping requirements placed on the public schools.

The debate over the law was filled with free-market rhetoric about the need to force the Milwaukee Public Schools to compete if they were to improve, about "empowering" parents, and about the importance of seeing whether students attending private choice schools would improve academically. Accordingly, the law called for yearly comparisons of the academic achievement of students attending choice schools with that of comparable students attending Milwaukee's public schools.

The Wisconsin legislature created Milwaukee's choice program as a five-year experiment. However, the governor, Tommy Thompson, vetoed that provision. The law's constitutionality was challenged, but the law was ultimately upheld by the Wisconsin Supreme Court on the grounds that it was narrowly drawn to affect a small of number of children living in poverty and did not include religious schools.[17]

By 1995, there had been four yearly evaluations of the Milwaukee voucher experiment. Conducted in accordance with the terms of the law by University of Wisconsin political science professor John Witte, none of these independent evaluations was able to find statistically significant differences in the achievement of students attending choice schools and that of a comparable group of students attending the Milwaukee Public Schools. The evaluations did find a high degree of parental satisfaction with the choice schools. However, more students left the choice schools each year than changed schools in the comparable group of public school students.[18] Witte's research findings were consistent with international research on choice programs. They hardly argued for expansion of the program.[19]

Witte's findings were attacked in 1995 by Harvard professor Paul Peterson.[20] Peterson's report was remarkable less for its substantive points, which appeared to be weak, than for its tone of personal attack on John Witte. According to Witte, the animus on display in Peterson's critique may have been the result of Witte's previous stinging criticism of methodological flaws in *Politics, Markets and America's Schools*, written by two Peterson protégés, John Chubb and Terry Moe, while they were at the Brookings Institution working with Peterson.[21]

Regardless of the weaknesses of Peterson's arguments or any personal motives he may have had, his report was immediately sent to every member of the Wisconsin legislature on the eve of debate on the governor's 1996–1997 budget, which included expansion of the Milwaukee voucher program to include religious schools. This civic effort to keep Wisconsin legislators abreast of internecine battles in educational research was launched courtesy of Timothy Sheehy, president of the Metropolitan Milwaukee Association of Commerce (MMAC). Sheehy began his cover letter to the legislature: "School choice programs are working in Milwaukee and should be expanded. Milwaukee employers have made it their number one legislative priority."[22]

It is impossible to know what Sheehy meant when he said Milwaukee's choice program was "working." What does seem clear is that there was a high level of coordination among conservative supporters of vouchers and the MMAC. In fact, Sheehy's letter to the legislators was sent at least four days before the Peterson critique was officially released.

The same month Peterson's report was released, the Wisconsin Legislative Audit Bureau, the research arm of the legislature, released its own report on the Milwaukee program. It contended that no conclusion could be drawn about the academic performance of children attending private schools under the voucher program and a comparable group of students attending Milwaukee's public schools.[23]

Witte responded to Peterson's criticisms in his own letter to the legislature, making a strong scientific case.[24] However, as was no doubt intended, the Peterson report succeeded in muddying the evaluation of student achievement under the Milwaukee voucher program so that both supporters and opponents could claim the data supported them. In such a situation, a reasonable person might expect legislators to tighten up the annual evaluations to try to clarify what effect, if any, the voucher program had on student achievement. Instead, voucher supporters succeeded in killing the annual evaluations entirely. As an alternative, the Legislative Audit Bureau was given the responsibility for providing an evaluation of the program in the year 2000. By that time, of course, any embarrassing results would be less of a political liability for those who had pushed for expansion of the program.

Demonstrating increased student achievement was not the only problem for the Milwaukee voucher program. It also had failed to attract all the students eligible to participate under the law. In fact, almost 25 percent of the participating students were enrolled in kindergarten. The high kindergarten enrollment is significant because the Milwaukee Public Schools are unable to accommodate all the kindergarten-age children in the city because of space limitations. It is likely, therefore, that many low-income parents sent their children to choice schools not because they were seeking an alternative to the public schools but simply because there was no room in a public kindergarten.[25]

In 1995, despite the choice program's failure to achieve its promised results, the Wisconsin legislature—under intense lobbying pressure from the Milwaukee business community and Governor Thompson—expanded the parental choice law to make religious schools eligible to participate and to increase the number of students who could attend choice schools to 7,000 children in 1996. Since the legislature included religious schools, the constitutionality of the new law was immediately challenged in a suit brought by the American Civil Liberties Union (ACLU) on behalf of fourteen parents and clergy. The ACLU argued on the traditional grounds that had always proved fatal to plans to allocate public funds to religious institutions—that it would breach the constitutional wall separating church and state.[26] The state supreme court agreed to hear the case and issued an injunction preventing the law from taking effect during the 1995–1996 school year. On March 29, 1996, the supreme court sent the case back to circuit court for trial, leaving the program in legal limbo for at least another year.[27]

An Unpopular Reform

Private school voucher proposals are often characterized by their supporters as a popular grassroots reform pushed by parents trying to seize the power now jealously guarded by bureaucrats and patronizing liberal elites. In fact, private school vouchers have been enormously unpopular with the voting public. Since 1978, four states have held referenda on voucher plans: Michigan in 1978, Oregon in 1990, Colorado in 1992, and California 1993.[28] In each case, the vouchers went down to defeat by at least a 2-to-1 margin.

Attempts to put a "regulated" voucher plan in place via a ballot initiative were rejected in California in 1980 and 1982.[29] In 1993, after 70 percent of California voters rejected yet another voucher initiative,[30] backers vowed that they would be back in 1996. Yet by 1995, support for the idea was still so thin among Californians that voucher supporters decided to shelve the idea until at least 1997.[31]

In 1995, even a popular governor like Christine Todd Whitman of New Jersey found support for her proposed voucher plan for Jersey City was so weak that she withdrew the measure.[32] Governor Whitman then handed the hot potato to a commission whose report was not due until sometime in 1996.[33]

The frequently touted Wisconsin parental choice legislation was never put to the voters in a referendum. In fact, it never even had to face an up-or-down vote in the full legislature. When the bill was originally adopted in 1990 and again when it was expanded to include religious schools in 1994, the measure was part of an omnibus budget bill. Procedural maneuvers effectively shielded the legislation from what, in all likelihood, would have been certain defeat. That's clever politics, but it hardly constitutes popular support.

In fact, a good deal of energy among groups supporting private school vouchers is devoted to figuring out how to "sell" the idea to a skeptical public. Focus sessions were conducted for one such group—the American Alliance for Better Schools—in Cleveland and Chicago by Public Opinion Strategies of Alexandria, Virginia. The sessions produced a litany of concerns about voucher programs: "Participants were reluctant to support any proposal which could potentially hurt public schools"; "parents feared chaos in schools, and questioned how such a program would be funded and administered"; "although empowerment of parents could be an effective tool to strike at education bureaucrats, participants [in the focus session] were able to cite instances where empowerment resulted in racial favoritism, or unfair practices—two themes participants were very sensitive to"; "although competition language is a popular notion among some . . . parents were inclined to see risk, often believing students—especially those who are younger or disadvantaged—as worthy of protection and more 'nourishing' environment."[34] Faced with these attitudes about damaging public schools, it is small wonder that private school vouchers are often actually pitched these days as an attempt to "strengthen" the public schools.

Despite the lack of enthusiasm among the general public, there is no doubt the voucher pot is boiling on the political front burner. In 1993, Puerto Rico adopted voucher legislation that provided a voucher worth $1,500 for parents earning less than $18,000 a year to send their child to any private school in Puerto Rico that would accept him or her—including religious schools.[35] The private school portion of the law was struck down by the Puerto Rico Supreme Court in November 1994, leaving Puerto Rico with a public school choice program.[36]

In addition to Wisconsin, voucher legislation was introduced in California, Illinois, Indiana, North Carolina, Ohio, Oregon, and Pennsylvania in 1995.[37] Minnesota Governor Arne Carlson promised to introduce voucher legislation in 1996.[38] In addition, constitutional amendments have been proposed in Michigan and Missouri to permit the creation of private school voucher plans.[39]

Yet in spite of all the legislative activity, only Wisconsin and Ohio had enacted voucher laws by the end of 1995. Ohio's law, intended to go into effect in autumn 1996, has created a pilot program modeled after Wisconsin's voucher legislation, called the Cleveland Scholarship and Tutoring Program. It provides vouchers that eligible low-income parents in Cleveland can use to send their children to private (including religious) schools. The constitutionality of the law was challenged by the Ohio Federation of Teachers and others in a January 1996 suit filed in Franklin County Court.[40] Besides Wisconsin and Ohio, support for a voucher law in 1996 appeared strongest in Pennsylvania. However, after a stinging rebuke in 1995, it was unclear whether Governor Tom Ridge would be able to muster the necessary votes in the legislature to pass voucher legislation in the 1996 session.[41]

The Apparatus of the Right

The continuing political life of this unpopular idea can be traced to very effective, highly placed efforts to influence politicians, policymakers, and media opinion leaders. Among the most visible groups are the Chicago-based Americans for School Choice and Empower America, which has strong ties to the Republican party.[42] These groups have an overlapping cast of characters (Bush's former education secretary, Lamar Alexander, for example, is associated with both) and a distinctly conservative, market-oriented slant.

The influence of Americans for School Choice and Empower America is amplified by a massive marketing effort in support of the private school vouchers by a well-financed, conservative public policy and media apparatus and a self-interested business community. Once again, as with so many other parts of the conservative school reform debate these days, a surprising number of intertwining roads lead to Milwaukee, Wisconsin.

Many people are accustomed to thinking of Wisconsin as a progressive state in the tradition of "Fighting Bob" La Follette; others have long considered Milwaukee, which boasted a socialist mayor until 1960, as a hotbed of trade unionism. But these people might have trouble recognizing the state and city that are now centers of far-right social experimentation.

The reasons for the transformation are manifold. The state Democratic party gradually slid into the same corporate arms that embrace the party nationally. The three-term Republican governor, Tommy Thompson, successfully remade himself from a small-town backslapper into one of the most powerful state politicians in history. And politicians from both parties have joined the power elite in a conspiracy of silence to avoid addressing the racial divisions that make Milwaukee one of the most intensely segregated cities in the country.

Battered by a decade of devastating job losses and white flight to the suburbs, Milwaukee offered plenty of opportunities that a well-focused, heavily bankrolled ideologue could exploit to change the direction of state politics. Enter Michael Joyce. Joyce, a hard-edged neoconservative and a devout Catholic, has been president of the militantly conservative Bradley Foundation since 1985. Nationally, he is considered a leading member of what has been called a conservative "attack machine,"[43] ready to pounce on any sign of menace to right-wing orthodoxy with op-ed pieces, news leaks, public policy reports, and political threats. In fact, Joyce is more than a member of the reactionary hit squad. He helped create it, and he helps underwrite it.

As president of the Bradley Foundation, Joyce helped set up the Philanthropy Roundtable, which he chairs. The roundtable consists of conservative foundations that use the organization to coordinate their contributions and leverage their influence. Thanks in no small part to the members of the Philanthropy Roundtable, there are now thirty-one conservative state and local think tanks and over a hundred organizations that conduct and distribute "market-oriented research and commentary on state and local public policy issues."[44] This is the sort of network that helped make a weak book advocating private school vouchers, *Politics, Markets and America's Schools* by John Chubb and Terry Moe,[45] a best-seller in 1990. Although the so-called liberal foundations such as MacArthur, Rockefeller, Ford, and Carnegie have much greater resources, they do not invest their funds as part of a strategic plan to win national policy debates.[46]

Joyce came to the Bradley Foundation from the conservative Olin Foundation. He was selected for the job at Olin by none other than William E. Simon, secretary of the treasury under Presidents Nixon and Ford. Simon is well known for his reactionary political views. He is perhaps less well known as one of the earliest practitioners of the modern art of the leveraged buyout. Thanks to his gift for exploiting the advantages of accumulating corporate debt in tax laws, Simon managed to become one of America's richest men and, in the process, helped destroy the livelihoods of thousands of American workers. His methods are described in detail by *Philadelphia Inquirer* reporters Donald Barlett and James Steele in *America: What Went Wrong?*[47]

Not content to simply put the boot to as many workers as possible while grabbing the boodle for himself, Simon also fancied himself a political visionary. The credo Simon preached was simple: Corporations should not fund their enemies—which meant anyone who criticized business or was insufficiently anti-Communist. With the end of the Cold War, this animus seems to have been transferred to a more diffuse category: liberals in general.

In the mid-1970s, Simon and a group of like-minded industrialists, including Joseph Coors and John Olin, began to cast about for ways to implement Simon's "vision." It didn't take long. In 1978, Simon and Irving Kristol set up the Institute for Educational Affairs for the purpose of helping corporations be sure their money was getting into the right hands. Michael Joyce was hired as the institute's first director. Simon was so impressed with Joyce that within a year, he made him executive director of the Olin Foundation.[48] In 1985, Joyce moved to Milwaukee and took over as president of the Bradley Foundation, where he now controls about three times as much money as he did at Olin.[49]

It wasn't long before Milwaukee and Wisconsin learned that there was a new kid on the block and that he played hardball. Joyce heavily funded the Wisconsin Policy Research Institute (WPRI), the Milwaukee Parental Assistance Center (founded by State Representative Annette "Polly" Williams, author of the Milwaukee parental choice legislation), and the Center for Parental Freedom in Education (headed by Quentin Quade, a former administrator at Marquette University, a private Catholic institution). All are highly visible and aggressive supporters of private school vouchers.[50]

Money matters. Before long, highly paid consultants were cranking out WPRI reports critical of the Milwaukee Public Schools and in favor of private school vouchers. For one 1994 report, "Why MPS [Milwaukee Public Schools] Doesn't Work," WPRI is reported to have paid its author, Susan Mitchell, $78,000.[51] Not surprisingly, some of the best "revolutionaries" money could buy were soon thinking and talking about the problems with public education in Milwaukee and describing the promise of private school vouchers in glowing terms.

The national and local spending priorities of Joyce's multimillion-dollar foundation feed off each other. While using Wisconsin and Milwaukee to test-market conservative political strategy, he also funds a wide array of reactionary intellectuals (e.g., Charles Murray, coauthor of *The Bell Curve*), magazines (e.g., *American Spectator, Commentary*), policy institutes (e.g., the American Enterprise Institute and the Hudson Institute), and other organizations (e.g., the Educational Excellence Network, the National Association of Scholars, and a self-described right-wing "battle tank," the Center for Popular Culture). The national commentary is cited to justify setting up conservative pilot programs locally, and then alleged local success stories (regardless of any actual success) are trumpeted nationally by the same network of commentators.

If you're a sufficiently compliant politician, Joyce will even provide you with a lawyer. The Bradley-supported Landmark Legal Foundation successfully defended the 1989 Milwaukee parental choice law against a legal challenge.[52] The attorney who won the case for Landmark, Clint Bolick (now at the Institute for Justice—also funded by Bradley), helped craft the expansion of Wisconsin's parental choice law to include religious schools in 1995.

When the constitutionality of the law was challenged, Wisconsin Governor Thompson refused to allow the state's attorney general, a Democrat, to defend the law. Instead, he turned to Michael Joyce. Joyce didn't let him down. The Bradley Foundation provided most of the $150,000 the governor raised from "private sources" to pay for the state's defense of the law. With the help of the Bradley Foundation, the governor assembled a legal "dream team" that included Whitewater special prosecutor Kenneth Starr.[53]

Joyce's zealous support of private school vouchers seems, at times, to spring almost as much from Catholic mysticism as from his professed neoconservative ideology. On August 30, 1995, he told one audience, for example, that "the Lord God" had led him to support State Representative Williams in her quest for a private school voucher law.[54] Although he often cloaks his support for vouchers in populist "empowerment" rhetoric, one critic observed that in Joyce's view, parental power has rather severe limits: It is "the power to decide where one wants their child to go to school—if one has enough money, if the school is close enough, if one likes the school, and if the school accepts the child."[55]

The August 30, 1995, public meeting at which Joyce announced the support of the Lord God for private school vouchers came immediately after the

Wisconsin Supreme Court enjoined the implementation of Wisconsin's new parental choice law expanding the program to include religious schools. Joyce announced the Bradley Foundation would provide a $1 million special grant to a fund (Parents Advancing Values in Education [PAVE]) that privately financed vouchers for poor children.[56]

On September 4, 1995, PAVE sent out a media advisory announcing that Michael Joyce's pals Lamar Alexander and William Bennett would be visiting Milwaukee the next day to promote private school vouchers. They made media appearances at two religious schools and were interviewed by a local conservative radio talk show host, Charles Sykes, who broadcast his show from one of the schools.[57] Sykes, it turns out, is also connected to Michael Joyce's Bradley Foundation. He edits *Wisconsin Interest*, a magazine published by the Bradley-funded Wisconsin Policy Research Institute.

Business Unlocks the Door

Wisconsin may not have become the spearhead for private school vouchers without the money Michael Joyce throws around. However, Joyce still probably could not have succeeded without the support of Milwaukee's business community. The importance of business support is, in part, illustrated by the success of voucher advocates in Wisconsin compared to the disastrous failure of a California voucher initiative in 1993. In California, the business community, perhaps fearing (with good reason) that the long-term effect of enacting a massive private school voucher scheme might be to increase education costs astronomically, sat on its hands during the campaign to pass the initiative. For this, they were assailed by "liberal" columnist David Broder. In the business community's failure to get behind Initiative 174, Broder saw "something significant—and shameful—about the condition of conservatism in this country."[58] Apparently, Broder bought the conservative cover story that vouchers have something to do with the welfare of poor children.

A much more likely reason for business to oppose private school vouchers was a fear that the way the California initiative was framed would have led to an enormous increase in the cost of education. Right now, a large number of parents voluntarily choose to send their children to private or religious schools at their own expense. Every time they do, taxpayers save money. If every one of those children got a government grant equal to the amount of money spent on a child in the public system, the cost of the status quo would explode.

In part to allay that fear, California governor Pete Wilson proposed a more limited voucher plan in January 1996. Wilson explained that he had opposed the broader California voucher initiative on grounds of cost even though he was not opposed to vouchers generally.[59] In shifting to a more focused voucher plan, Wilson was, in effect, adopting the Wisconsin strategy. Wisconsin's white voters and members of the legislature were willing to support a voucher plan as long as it was carefully drawn to affect solely Milwaukee, the only district in the state with a majority of African American students.

However, even if voucher plans are carefully structured to keep existing spending inequities in place, the fear that they might lead to an explosion in costs is not farfetched. If, for example, the Milwaukee and/or Cleveland voucher plans pass constitutional muster and are used to provide public funds for poor children attending private nonsectarian and religious schools, a constitutional argument could be made that equal treatment must be given to every child regardless of his or her economic circumstance.

If such a claim succeeded, the political fight would then center on whether to increase education funding dramatically to pay for all the new tax-supported private school students or whether to try and spread around existing funds that much more thinly. No doubt, the support of many businesspeople hinges, in part, on their judgment about which outcome is most likely. In either case, however, the result would not benefit poor children.

Although the corporate-conservative tide is clearly with vouchers, neither the business community nor political and social conservatives represent a monolithic block. The range of views among these groups, depending on the issue, spans the distance from civic-minded pragmatism to right-wing revolutionary ideology. Voices of dissent have, for example, been raised among conservatives in opposition to private school vouchers. Charley Reese, a conservative columnist for the *Orlando Sentinel*, has openly chastised the neoconservative Bill Bennett–Jack Kemp crowd for seeking vouchers to convert a portion of the public school system into "their own tax-paid private school system."[60]

In the conservative magazine *The American Spectator*, Charlotte Allen offers up "Choice: A Burkean Dissent," attacking vouchers for ushering in increased government regulation and "the creation of another client for the welfare state: the private school system."[61]

This view is shared by more than a few conservative politicians. William Goodling, chair of the House Committee on Economic and Educational Opportunities, for example, does not support vouchers because of concern that government control inevitably follows government dollars. In 1995, voucher plans backed by John Rowland, Republican governor of Connecticut, and Tom Ridge, Republican governor of Pennsylvania, were defeated by the active opposition of Republicans in their state legislatures.[62] On the surface, no group would seem more likely to embody this traditional conservative point of view than Milwaukee's corporate elite. Typically a little behind the curve, Milwaukee business leaders were slow to catch the reform fever sparked by *A Nation at Risk* nationally. It was only at the insistence of Charles McNeer, CEO of the Wisconsin Electric Energy Corporation, that the Greater Milwaukee Committee (GMC), the organizational home of Milwaukee's business movers and shakers, established a committee on education in the mid-1980s.[63] The GMC education committee, in turn, spawned the Milwaukee Idea Committee to facilitate cooperation between business, community organizations, and educators. The Idea Committee evolved into the Milwaukee Education Trust in 1989.[64]

Although the Education Trust was the focus of a 1990 CBS *Good Morning America* back-to-school special on school-business cooperation, it was, in fact, already falling apart by that time. This was partly because of a general lack of interest and financial support from the business community for anything much more than a low-cost Teacher Awards Program and partly because of an ill-conceived mentoring program called One on One. The One on One program matched primarily white, middle-class executives with inner-city students. The Education Trust's own evaluation showed that the grade point average of students in this program actually declined.[65]

In 1993, the Metropolitan Milwaukee Association of Commerce, which had taken over responsibility for funding the trust, announced a final donation of $500,000 and withdrew.[66] Despite the fact that the tight-fisted Milwaukee business community hadn't even raised enough money to support its One on One mentoring program and had to hit up the state for $200,000 in public money to keep it afloat, the talk in 1993 was of spending too much money and getting too few results.[67]

The Education Trust, with its broadly based board of directors, has never taken a position on private school vouchers. It has, however, called for a more equitable funding formula for schools, something that would benefit districts such as Milwaukee that serve large numbers of poor children. Such a proposal is anathema to the corporate heavy hitters at the MMAC.

So it was that by the early 1990s, Milwaukee's historically tradition-bound and cautious business community was on the verge of throwing its weight behind a radical idea: private school vouchers. In part, this was possible because the composition of Milwaukee's corporate elite had changed. The number of large businesses presided over by a paternalistic management with deep roots in the community had dwindled. The sale of the privately held Allen-Bradley Corporation to Rockwell International in 1985 for $1.65 billion,[68] for example, reflected the shift to outside control that was rippling through Milwaukee's business establishment. Coincidentally, it also provided most of the Bradley Foundation millions that Joyce now throws at conservative causes. Milwaukee's corporate elite was ready to take a "revolutionary" path. And Michael Joyce, anxious to turn the city into a showcase for conservative educational and social engineering, was there to help show them the way.

In Milwaukee and across America, as corporate political power has grown throughout the 1980s and 1990s, the social and economic agenda of big business has increasingly overtaken its publicly proclaimed support for *A Nation at Risk* reforms. There is no way to get the high-quality, high-tech schools business leaders loudly proclaim they need and leave intact the social and economic policies corporate America fought so hard for in the 1970s and 1980s.

The political dynamics of the mid-1990s have turned a business drift to the right on education reform into a headlong rush. With a pack of self-proclaimed Republican revolutionaries controlling both houses of Congress, business can look forward to continued massive cutbacks in all forms of social spending, the prospect of further reductions in taxes on corporations and upper-income taxpayers, and increased freedom from government regulation and oversight.

As their narrow self-interest and short-term opportunity have become more clear, many corporate leaders have put aside qualms about the potential financial risk involved and begun signing on to the private school voucher crusade. To be sure, executives continue an array of piddling acts of educational good work—teaching awards, mentoring projects, the sorts of things a CEO can fund out of the chump change in his or her desk drawer. But business also amplifies the steady drumbeat of criticism of the public schools and lets loose a barrage of dire pronouncements about the hopelessness of reform that is anything less than "revolutionary"—by which corporate leaders mean "market-based."

The opinions of the business community are often rooted in mythology. Some of the most common myths include: We spend a fortune on public education; the schools are performing less well now than twenty years ago; education reform has been tried, and it hasn't worked; schools don't need more money; spending more money would be throwing good money after bad; the system can't be reformed because it is dominated by special interests—the educational bureaucracy and organized labor, otherwise known as management and staff.

In truth, as a percentage of per capita income, the United States ranks 14 out of 16 industrial countries in spending on K–12 education.[69] There's also been a consistent misrepresentation of test data with regard to the performance of the schools. For the most part, the data actually show that the public schools have been educating a more diverse, more impoverished student population to higher levels of academic achievement.[70] But the facts of the matter have never been the issue. That reality leaves many educators and social scientists scratching their heads at how little difference data seem to make in the debate because fundamentally, the private school voucher debate is largely about political ideology.

Consider the performance of Milwaukee's business community compared to that of its schools. By any measure, the business community's record has been abysmal in creating jobs that pay a living wage, especially for minority workers. A University of Wisconsin–Milwaukee Center for Economic Development analysis of job creation in the city between 1982 and 1992 found that 63.9 percent of the jobs paid below $20,000; 49.5 percent of the jobs went to people who did not live in the city; 88 percent of people employed in firms created since 1982 were white; and 95 percent of African Americans and Latinos employed by these firms earned under $20,000 a year.[71]

In comparison, the performance of the Milwaukee Public Schools is quite good. Despite the fact that Milwaukee has been devastated by the loss of family-supporting jobs and that students are much worse off economically than just a decade earlier, test results show the performance of students from poor families has remained stable and those of children who are not poor has improved considerably—even using the data of some of the system's harshest critics.[72] Furthermore, the Milwaukee dropout rate is declining.[73]

The private sector's failure to create jobs that pay a living wage in Milwaukee and throughout the country raises serious questions about what the business community really hopes to gain from private school vouchers. The corporate line is: Business has an interest in public education because it needs high-skilled, high-tech workers for the workplace of tomorrow. But either the people expressing that rationale are ignorant of the data or they're cynically advancing a phony argument as a cover for their true motives.

The 1995 study of the poorest areas of Milwaukee conducted at the University of Wisconsin–Milwaukee found there were thousands more job-seekers than available jobs, with the prospect of the gap widening even more if the governor succeeded in passing a requirement that all welfare recipients work. Most of the available jobs were in lower-wage occupations, such as short-order cook, janitor, and security guard.[74] These are hardly the highly skilled jobs business says it is trying so desperately to fill.

In fact, since the largest number of jobs available are minimum-wage, low-skilled jobs without benefits, it would appear that business would be perfectly well served by a minimal public education system that produced obedient low-wage clerks, waitresses, and floor-washers. In that case, school vouchers could be nothing more or less than a fig leaf to cover up an attempt to disinvest in poor, primarily African American and Latino kids.

Business leaders would never dare openly acknowledge such motives, of course. But what they do say out loud defies belief—that the corporate business establishment favors nothing less than dismantling one of America's basic public institutions in order to improve it for poor children. When the members of the Association of Commerce start talking "revolution" on behalf of the poor, there's something they're not telling us.

Confusion on the Left

In seeking private school vouchers, these unlikely corporate bomb-throwers help provide the political muscle for a volatile coalition that includes free-market advocates, black nationalists, the Catholic Church, and even a few "progressives."

Consider the strange case of John Norquist, mayor of Milwaukee. Before being elected mayor in 1988, Norquist was a long-time Democratic state legislator with a reputation as a progressive. Nevertheless, he also has solid business support because he is devoted to the "market." While in the legislature, for example, he helped kill Wisconsin's hospital rate-setting commission in 1987. As a result, Wisconsin enjoyed a boom in hospital overconstruction that helped fuel soaring medical care costs.[75] Now Norquist wants to bring the same market advantages to education. He loves private school vouchers and sees nothing wrong with state funds going to religious schools. And he never tires of attacking an education bureaucracy he seems to regard as the root of all evil.

Norquist's logic often seems muddled. In a policy paper published by the conservative Reason Foundation he wrote:

> [Few people] immigrate to this country for our K–12 public education. Yet we're the top country among industrial nations when it comes to higher education. . . . The single variable that makes the biggest difference is school choice. . . .
>
> The K–12 people say, "We are surrounded by all these problems." Well, the University of Chicago is surrounded by problems and it's one of the very best.[76]

The logic of comparing public schools, with their mission of educating everyone, to an elite, private university might escape many. But Norquist's reasoning is less important than the fact that he supports vouchers. In doing so, he helps voucher advocates claim the bipartisan high ground and undermine the criticism that they are right-wing zealots.

Progressives drawn to Norquist's position have to ignore the reality that education activist and writer Allen Graubard pointed out over two decades ago in his criticism of left-wing romantics who wanted to "de-school" society. In his 1972 book, *Free the Children*, Graubard argued that: "Schools didn't create class hierarchies, privilege, and vastly unequal distribution of wealth and power. And these conditions cannot be changed by talking about abolishing schools."[77]

The charitable explanation for a "progressive" like Norquist supporting private school vouchers is that he is hopelessly naive. A less kind view is that he is just another career politician who finds himself unable to affect the important institutions that control the life of the city he governs and so has latched onto the public schools as a handy scapegoat. Another explanation is uglier. Perhaps the real political calculus behind the Milwaukee mayor's advocacy of private school vouchers is revealed by his support for removing the income restrictions for participation in a program and the expansion of the program to include religious schools.

If adopted, the likely effect of Norquist's proposals would be to re-create the Catholic schools in Milwaukee as tax-supported sanctuaries for white students whose parents might otherwise flee to the suburbs rather than face the prospect of sending their children to Milwaukee's majority African-American public schools.

Consider that the greatest capacity for expanding the voucher program is in Catholic schools. Consider that most Catholic schools are on the south side of Milwaukee and serve primarily white students. Consider that removing income caps for participation in the program would, without a doubt, attract still more white parents to these schools and help hold current students in place. Consider that under a tax-supported voucher plan, Catholic schools would not have to keep enrolled any student they deemed disruptive or for some reason undesirable—guess which students those would be? And guess where those students would go when they were rejected by a Catholic voucher school?

The voucher program Norquist champions would make the Wisconsin experiment look suspiciously like the attempts by southern states to funnel public tax dollars to the all-white "freedom of choice" academies that sprung up following the *Brown* v. *Board of Education* Supreme Court decision that struck down legally sanctioned segregated schools.

Nevertheless, the mayor seems determined to transform Wisconsin's voucher experiment, originally a way of keeping well-established community schools, primarily in African-American neighborhoods, from closing, into a political device for stemming white flight by creating racial enclaves for south-side white students.

If Norquist gets his way, any remaining glimmer of hope for integration in Milwaukee will be further dimmed, and the pressure to keep down spending for an ever more poverty-stricken public school system serving higher and higher percentages of desperately needy students will intensify.

Milwaukee is already one of the sixteen areas in the United States considered "hyper-segregated." Nowhere else in the country are African-American citizens so likely to live in completely African-American neighborhoods that are geographically concentrated in a core area.[78] Moreover, the unemployment rate for blacks in Milwaukee is six times that of whites—a gap that has doubled since 1980. Not surprisingly, the black poverty rate increased 125 percent in the same period. And, regardless of income level, an African American in Milwaukee is three times as likely to be turned down for a home mortgage as a white Milwaukean.[79]

The mayor could express anger and outrage about the economic, social, and political priorities that have inflicted these profound wounds on Milwaukee's body politic. He could say something honest about the central role that racism continues to play in the ongoing decline of the city he was elected to lead. Instead he continues to lobby for private school voucher proposals guaranteed to sharpen Milwaukee's racial divide. How ironic that a "progressive" northern mayor is taking private school vouchers back to their racist roots.

Left-wing romantics who might be drawn into the camp of politicians such as John Norquist, with a dream of constructing a more just world over the rubble of public education, constitute a tiny segment of the people supporting the reform. Most of the reasons for supporting private school vouchers are decidedly not progressive.

The Market Myth

Allegiance to the "free market" is the reason most frequently offered. This reasoning is distinct from practical complaints about educational quality. The free-market argument is much more ideological or perhaps even theological. It also deserves much closer scrutiny than it usually receives.

People advancing this point of view seem to believe that because the market can do some things, the market can do everything. Using the analogy of the market, they look at private school vouchers as a way of allocating educational resources more effectively and providing rewards and incentives for high performance: If you produce a product that people don't want, they don't buy your product and you fail. To them, that's accountability.

One of the things that seems baffling is the willingness of so many supposedly tough-minded conservatives to ignore the need for accountability in the use of public funds. Taxpayers are accustomed to seeing a strict and detailed accounting of how public funds are spent. The rules and procedures governing public expenditures require open records and open meetings to guarantee public access and evaluation of performance. But for free-market advocates, that's largely irrelevant. Some may occasionally support public accountability measures, but what they see as the ultimate check on unwise or wasteful spending is the competitive discipline of the marketplace. To them, it is the market, not government oversight, that imposes accountability.

Unfortunately, the sort of educational market that would exist under a school voucher system would most likely resemble the deregulated savings and loan market in the 1980s. In such a market, the entrants into the economic activity—private and religious schools—would have access to a steady and stable flow of public moneys, with few if any public controls in place to see how the funds were actually spent and to what effect. The public would thereby assume an enormous public financial obligation with few effective ways of ensuring a public benefit. But then, as far as free-market advocates are concerned, schools are accountable only to their customers. They are not accountable to the general public at all.

Free-market advocates of private school vouchers tend to deify parents in a way that would bring tears to the eye if it weren't so suspect. Never mind that child abuse very often occurs at home.[80] Never mind that many children in the schools today don't even have parents in the traditional sense; they may be raised by another kind of adult caregiver who may or may not provide the same degree of supervision as the idealized family conjured up by voucher fans. Those fans often talk as if all children were being raised by Ward and June Cleaver—parents who (aside from representing the conservative image of a family) are always closely involved, wise, compassionate, and endlessly energetic, as well as willing to shop to the ends of the earth to find just the right educational program for their child. Anyone who suggests that the real world might be just a little more complex is immediately attacked as a patronizing and controlling elitist.

In the world according to many free-market advocates, attempts to improve the circumstances of America's poor children through government intervention arise from a malignant desire to control those children and their parents. In their view, the market is better at respecting the rights and promoting the welfare of individuals than the government is.[81] These high-minded advocates of respecting the poor by doing less talk very differently when discussing welfare reform. When the subject is welfare instead of school vouchers, poor parents are said to breed like rabbits, to have no values at all, and to cruelly neglect the children they brought into the world solely to increase the welfare payments they suck out of the pockets of responsible, working people.

Aside from the obvious hypocrisy, there's a basic public policy problem with this convenient deference to parents. With private school vouchers, the only people with standing to say anything about schools are the parents who send their children to those schools.[82] That's very different from the democratic tradition of community citizenship in which each person has standing to debate what his or her schools ought to teach, what they should stand for, how much should be spent on them, and what kind of young adults they are to educate.

Under private school vouchers, citizens lose all standing to directly control public education. If parents choose a school, that school is, by definition, the kind of school that tax dollars should support. The only function of a citizen who doesn't have a child in school is to pay taxes. He or she has no other role.

The goal of getting tax dollars without government oversight is very clear in the 1994 Christmas letter of Paul DeWeese, the chairman of the TEACH Michigan Education Fund, an organization that describes itself as one of the most influential statewide groups promoting choice in the country. DeWeese writes: "TEACH Michigan Education Fund now stands poised to lead a *second revolution* in education policy in Michigan. We believe the infrastructure has been created which will ultimately allow private and religious schools to be chartered, while remaining *independent* of government control."[83] You don't need an MBA to see there's something out of whack with a market in which one party provides all the revenue and another party receives all the services and decides what the nature of those services should be.

Childless taxpayers shouldn't get too upset about the all-powerful role of parent-consumers, though. In reality, the power of parents in voucher schemes is pretty illusory, too. That's because decisions by the providers of education in a private market would be made far differently than they are in the current public system.

In Milwaukee, as in many other communities, innercity parents have successfully rallied in recent years to keep open schools that the educational bureaucracy had planned to close. During the same period of time, decisions were made to close private sector institutions, which meant devastating losses to the community. In Milwaukee, for example, a large department store that had anchored the major shopping center in the African American community closed in 1995—not because it wasn't profitable but because it wasn't considered profitable enough. The decision was made in a distant corporate headquarters, based on considerations that had nothing to do with the good of the community in which the store was located. The community wanted the business badly, but the stores were shut down anyway because the community had no political mechanism to force its views to be taken into account.

In a so-called free market in education, the decision whether a school should open or close is also taken out of a political process in which community members have standing to participate without any question or equivocation. Instead, it becomes a private matter without the requirement that the public be heard or that the school take the good of the community into account.

If a multinational conglomerate set up a school in the inner city, who would protect the rights of the parents? A decision could be made in London or in Singapore or in the Netherlands to close down that school based on cash flow decisions having nothing whatever to do with the community. This is similar to what has happened to many towns after a Wal-Mart moves in and sets up shop just off the interstate. The downtown business district that is the economic and social core of the community often goes belly-up. Suddenly, the town is held hostage by a corporation whose investment decisions have nothing to do with the well-being of the local community.

Another basic fallacy in applying the free-market argument to our schools is the seemingly unquestioned assumption that the most successful product competing in the marketplace is the one of the highest quality. The network television schedule refutes that hourly. The marketplace is filled with examples of corporations that compete very successfully without any relationship to the quality of their products. Can anyone in the world tell the difference between Jell-O and a no-name-brand gelatin dessert? The answer is, probably not. Success is often a direct result of marketing and a multimillion-dollar advertising budget. The idea of spending education tax dollars on celebrity spokespeople and jingles (or any kind of advertising for that matter) makes about as much of a contribution to the public good as the glossy commercials for health care providers who are attempting to attract customers who either aren't sick or have plenty of insurance.

Separate and Unequal

Contemporary corporate catchphrases about "empowerment" echo the slogans of black nationalism. Needless to say, black nationalists are driven by a very different ideology than the free marketeers. Their support for private school vouchers is most often the result of a deeply held conviction that African Americans need to control the institutions that dominate their community.

The 1989 Wisconsin law establishing "parental choice" for poor, primarily African American residents of Milwaukee's inner city cannot be understood without reference to the city's racial politics. In the late 1980s, black nationalist Democratic State Representative Polly Williams was casting about for a way to slap what she regarded as the arrogant and ignorant bureaucracy of the Milwaukee Public Schools and a racist, backward-looking teachers' union and, at the same time, help a handful of private, nonprofit community schools in Milwaukee's African American community. She managed to pull together a majority in the state assembly for her 1989 Milwaukee parental choice legislation.

Although Milwaukee's African American legislators were split on the issue, a number of Democratic representatives, apparently counting on their senate colleagues to kill the bill, voted yes on Williams's legislation. They didn't figure on State Senator Gary George. George, an African American legislator from Milwaukee and then-chair of the legislature's powerful Joint Committee on Finance, slipped the parental choice legislation into the state budget bill and thus effectively prevented senate Democrats from voting it down as a separate piece of legislation.

Suddenly, Williams—branded earlier as one of the ten worst legislators in Wisconsin by Bradley Foundation–supported conservative radio personality Charles Sykes—discovered that Sykes now thought she was an educational visionary.[84] And she found herself hauling in honoraria for addressing cheering groups of white conservatives all over the country.

Williams argued that black parents don't need to be told by white bureaucrats what is best for their children; that African American children necessarily learn best from African American teachers; and that universities, teachers' unions, and the public school bureaucracy had erected institutional barriers that kept African American adults from teaching their own children. According to Williams, these barriers are administered by patronizing white liberals for their own benefit. To her, private school choice was a mechanism for loosening the suffocating grip of white institutions on the African American community.

The unlikely Williams disciples at the conservative Bradley Foundation immediately recognized her as a crowbar sent from heaven to help them dismantle "liberal" institutions and discredit what foundation president Michael Joyce is fond of calling the "nanny state."

Williams's logic is similar to that of another nationally known black nationalist from Milwaukee—former Milwaukee school superintendent Howard

Fuller. Fuller, now a professor at Marquette University, a major Catholic university, has become a prominent spokesperson for private school vouchers. Like Williams, he argues that vouchers will "empower" poor African American parents who are denied the choices available to more affluent whites. Fuller's position is consistent with his attempt in the late 1980s to establish what would have been a virtually all-black school district in Milwaukee's inner city, arguing that such a district would empower poor African Americans by giving them control over the schools that educate their children.

The rhetoric of black nationalism has strong appeal within the minority community, even among those who do not consider themselves black nationalists. Unequal treatment within the present system has left the African American community with some of the poorest schools and the longest bus rides to achieve integration. Those are real problems that should be addressed for the benefit of all children. Vouchers, however, rather than correcting grievances within an integrated system, would break the system apart and officially sanction the devolution of society into exclusive camps based on race and class.

It is not a matter, as some argue, of giving poor, black children the same opportunities as children from wealthier families to attend private or religious schools. The voucher isn't worth that much and never would be. When Milton Friedman originally proposed vouchers, he described them as affording a "minimum" level of schooling provided by the government, which could be supplemented by the personal resources of individuals if they wanted a higher level of education.[85] Following Friedman's logic, no matter how badly poor parents might "want" a higher level of education, if they couldn't pay for it by supplementing their child's voucher (currently $3,600 in Milwaukee), they would be out of luck. But then, that's the beauty of the market—everyone has a niche.

Even if Milwaukee parents participating in the voucher program got vouchers for the full amount spent on a child in the public schools (rather than just the state's portion, as they currently do), they still would be among the poorest of parents. They would be the least able to supplement their child's education. And there also would be no guarantee at all that they could find private schools that would take their children.

Race permeates the issue of vouchers. In cities like Milwaukee where the teaching staff is predominantly white and the student body predominantly black, the issue also helps create a climate of suspicion and mistrust that pushes African American parents toward black nationalists and white conservatives. For example, black nationalists often join right-wingers like Michael Joyce in spouting statistics about where public school teachers do and do not send their own children; the point that is often made is that the public schools are not good enough for the children of white teachers but are acceptable for black students.

For the most part, the source of these statistics is Denis Doyle's book *Where Connoisseurs Send Their Children to School.* In the book, published by the conservative Center for Education Reform, Doyle writes that teachers "choose private schools for their children when it serves their interest best."[86] He goes on to say that "the truth is self evident: while they work in public schools they choose private schools for their own children because they believe they are better."[87]

Unfortunately, Doyle's own data don't support his argument. *Public school* teachers send their children to private schools at a rate lower than the general public (12.1 percent to 13.1 percent), despite having higher educational levels and incomes than the general public. Indeed, one might, as one reviewer has, turn Doyle's logic on him and ask why 67.3 percent of private school teachers send their children to public schools.[88]

It is easy to understand that many in the African American community would choose to see vouchers as a way of gaining control of their own destinies. African American neighborhoods have been under economic siege for over two decades, and white America continues to be almost willfully ignorant of the crisis confronting black Americans.

In times of crisis, African Americans have historically looked inward for a source of strength and protection from a hostile, white-dominated society. In the 1880s, with the promise of post–Civil War reconstruction a fading dream, Bishop Henry Turner touched off "Africa fever" among African Americans. During the evil days of lynching and "separate but equal" treatment, Booker T. Washington preached self-help. Amid the strife and racial turmoil following World War I, Marcus Garvey organized the largest black organization in U.S. history, the Universal Negro Improvement Association.[89] And in 1995, Nation of Islam's leader Louis Farrakhan organized the Million Man March, in part to dramatize the need for African Americans to take charge of their own destiny.

However understandable, attempts to fit private school vouchers into a framework of empowerment may prove to be yet another painful dead end for the African American community. In the context of 1990s America, the politics of vouchers threaten to legitimate the kind of logic that produced Bantustans and native homelands under apartheid in South Africa.

There is precious little in U.S. history or current circumstance that suggests that giving the most segregated or impoverished segment of our society in the inner cities nominal control over its own school district or giving impoverished adults an educational "voucher" would lead to anything but more misery and destitution. The resources and power available to African Americans are too small in relation to the larger white community. It has nothing to do with the individual characteristics of the people involved and everything to do with the way economic and political power is distributed.

Williams and Fuller claim they would only support a voucher plan that applied exclusively to poor children and did not shift resources to the already privileged. This assertion seems to assume that poor children and their allies can somehow control the political debate. But there is simply no evidence to support this assumption and considerable evidence in the other direction.

It should serve as warning that the expansion of the Wisconsin parental choice legislation to include religious schools passed in 1995 was not crafted by Williams. It was written by a well-paid, white suburbanite under contract to the Metropolitan Milwaukee Association of Commerce—Susan Mitchell. That's the same Susan Mitchell who received $78,000 for writing the 1994 attack on the Milwaukee Public Schools for the Wisconsin Policy Research Institute.

The MMAC, most of whose members are white and live outside the city, didn't just draft proposed changes in the law. It also funded its own "grassroots" support in Milwaukee's inner city in the form of Parents for School Choice, a group headed by Zakiya Courtney, the former principal of a choice school. Although Courtney claimed to speak for 3,500 parents, her organization was, in fact, considered by many observers as little more than a mail drop, an answering machine, and a fax machine paid for by the business community. An articulate spokesperson, Courtney became a fixture in the local media and sometimes appeared in the national media as a "parent activist." In August 1995, with the battle to expand the voucher program won in the Wisconsin legislature and signed into law, the MMAC pulled the plug on Parents for School Choice, and Courtney reportedly went on to a new job at Mount Mary, a local Catholic women's college.[90]

No one criticized Parents for School Choice more harshly than Polly Williams. According to Williams, "The business community hired a consultant to promote school choice legislation. The people in the community didn't hire them. The business community did. They put a group in our community and said they represent parents. . . . 'Parents for School Choice' is just in the way."[91]

Looked at another way, it could be said that it was Williams who was suddenly in the way. She had served her purpose and provided an opening for the Bradley Foundation and the Milwaukee business community. Then, she was shoved aside as the foundation pursued what seems to be its real political agenda—dismantling the public school system and creating an educational "market."

As she found herself on the outside, Williams began fighting elements of the choice program that made it increasingly obvious the program was not, at heart, aimed at benefiting the poor. She publicly complained about registration fees at choice schools, ranging from $50 to $350,[92] and requirements at some private schools that parents contribute to fund-raising efforts with either time or money—both of which are in short supply among the working poor.[93] She even began lobbying the Wisconsin Department of Public Instruction to issue regulations to curb these practices.

By the end of 1995, it was becoming harder and harder to avoid the conclusion that the real effect of Wisconsin's private school voucher legislation would likely be to make poor parents more vulnerable, not less so. The voucher plan threatened to weaken the public school system, one of the few remaining large public institutions capable of blocking, to some small extent, the cold wind of the market for those with the least power in the marketplace. Whatever else the public schools may be, they are a large institution with broad reach in the community. They have to be taken into account.

If the Milwaukee voucher experiment were to become a national model, the ability of African Americans to use school systems as institutional vehicles for promoting the interests of their community will have been lost. African Americans have finally assumed leadership positions in city school systems across the country, yet now the talk is of dismantling those systems.

In the sort of radically decentralized education system that voucher advocates envision, the fifteen or twenty poor parents who succeeded in getting their kids into any particular school wouldn't have to be taken into account at all. Perhaps some people see that as a return to the natural order of things.

White conservative supporters of private school vouchers most often use a newfound concern for schools in the black community as their social justification. However, in Milwaukee, for example, vouchers also have some support in the Hispanic community. In part because many Latinos are Catholic, the idea of being able to choose to attend Catholic schools with a state-funded voucher is, on the surface, an attractive option.

Old-Time Religion

The use of private school vouchers to avoid racial integration in the South in the 1950s was often accomplished by means of all-white religious academies established by fundamentalist groups. In recent years, the increasing power of the Christian Coalition and other political-religious pressure groups on the Right has moved the tactics of anti-integration religious conservatives from the deep South onto a national level. At the Christian Coalition's national conference in 1995, a workshop called "School Choice—The Next Victory" outlined legal and political strategies for creating private school voucher plans that could rescue children from the "socialist training camps" of the public system.[94]

Another tireless religious champion of vouchers has been the Catholic Church. At least the Catholics' motive is straight-forward: They want the dough. The recent revival of political interest in vouchers came just as many Catholic schools across the country were preparing to close their doors. Until Wisconsin politicians started pushing school voucher legislation, the archbishop in Milwaukee wanted to get out of the business of educating kids. Enrollments were declining. Schools were closing. People weren't supporting the Catholic school system.

The biggest problem for Catholic systems across the country is soaring costs, a direct result of the dramatic drop in the number of men and women entering religious orders; their more numerous predecessors had always provided a pool of cheap teaching labor. By 1991, nearly 90 percent of teachers in Catholic schools were laypeople, and they expected real salaries. In response, the church launched a nationwide Discover Catholic Schools multimedia promotional campaign. The campaign came just as President Bush was pushing for more parental choice, and it was billed as an effort to "promote the rights of parents to select the best school for their children."[95]

To Catholics, the basic issue is economic survival, and their appeal is to fairness. Their argument is: We're providing a service and reducing public costs by educating children who otherwise would be in the public system. Our parishioners are picking up the tab even though most of the children who attend our schools in cities aren't even Catholic anymore. Since we are providing a public good, we should receive public funds.

The Catholic effort becomes a little less straightforward in some of the political support groups that now pretend to have more secular motives. In Milwaukee, this includes the PAVE Foundation, founded in 1992. PAVE is sometimes described as part of a nationwide philanthropic network of privately funded school choice plans. Whatever it claims to be now, PAVE started out in 1987 as a good, old-fashioned Catholic charity. It was then called the Milwaukee Archdiocesan Education Foundation and was endowed by the bishop of Milwaukee with $1 million.[96] However, when it was unable to raise enough money from businesses and foundations to keep Milwaukee's Catholic school system intact, PAVE became a "private scholarship program," headed by the same executive director as the former Milwaukee Archdiocesan Education Foundation. By becoming a private scholarship program, PAVE could claim a broader public purpose and, perhaps more important, collect tax-free contributions from corporations that might shy away from supporting only Catholic schools.

PAVE helps illustrate the connection that pulls together the conservative Bradley Foundation, the Catholic Church, and the business community to push for private school vouchers in Milwaukee. PAVE established what it calls the Partnership for Educational Choice, a program that provides half the tuition (up to $1,000) to any private school, sectarian or nonsectarian, selected by participating low-income parents. It started with an initial endowment of $500,000 from the Bradley Foundation and $100,000 each from Wisconsin Electric Power Company, Johnson Controls World Services, Inc., and Northwestern Mutual Life Insurance Company (the "quiet company").[97] Three years after forming the Education Trust to improve public education, the Milwaukee business community was committing the bulk of its educational funding to a program designed to support private schools.

The PAVE program is not unique. It is one of twenty-two privately funded "choice" programs across the country.[98] They are primarily supported by corporate and conservative interests. CEO America, for example, based in Bentonville, Arkansas, has received a $2 million, five-year grant from the Walton Family (of Wal-Mart fame) Foundation.[99]

The granddaddy of all these "private choice" programs is the Educational CHOICE Charitable Trust program set up in 1991 by J. Patrick Rooney, chairman and CEO of the Golden Rule Insurance Company of Indianapolis. Rooney and Golden Rule are described by John Judis in a *New Republic* essay this way: "Golden Rule is the kind of company that any reasonable national health care reform would have doomed to extinction. . . . *Consumer Reports* ranked it 'near the bottom' of insurance companies because of its inadequate coverage, frequent rate increases, and readiness to cancel policies. . . . Failing in the market, Golden Rule and its chairman Pat Rooney . . . sought government help to boost their business."[100]

Rooney is a big-time supporter of GOPAC, the organization set up by Newt Gingrich to fund the foot soldiers in his revolution. Since 1991, Golden Rule has invested more than $250,000 in lobbying. What Rooney wants is, among other things, something called a "medical savings account"—a scheme to attract money from the healthy that Consumers Union has called the antithesis of what health insurance should be. Not surprisingly, the Rooney-inspired medical savings account turned up first as part of the Republican plan to "reform" Medicare.[101] When that failed, it was made part of the health insurance reform legislation passed by the House on March 28, 1996.[102]

While Rooney was spreading money around in an attempt to get the federal government to turn on the cash spigot for Golden Rule, he also was waxing eloquent about what the market could do for schools. In an article entitled "Golden Rule—Living Up to Its Name," Rooney raised paeans to the need for "families to experience a sense of control over their future."[103] He was, of course, talking about the virtues of the privately funded school choice program (CHOICE Charitable Trust) that he had just set up in Indianapolis.

If private choice programs are, in fact, little more than the standard sort of charitable activity that businesses and foundations have engaged in for years, one might ask: What's in a name? The answer is, plenty. The name reveals the well-coordinated strategy behind the program: to build support for private school vouchers by claiming that parental acceptance of the private "choice" money reflects a surging popular demand for publicly funded private school vouchers.

More than a hundred participants at a November 1992 national conference of these groups in Indianapolis received a 181-page manual on how to organize a private voucher plan. It included the admonition to "conduct its entire developmental stage in secrecy" and "to be sure to present the program in a way that undercuts opposition."[104]

The conservative zealots who support school choice know, as Michael Joyce said in his speech announcing a $1 million gift to PAVE in 1995, that private charity cannot accomplish what they want. However, it can be a useful crow bar to try to pry open the public treasury to fund their market-driven vision.

PepsiCo, apparently unaware of the deeper political meaning of the phrase *private voucher program,* got caught in the political cross fire in New Jersey. After announcing a private voucher scholarship plan with the mayor of Jersey City on the steps of the city hall in October 1995, the company found itself engulfed in controversy. A few weeks later, in announcing that PepsiCo had shelved the program, Edwin Glasspool, a company spokesperson, said, "It kind of came out as 'Pepsi supports vouchers.' That's not what we're about. We just wanted to finance some scholarships for some urban kids."[105]

Joyce and others who try to transform private scholarships for the poor into public funding of private schools frequently use the justification that Catholic schools get better results for less money. The performance of Milwaukee's Catholic schools roughly follows the national pattern—although it is often hard to make reliable comparisons because private schools, religious or otherwise, do not have to reveal their test results. But in 1991, a Milwau-

kee newspaper reporter successfully prodded the Catholic archdiocese to release the test scores of children in its schools. The results should have come as
a shock to supporters of private school vouchers, many of whom claim that
children who attend Catholic schools get a better education for far less
money. The results showed that when the performance of children from similar social and economic backgrounds were compared, the Catholic schools
in the Milwaukee archdiocese did no better and perhaps a bit worse than the
much maligned Milwaukee Public Schools.[106]

An equally interesting picture emerges when the costs of Catholic and public school education are compared. In 1994, when the archdiocese began closing its central-city elementary schools, the Catholic school system had a
deficit of $100,000, largely because of a per-pupil tuition of approximately
$4,000 a year at the four schools. In the 1992–1993 school year, when ex-
cluding centrally budgeted items such as fringe benefits and transportation,
each elementary school in Milwaukee received, on average, approximately
$2,958. Even when the centrally budgeted items are included, the public
schools only spent approximately $4,645 per student.[107] And for that price,
the public schools took all students who showed up at their door, paid their
employees a livable wage with benefits, and provided a much more complete
educational program than the Catholic schools offered.[108] All of which suggests that the substantial amount of energy put into private school vouchers
has little to do with trying to provide a high-quality education for every child.

The real issue in school performance, not surprisingly, is not a religious
versus nonreligious or even a private versus public issue. Rather, it is a matter
of advantaged versus nonadvantaged children. A national study of student
performance published in *Money* magazine in 1994, "Why Private Schools
Are Rarely Worth the Money," found achievement in public schools serving
high-income areas and in elite, private prep schools was very similar. Perhaps
because of higher salaries, public school teachers had stronger academic qualifications than their private and religious school counterparts.[109] *Money*'s advice to its readers was: Send your children to public schools.

Reform Without Content

Something obvious needs to be said about private school vouchers. Despite
being touted as an educational reform, a voucher plan has absolutely no educational content—none. If the strongest supporters of private school vouchers were asked to describe a so-called choice school, they couldn't provide an
answer. There is no distinctive curriculum. There is no distinctive instruc-

tional style. There is no distinctive organization. There is literally no educational content attached to a school that would be funded by private school vouchers. It could be anything.

Confronted with this paradox, the political right wing and captains of industry parrot the rhetoric of CEO Mao and the great cultural revolution of China: "Let a thousand flowers bloom." The paradox has turned some segments of the business community comically schizophrenic. Corporate heavyweights entered the debate over public education demanding world-class standards. Our very survival as a nation was at stake unless we raised the standards of our public schools, they said.

The problem is that many have also been convinced by neoconservative deep thinkers that they should put their power behind radical decentralization of the entire educational system. But when you give control of the educational program to each school participating in a radically decentralized system, it's like herding cats: It becomes virtually impossible to gather and disseminate meaningful information about the overall performance of the system or even about which schools are doing well and which are doing poorly according to some common standard. It is conceivable that hundreds of innovative ways for schools to perform poorly would be discovered without any school being held accountable.

A final point is a sad one. Using vouchers to decentralize the public school system is a proclamation that, as a nation, we no longer aspire to provide a high-quality education for all children. Instead, those children who are smart enough to choose parents who are smart enough to negotiate a decentralized system to their advantage are given a chance to maybe—just maybe—get a better education.

Poor parents are being offered an illusion of hope, but what really is being created is a lifeboat mentality. Parents who don't like their schools are not encouraged to organize, take them over, and demand a better education for their kids. Instead, voucher supporters shout that the ship is sinking and there are only enough lifeboats to save a small percentage of our children. You'd better make sure your kids get in the boat fast.

6

Charter Schools:
The Smiling Face
of Disinvestment

Charter schools are the hottest reform of the 1990s. Everyone, it seems, loves them. *Time* magazine says they are the "New Hope for Public Schools."[1] *The Economist* proclaims that schools are "Free at Last."[2] The Democratic Leadership Council journal, *The New Democrat*, says advocates are "Rebels with a Cause."[3] And the *New York Times* (introducing an unusual note of irony) calls them the "Latest 'Best Hope' in U.S. Education."[4]

By anyone's reckoning, the rise of charter schools to the top of the educational reform agenda has been spectacular. Barely five years old, the charter school movement has its own organization, the National Association of Charter Schools, its own newsletter, the *Charter School Chronicle*, and even (as evidence of serious, long-term aspirations) a fledgling scholarly journal, the *American Journal of Charter Schools*. It has strong support from well-placed politicians such as former Bush administration secretary of education Lamar Alexander; Roy Romer, the Democratic governor of Colorado; William Weld, the Republican governor of Massachusetts; and even President Bill Clinton.

Throughout the 1980s, the school reforms capturing most of the attention were those associated with the *Nation at Risk* report: private school vouchers and public school choice. Then, in a 1988 National Press Club speech, Albert Shanker, president of the American Federation of Teachers, pushed a new reform idea. He called for empowering teachers by creating "charter" schools that focused on professional development and had a clear commitment to improving student achievement.[5] To many educators, parents, and politicians, the charter school idea represents a public education alternative to private school voucher proposals. It is an idea they can embrace enthusiastically because it seems to both protect public education as an institution and, at the same time, provide for fundamental reform and systemic "restructuring." As a bonus, charter schools have more media sex appeal than, say, site-based management.

In the early 1990s, a number of factors helped accelerate the rush to charter schools. The *Nation at Risk* reforms were increasingly abandoned by important segments of the business community and under attack as little more than costly tinkering with a failed educational status quo. School vouchers hit a wall of sorts when three voucher referenda between 1989 and 1993 (in Oregon, Colorado, and California) lost by better than 2-to-1 margins, and the defeat of George Bush in the 1992 presidential election removed a powerful voucher advocate from the White House.

These developments, coupled with the general deregulatory trajectory of American politics and policy, virtually assured that charter schools would become the next education "revolution." And indeed, by the mid-1990s, a volatile mixture of proposals that were often very different in spirit from the ideas expressed in Shanker's National Press Club speech were advancing under the banner of charter school reform.

Tom Watkins, the director of the Detroit Center for Charter Schools, has found that charter school advocates are usually one of three types. The zealots, he says, are those who believe: "Private is always better than public, the market system is inherently superior to the public system, unions are always the problem, and private and religious schools out-perform public schools even when socio-economic differences are taken into account."[6] A conservative supporter such as Jeanne Allen, a former Heritage Foundation policy analyst and founder of the Center for Education Reform, falls into this category.

The second group of charter school supporters, according to Watkins, are entrepreneurs. They want to make money running schools or school programs. In the Edison Project schools operating in Mount Clements, Michigan, and Boston, Massachusetts, for example, private entrepreneurs are using charter school legislation as an opportunity to turn a profit.

The third group consists of what Watkins calls child-, parent-, and teacher-centered reformers. These reformers support charter schools because they are interested in expanding public school options and providing the sort of creative tension they believe will help improve all schools. Watkins places himself in this camp. It is this group—perceived as representing a kind, moderate, educational middle—that generates most of the favorable press reports about dedicated individuals struggling to make a difference in the lives of America's schoolchildren. These are the people who have given the charter school movement its air of mainstream respectability.

Despite the rosy image provided by the child-centered reformers, there isn't much question that most of the money and political influence driving the charter movement has been provided by the zealots and the profiteers. They have co-opted the language of the child-centered reformers to lend social acceptability to their attacks on any adult who would attempt to stand in the way of their ideology or their profits. Their goal is not nearly as caring as their rhetoric. Bluntly put, it is to dismember public education and feed off of the carcass.

Prairie Fire Reform

Most charter school reformers aim their rhetorical firepower at those ever popular sources of all evil in American public education: "overregulation" and unresponsive bureaucracies. Remove the regulation and dismantle the bureaucracies, their logic goes, and—voilà—a thousand flowers cultivated by the unfettered ingenuity, energy, and commitment of parents and teachers will bloom. The idea is simple, direct, and appealingly libertarian. It also fits nicely with the received wisdom that public schools are so bad almost any experiment is worth trying, as well as with the ongoing effort to restructure public education by devolving more decisionmaking authority to individual schools. It is small wonder that by 1991, the charter school bandwagon was in the bipartisan political fast lane and gaining speed.

In 1991, Minnesota became the first state to pass a charter school law. The Minnesota legislation enabled school districts to "charter" schools organized by teachers. These schools were freed of most state and local regulations and operated as nonprofit cooperatives that were legally autonomous. Existing nonsectarian private schools also were allowed to apply for charter status. For the most part, the Minnesota legislation met Shanker's criterion of empowering teachers.

Within fours years, charter school laws had been adopted from one end of the country to the other. At the end of 1994, 11 states had some form of charter school law on the books and 134 charter schools had been approved.[7] By spring 1995, the number of states that had passed charter school legislation had risen to 20, and the number of charter schools approved had jumped to 200. Of those, 110 schools were up and running.[8]

A survey of the 110 charter schools open nationwide, published in August 1995, found that about 27,500 students were enrolled. Most of the schools they attended were small (with about 250 students—or only 140 if California charter schools were excluded). The schools were most often located in "leased commercial space" (in Hull, Massachusetts, for example, this meant eight rooms in the Seashore Motel). Two-thirds wanted to attract a cross section of students, and about half were intended to serve "at-risk" students. Their academic focus was primarily on "integrated interdisciplinary curriculum," or "technology," or a "back to the basics" program.[9]

Although charter school legislation has indeed swept the nation, the practical meaning of the term *charter school* varies considerably from state to state. The political struggle between charter school advocates with different agendas is evident. At a minimum, however, all states define charter schools as public schools that operate under a special contract or charter. Depending on the state, the sponsor granting that charter can be a school district, a university, a state education board, or some other public authority. Instead of having to meet most state or district regulations, a charter school is accountable for such matters as educational programming, academic results, and fiscal affairs under the terms of its contract with its sponsoring organization.[10] The sponsoring organization is, in turn, responsible for guaranteeing compliance with the contract. In almost all cases, charter schools are to be nonselective, tuition-free, nonsectarian, and based on choice. Funding depends directly on the number of students enrolled.

One of the most significant differences among the various charter school laws is the degree of autonomy they grant to the schools. Arizona, California, Colorado, Massachusetts, Michigan, and Minnesota have what are sometimes characterized as "strong" charter school laws because they allow the schools to operate as legally independent entities with a high degree of autonomy. In contrast, the "weak" charter school laws passed by Georgia, Hawaii, Kansas, New Mexico, and Wyoming grant charter schools little more autonomy than other public schools.[11] Most, but not all, states place limits on the number of charter schools allowed.

Obviously, the definitions of "strong" and "weak" in this context are in the eye of the beholder. Given the variety of reasons offered for embracing the charter school concept—encouraging innovative teaching, creating new professional opportunities for teachers, promoting community involvement, improving student learning, and promoting performance-based accountability, among others[12]—it is not surprising that charter school legislation varies considerably. The different legislative formulations each has its advocates. But an important rhetorical battle already has been won by those who would use such laws for their own profit when laws that loosen regulation and oversight are characterized as "strong."

A Curriculum-Free Franchise

The second annual charter school conference, hosted by Wisconsin's Republican governor Tommy Thompson in Milwaukee in April 1995, offered an insight into the tenor of the charter school movement. The people at this meeting were on another planet compared to the long-haired, jeans-clad free-schoolers of the 1960s and 1970s who dominated alternative education meetings with passionate discussions about the role of schools in promoting social and economic justice.

The group gathered in Milwaukee was overwhelmingly white, well groomed, polite, upbeat, earnest, decidedly middle-class, and very *entrepreneurial*. The meeting had an air of good-natured self-congratulation and determined enthusiasm that might be expected at a convention of fast food franchisees, software vendors, or health care product merchandisers.

Vendors offered their help to get *your* new charter school off the ground ("Take a look at what GRANT$LINE INC. has to offer"). State government officials described the charter laws in their states, and charter school operators shared their experiences. The National Education Association was represented, and so was the for-profit Edison Project. The San Diego Chamber of Commerce sent someone to explain why the business community should support charter schools. The conservative Goldwater Institute made a presentation. There also was a sprinkling of academics, parents, and school superintendents.

Despite the appearance of a representative from Bill Clinton's Department of Education, who explained federal charter school legislation, the meeting had a distinctly Republican flavor, albeit "big-tent" Republican. There was no doubt that, as far as the organizers of the conference were concerned, charter schools were at the cutting edge of American school reform. Much less clear was what was to be taught in these revolutionary new schools.

Since charter schools represent a structural reform in how schools are governed, supporters are not hampered by any need to establish a common view of what constitutes a high-quality education. Their motto, "let a thousand flowers bloom," probably accounts for a good deal of the reform's political cachet. Having to agree on little more than the term *charter schools*—a term that is subject to manifold interpretations—gives politicians of every stripe the opportunity to become wholehearted backers of reform.

Within the charter school movement, the lack of definitional precision makes it easier for supporters to form working coalitions with others who may have very different educational views. However, as the charter school bandwagon rolls on, it is almost guaranteed that much of the sunny camaraderie that pervaded that movement's early days will dissolve into arguments over which faction's views represent the "real" charter school reform ideal. Already, some charter school policy documents warn that "opponents" of charter schools are getting smarter and attempting to kill the idea by supporting "weak" charter school laws.[13]

From the standpoint of figuring out how effective charter schools are at improving the academic performance of public education, the lack of a common educational view presents lots of problems. Since charter schools can be held accountable for many different things, measuring their performance against a common set of academic standards is not possible. Although charter school reform is based on the premise that public schools are failing, the vagueness of the reform with regard to education makes it virtually impossible to know whether charter schools are succeeding.

An Attempted Evaluation

By mid-1996, no national evaluation of the effectiveness of charter schools has been completed. However, the Pew Charitable Trusts are funding a national Hudson Institute study being conducted by Chester Finn and Louann Bierlein. And an evaluation commissioned by the U.S. Department of Education should begin reporting its findings by 1998 or 1999. A 1995 report, "Charter Schools: Legislation and Results After Four Years," issued by the Indiana Policy Center, found little in the way of systematic evidence that suggested charter schools increased student achievement. According to Mark Buechler, the report's author, this was at least in part because many charter schools had not developed rigorous expectations for performance or detailed how performance was to be measured.[14] These are disquieting shortcomings for a reform sold to the public on the basis of its ability to improve educational accountability.

In December 1994, the House Research Department of the Minnesota legislature released a report on that state's charter schools. The report did not try to judge the success or failure of the charter experiment, for the authors felt it was too early for that. However, it did highlight a number of problems that threw into question the idea that charter schools would provide a model for public school reform.[15]

Since Minnesota charter schools were free of all legal requirements placed on public schools except those clearly spelled out in their charters, the schools didn't necessarily have to operate in open meetings or otherwise be subject to public scrutiny. That made it difficult for the public to hold them accountable for proper and efficient conduct of their activities. Accountability was further compromised by a finding that school boards granting charters could be unwilling or unable to adequately evaluate charter school outcomes or student success.

One of the biggest problems Minnesota charter schools faced was financing. As a result, they relied on experienced teachers to accept low salaries and take on administrative and other responsibilities so the schools could afford to do things such as reduce class sizes. Charter schools also had difficulty finding facilities and paying for even the most basic equipment, such as books and desks, without additional income from private sources that could not be relied upon to provide continuing, long-term support. The financial problems faced by Minnesota's charter schools are not unique. A 1995 survey of charter schools around the country found that financial support and the lack of start-up funds were the most frequently mentioned problems.[16] The authors of the Minnesota House Research Department report concluded that without increased support, "it is not clear that charter schools will be able to function as anything but educational reform 'on the margin.'"[17]

Despite the report's perfectly reasonable conclusion, most charter school supporters would be the last ones to admit publicly that they are backing a reform that has no demonstrated ability to increase academic achievement and that will cost lots of additional money to get off the ground and stay aloft. Most would rather claim that the market will somehow provide. That is why charter school advocates often prefer to frame the issue of accountability the same way voucher supporters do. Real accountability, they say, is imposed by the market. Market competition will attract parents who "know what they like" and who are "empowered" to choose the school their children attend. In other words, charter schools are accountable because if parents think a charter school's program is good, they will send their kids, and if they don't, they won't. This view assumes parents know an effective school program when they see one and could not possibly be satisfied with an ineffective school.

Undeniably, this position has lots of populist appeal. In practice, however, parents' decisions about where to send their children are much more complex than a simple judgment about a school's academic program. Considerations such as proximity to the school, work schedules, availability of after-school care, and extracurricular activities get thrown into the mix. Also, if choice is to be a real option, as opposed to a rhetorical one, parents must have more than just the freedom to walk away from schools they don't like. They also have to be able to get their children into the schools they prefer.

The chance of a market creating a multitude of options for all parents, especially those in most impoverished urban areas, is so small as to be nonexistent. That is no doubt why, as yet, no one has explained in concrete, practical terms how the surplus educational capacity needed to give parents such an opportunity would be created. Who pays to keep a vast network of partially filled schools at the ready should a dissatisfied parent decide to switch schools? In the real world, as opposed the miraculous world of the educational "market," financing already limits a parent's choices. Charter schools do nothing to change that basic fact.

Real World Problems

Many people are learning that operating a school outside the existing public school system is much harder than it sounds. That is not because of bureaucratic obstructionism. It is because of real logistical problems, space needs, and, most important of all, capital costs. The problem of capitalizing charter school reform without spending additional tax dollars is what made the promises of the for-profit firms Education Alternatives, Inc., and the Edison Project so attractive at first blush. However, as anyone who has run a business knows, capital doesn't come cheap.

The EAI contract with Baltimore, for example, virtually guaranteed that its up-front investment was a risk-free one that would be repaid with handsome dividends.[18] Although this setup helped ensure EAI's profitability in Baltimore, it also meant that unless there was an increase in school funding, EAI would have to be paid off by reducing expenditures on children attending Baltimore's non-EAI schools.

Nonprofit groups running independent charter schools face similar financial problems and equity issues. The experience in Massachusetts illustrates the point. Although the state set aside an additional $2.5 million of new state money and received $829,000 from the federal government under the 1993 Education Reform Act to help defray the start-up costs of charter schools, it was not nearly enough to meet their capital needs by 1995.[19]

Besides not providing sufficient funds (which would be politically impossible for a supposedly "cost-neutral" reform), the funding formula for charter schools established by the Massachusetts law creates another problem. It provides the same amount of money for each student regardless of grade level, ignoring the fact that secondary education is more expensive than elementary education. As a result, the operators of elementary charter schools in Massachusetts are relatively fat and happy while the secondary charter schools are pressed for cash.

The popularity of charter schools seems to demonstrate America's enduring faith that major educational reforms can be accomplished on the cheap. Charter school reformers in Massachusetts and elsewhere have sold the idea that their schools won't cost anyone any money—a real "win-win" reform. This fiscal miracle is accomplished by a budgetary sleight of hand. The money provided to educate charter school students is taken out of the state aid to the district in which the student lives.

On the surface, such a system may indeed seem "cost neutral." However, this system of funding serves to harm students who remain in the public school district that is footing the bill. In Boston, for example, the public schools lose $7,000 per student in state aid for each student attending a charter school. The district only spends approximately $5,851 on its own students. In addition, Boston and other public school districts are required to pay for the transportation of charter school students and the cost of fringe benefits for any public school employee who chooses to work in a charter school.

The Boston Public Schools lost approximately $6 million in operating revenues for the 1995–1996 school year as a result of the Massachusetts charter school law. Since children attending these schools in Boston do not come from the same school or classroom originally but are instead drawn from all over the district, there is little or no possibility for the Boston public school system to realize enough savings in its operating costs to make up for the money lost.

To make matters worse, public schools in Massachusetts are also required to pay charter schools for children in their district who were not previously students in the public schools. For example, of the nearly 630 students attending the Renaissance charter school run by the Edison Project in Boston, about 200 had not been students in the Boston public schools. Nevertheless, the Boston system had to pony up almost $1.5 million to pay for their education at Renaissance.

During the 1995–1996 school year, Massachusetts reimbursed the Boston public schools for about half of the $6 million in state aid it lost as a result of the charter school law. The city of Boston picked up the rest. It is anybody's guess where the extra money will come from in the future. One thing is certain, however: If the lost revenue is not replaced, the people who will wind up paying for the "cost-neutral" charter school reform in Massachusetts are the children left in the public schools. That makes charter school laws like the one in Massachusetts look more like unfunded mandates than serious educational reform.

Watching the Money

How to raise the necessary money is one of the financial problems facing charter school reformers. How to keep track of it after it has been raised is another. Few of the institutions legally empowered to grant charters are likely to have either the expertise or the resources to monitor and enforce those charters. If the experience with educational performance contracting during the Nixon administration and the more recent contract problems between Education Alternatives, Inc., and the Baltimore and Hartford school systems are any indication, there will soon be more scandals about mismanagement and educational short-sheeting at charter schools.

One California charter school, Edutrain, went belly up in 1994 without accounting for over $1 million in public money. Apparently, the school administration had been spending funds to help pay the principal's rent and lease him a sports car, hire a bodyguard, and pay for a $7,000 staff retreat in Carmel—even while teachers lacked textbooks and supplies.[20]

To some charter school supporters, the failure of Edutrain is an example of the educational market imposing its discipline. The only problem with this logic is that an educational "market" did not punish the people who set up Edutrain the way a financial market punishes investors in stocks and bonds when share prices plummet or a bond issuer defaults. The people punished in the Edutrain fiasco were the children who attended the school and had their education disrupted and the taxpayers and students in the Los Angeles Unified School District who were out the money and received nothing in return. The charter school market feeds on the revenue provided by taxpayers even in failure. It is a market in which the financial risks are socialized and the financial gains are privatized.

In spite of all the rhetoric about accountability, early reports of the "success" of charter schools often rest on little more than the fact that they are open and the people involved are happy. This gives charter schools the kind of "feel-good" standard of performance that is firmly rejected by critics when applied to public schools. Louis V. Gerstner Jr., the CEO of IBM, for example, actually complains about poll results showing a high degree of parental satisfaction with the public schools their children attend. He argues that parental satisfaction with public schools is an impediment to educational reform because it allows educators to believe they are doing a good enough job.[21]

The Demonizing of Teachers

The lack of a common educational vision assures that the argument for charter schools (like the argument for private school vouchers) is dominated by economic, not educational, ideas. Central to the logic of both vouchers and charter schools is the idea that competition will force public schools, which now have a monopoly in providing educational services, to improve or perish as parents choose to send their children to better schools. Unfortunately, *how* competition will result in better teaching and more learning is never specified.

The assumption is that educators have grown fat and complacent in the warm embrace of a government monopoly and that a threat to their now-secure futures will force them to figure out how to do a better job. In this scenario, teachers' unions are considered self-interested culprits responsible for driving up the cost of education without being willing to accept accountability for improving student achievement.

Charter school zealots such as Jeanne Allen ridicule the idea that schools (particularly in poor, urban districts) might need more money to improve. Any increase in funding would, from their perspective, be throwing good money after bad. In what has become the conventional wisdom in the charter school movement, the enemies of school improvement are rigid union contracts, bloated and unresponsive bureaucracies, and overregulation, not fiscal constraints.

This construction of the problem puts conservative charter school advocates like Allen in the odd position of calling for teacher empowerment while at the same time railing against teachers' unions. Taking the next logical step, they often assert that teachers are victimized by their unions and, therefore, that the way to liberate teachers and improve education is to dismantle their unions. As Allen darkly warns readers of her *School Reform Handbook*: "A public school teacher who will openly support your position brings credibility and an air of non-partisanship and fairness to your organization. But, be understanding of the fact that a teacher willing to do so may be taking both professional and personal risks."[22]

In some ways, this logic is reminiscent of Margaret Thatcher's support for the Polish union Solidarity during its clash with Poland's Communist government in the 1980s. While supporting Solidarity in Poland, Thatcher was doing everything she could to crush the power of trade unions in Great Britain—in the name of helping British working people.

Hostility toward teacher unions and the teacher certification requirements they have achieved is built into some so-called strong charter school laws, including those in Arizona, California, and Massachusetts. Under those laws, virtually any adult with "qualifications" is allowed to teach in a charter school—or administer one for that matter—without the need for certification. This approach is, in some ways, analogous to trying to solve the problem of access to health care by allowing anyone who can attract patients to practice medicine.

The 1995 revision of Wisconsin's charter school law is another example of how teachers unions' have been identified as enemies of school reform and obstacles to improving school performance. In the Wisconsin law, there is now an explicit prohibition against teachers in Milwaukee charter schools belonging to the union local that represents their colleagues in the district. This provision not only makes it harder for charter school teachers to organize, it also assures that their bargaining position, should they nonetheless choose to organize, will be much weaker than it would be if they were part of a larger local.

For people who regard teachers' unions as the enemy, this is, of course, all to the good. Whatever one's views of teachers' unions, however, the issues that unions address are real and important to people who work in schools. They will not go away just because a charter school law makes it harder for unions to be organized. For example, a charter school survey in California found that regardless of their attitudes toward teachers' unions or union contracts, charter schools' staff members were most worried about issues such as tenure, pay, and job assignment.[23]

Edventures in Exploitation

The surge of interest in charter schools seems to have energized a fledgling movement seeking to increase the number of what are called "teachers in private practice." The American Association of Teachers in Private Practice was founded in 1990.[24] The group cosponsored Edventures 95 in July 1995, which was billed as a meeting for "Edventurers seeking new opportunities with the rapidly changing face of education."[25] Other meeting sponsors included Charter School Strategies, Inc., Designs for Learning, Education Investing, Inc., and the University of St. Thomas. Speakers included people active in the charter school movement and *lots* of entrepreneurs.

There is no doubt about it: "Teachers in private practice" is a movement for teachers who want to work as entrepreneurs rather than employees. The promotion of teachers as entrepreneurs is couched in the language of greater professionalism and independence for educators who are freed to work when and where they want and even free to set their own fees. To those who contend good teachers are too often yoked to incompetents by union protections, the idea also is presented as a chance for good teachers to take their competence to the marketplace and receive the greater rewards their talents will command.[26]

The prospect of becoming a teacher in "private practice" is probably appealing to a relatively small number of educators who, for one reason or another, don't have to rely solely on their teaching income and to those who think the risks and rewards of life in the marketplace will liberate their creative energies from the constraints imposed by the bureaucratic public education system. But for a number of reasons, the chances of the idea accomplishing what its proponents claim are pretty slim. In practice, the ability of professionals to set their own fees depends on how many others are competing in the marketplace. Since the money available for public education is tightly constrained, it is most likely that cost, not competence, will often be the most important factor in whether someone is hired. The combination of a large pool of potential teachers and tight school budgets guarantees that even John Dewey would find it hard to command a higher price for his talent.

The most likely outcome of changing state laws to make it easier to be a private practice teacher will be that large numbers of teachers will find themselves shut out of the more highly paying positions with fringe benefits that they might have had as school district employees in the past. These teachers will be involuntary teachers in private practice. If school districts are given the opportunity to hire teachers as private contractors without regard to union contract provisions, they will have a financial incentive to hire as many as possible on that basis. Furthermore, if teachers are private contractors, school districts won't have to provide them with fringe benefits, meet work rules negotiated by a union, or guarantee job security. Inevitably, the number of openings for teachers employed by the school district will shrink. As it does, the alleged professional independence of private practice teachers would mean little more than the freedom to do the same work for lower wages.

Such teachers would have few opportunities to raise their incomes, whatever their competence. This mirrors what has happened at public universities since the mid-1970s. As the amount of money available to hire professors in positions leading to tenure has steadily diminished, more "adjuncts" have been hired to work on year-to-year contracts at low pay with few, if any, fringe benefits.[27] A small number of educators might find this an acceptable arrangement because of some unique circumstance. Most, however, feel trapped in low-paying, dead-end jobs that undervalue their skills and their contributions. They are, as the outside critics argue, free to change careers. However, a system that consistently turns away talented people who otherwise would become the next generation of academic leaders undermines the quality of higher education in the long run. Ultimately, it robs students and society at large of the contributions those professors could have made.

Private practice teachers—along with other adults who, under some charter school laws, are allowed to teach without certification—also would provide a reserve labor pool that could be used to weaken the bargaining position of teachers' unions and hold down the wages of unionized teachers. Certified and uncertified teachers in private and religious schools are already in this battered boat. That's why large numbers leave those mythically superior schools as quickly as they can find decent-paying jobs in a public school system.

Sold as an appealingly libertarian idea, teachers in private practice would, in operation, probably best serve the short-term interests of school boards, corporations, and their political allies who want to drive down the cost of public education by reducing the earnings of people who work in schools. It also would enlarge the skilled labor pool of relatively low-paid workers for companies such as Sylvan Learning Centers, which contract with schools to provide specified educational services. The increased use of educational contractors employing a large number of private practice teachers at lower wages than they would receive as school district employees would further increase the pressure for public schools to privatize as much of their operations as possible. And this is exactly the point for the zealots and the profiteers.

However the various proponents of teachers in private practice may view themselves, an expanded use of such teachers would quickly become little more than a cover for lowering wages. This "cost saving" would be the mirror image of the private sector strategy of increasing profits by reducing workers' wages through contracting out with a vengeance in the 1980s and 1990s.

Most charter school supporters realize that their schools can never occupy more than a very small corner in American public education without either drastic reductions in the wages of school employees or huge increases in education spending. Such increases could only come from corporations and wealthy individuals since working people can no longer afford to pay a disproportionate share of taxes to maintain the public school system.

For the zealots and profiteers, charter schools are as much a vehicle for breaking up teachers' unions and lowering wages as an education reform strategy. That is why so much of their rhetoric demonizes teachers' unions and paints them as selfish enemies of reform. They attack the unions for backing "weak" charter laws (i.e., those that keep charter schools clearly accountable within the structure of public education). For all the profiteers' talk of rewarding excellence, the concept of teachers in private practice is just one more useful mechanism to protect corporate interests and wealthy individuals from the threat of education-related tax increases. They claim more educational funding would only benefit the adults who work in schools, as if the interests of students and their schools were somehow in competition.

The prospect of lower wages for teachers and other school employees may be very attractive to some hard-pressed communities, school boards, and administrators in the short term. However, in the long term, a continuing erosion of teachers' wages would threaten to drive many of the best prospective teachers into other occupations. The most likely effect would be to lower the overall quality of public education, inevitably harming the poorest children the most.

Storefront Education

One of the most hotly contested aspects of charter schools is who will run them. As originally proposed by AFT president Shanker, the idea was to "empower" certified teachers by freeing them from regulations so they could run the educational program of their schools more effectively. However, charter school laws in states that allow private and for-profit schools to operate without certified teachers open the door to some strange possibilities.

Consider the Gaddie family. The Gaddies have years of experience running private schools in Arizona. In the 1970s, they ran the John Hancock Academy to teach the McGuffey Reader to their own children and a few others. Later, they opened the Mountain States Technical Institute to serve high school and post–high school students. The Mountain States Technical Institute filed for bankruptcy and was closed in 1991 following investigations by the Internal Revenue Service, the U.S. Department of Education, and the Arizona State Board for Private Post-Secondary Education. The Gaddies stood accused of misusing government funds and a variety of other complaints.

Inspired by Arizona's "strong" charter school law, the Gaddies filed applications to open three charter schools. Mom and Dad Gaddie applied to open the McGuffey Basic School. Their daughters applied to open the Patrick Henry Basic School (submitting the same application minus the references to McGuffey). And their son Reed applied to open Arizona Apprenticeship Training School. Reed Gaddie, a graduate of his parents' Mountain States Technical Institute, planned to teach high school–age kids the heating and ventilation trade. His was the only application approved—pending a background and credit check.[28]

The Gaddies are only one example of the eager entrepreneurs unleashed by Arizona's charter school law. The state allows virtually anyone who can fill out an application, submit a business plan, pass a background and credit check, and pay the $32 cost for fingerprinting to have a shot at running a school. The law has produced a colorful profusion of applications (e.g., Global Renaissance Academy of Distinguished Education, Eduprise, Phoenix Academy of Learning, Global Academy for International Athletics, and EduPreneurship[29]) and a lot of offbeat, underfunded little schools.

Not all of the charter schools opened in Arizona or anywhere will be run by folks like the Gaddies. Some will be run by small groups of teachers and others trying to implement their vision of a high-quality education. Many will work long and hard to accomplish their goals, and some will have good results. However, many of these schools probably won't last long. People burn out, they move on, their kids grow up, and, for any number of reasons, the effort collapses.

The quick-buck operators, on the other hand, are likely to be much more durable. Attracted by the lack of regulations, effective fiscal controls, or academic standards and untroubled by any concern for the welfare of their students, they will be free to set up and close down over and over again, milking the system for as much as they can get. Their role models will be the scam artists who bilk postsecondary students out of their college Pell Grant money and student loans by opening up fly-by-night schools of "business" or "technology" or, perhaps, even "hair styling" and "nail" academies.

One of the paradoxes of the charter school idea is that the further the schools are outside the public school system, the more they rely on the idiosyncratic vision of a few people and the more exotic their methods of funding become. As a result, even if there are some individual success stories over the next few years, they may not serve as models for improving the education of children elsewhere because the circumstances will be unique.

The Public Debate and the Real One

Nevertheless, supporters and opponents will spend a lot of time debating the successes and failures of charter schools to suit their own purposes. There will be growing pains. For example, in Massachusetts, the Atlantis charter school was reportedly sinking. And by December 1995, the Valley Academy, an Arizona charter school, was on the verge of going belly up because of financial difficulties.[30] Charter schools will fail, fraud will be uncovered, and tax dollars will be wasted. But just as certainly, glowing testimony will be paid to the dedication and sacrifice of the selfless teachers and administrators at some "Chartermetoo" school who transformed the lives of their students and proved the success of charter school reform.

Free-market zealots will either claim vindication or argue their revolutionary ideas need more time to work. Supporters of public education will call the experiment a costly failure and marvel at the willingness to spend large sums on unproven alternatives while cutting resources for the public system that serves most children. With an absence of any uniform standards, the war of educational anecdotes and misleading statistics will remain "subject to interpretation." And all the while, the desperation of America's poorest children and their families will grow.

No state's charter schools, under laws strong or weak, will make an appreciable difference in the educational experience of most of these children. They are failing in public schools. They are failing in Catholic schools. They are going under. That is not because poor children cannot succeed. It is because they have been abandoned in an intellectual debate that masks selfish interests with calls for "market based" school reform without ever acknowledging the millions of children who have been shut out of the game.

Ill-fed, unhealthy, and growing up in economically devastated, unsafe neighborhoods, America's children of poverty are hardly in any position to play the market to their advantage. They need the sustained care and close attention of competent and nurturing adults. They need it in school and out. No amount of entrepreneurial zeal will make up for a lack of resources to provide for them. Indeed, it is the market that has destroyed the neighborhoods where these children live and knocked the pins out from under the adults on whom they rely. Unleashing the market on the public schools will only compound the harm.

Charter schools, like private school vouchers and for-profit schools, are built on the market-inspired illusion that our society can be held together solely by the selfish pursuit of our individual purposes. The charter school movement represents a radical rejection not only of the possibility of the common school but also of common purposes outside the school. The struggle is not, at its root, between market-based reforms and the educational status quo. Rather, it is a battle over whether the democratic ideal of the common good can survive the onslaught of a market mentality that threatens to turn every human relationship, inside and outside the classroom, into a commercial transaction.

7

What the Market Can't Provide

Lamar Alexander might be called many things. But no one would ever fault his political instincts or accuse him of a lack of ambition. Alexander served two terms as governor of Tennessee, put in a stint as president of the University of Tennessee, became President George Bush's secretary of education, and then spent much of the mid-1990s in a failed effort to win the 1996 Republican presidential nomination.

Education reform is an important part of Alexander's political persona. His views on education and social policy reflect an emerging consensus between neoconservative Republicans and so-called New Democrats. He is a tireless campaigner for the "systemic" restructuring of American public education. As secretary of education, he pushed the administration's "break-the-mold" school reform initiative to create a model innovative school in each congressional district. He also talked up the New American Schools Development Corporation set up at the urging of the Bush administration to channel corporate money to school reform projects. Alexander loves private school vouchers, charter schools, and for-profit management of public schools. And as an early investor in Whittle Communications, he made a lot of money from the selling of children to advertisers.

Despite Alexander's interest in school reform, there is a successful educational initiative from his past that he does not talk about these days, a reform that holds a greater potential for improving public school performance than virtually all the ideas he now supports. How surprising it is that he has been unwilling to trumpet his accomplishment.

When Alexander entered his second term as governor of Tennessee, education was at the top of his agenda. At the same time, influential leaders in state education were intrigued by what appeared to be positive results from a statewide effort in Indiana to reduce class size. Tennessee legislators were aware, however, that years of research on class size had produced inconclusive and sometimes contradictory results. As a result, they did not want to mandate reducing class size unless they had proof that smaller classes would mean greater student achievement.

A Reform That Works

The legislature hit upon the idea of commissioning a statewide study focusing on a specific question: What is the effect of smaller classes on student achievement and development in the early primary grades (K–3)? After some high-powered political wheeling and dealing, legislation funding the Tennessee Student Teacher Achievement Ratio (STAR) study was signed into law by Alexander in 1985.

From 1985 to 1989, researchers followed a group of more than 7,000 children attending 79 schools in 42 school districts throughout Tennessee, from kindergarten through third grade. The schools participating were in rural, urban, suburban, and innercity locations. In each school, children and teachers in the study were randomly assigned to either a small class (15 students), a regular class (24 students), or a regular class (24 students) with a teacher and a teacher's aide.

All three types of classes were used in every participating school, and all schools followed their normal practices in every other way. Results were measured on both standardized and criterion-referenced tests. A member of the research team was present during the administration of all tests to ensure that the testing situations were standard.

The study produced some remarkably clear-cut results. The researchers found, for each of the four years of the study, that students in the small classes scored significantly higher than students in the regular classes in the subjects tested—math and reading. In educational terms, the students in smaller classes were about two to six months ahead of their peers in larger classes.[1] Of particular significance for urban schools, children living in poverty and African American children (especially males) made the greatest academic gains as a result of being in smaller classes.[2] Smaller classes also seemed to prevent a gap in the achievement levels of minority and white children.[3]

The children who participated in the STAR study are still being followed by researchers in Tennessee under a follow-up project called the Lasting Benefits Study. Students involved in the original STAR study are now in high school. The latest available analysis of their educational performance (as of eighth grade) showed that the achievement advantage enjoyed by students who attended smaller K–3 classes narrowed somewhat in grades 4 and 5. However, in grade 6, students who had been in small classes once again began to widen the gap between their achievement and that of other students.[4] Besides performing better academically, students who were enrolled in smaller classes were more likely to participate in extracurricular activities and were more involved in their own education (i.e., they were taking a more active role in the classroom) than students who were in larger classes.[5]

In 1995, the American Academy of Arts and Sciences called the Tennessee STAR study "one of the great experiments in education in United States history" because of its scope, the rigor of its research design, and the significance of its findings.[6] Although the study was not initiated by Alexander, he was directly involved and had signed the related legislation. On the surface, it would seem odd that he has not sought to capitalize on its proven success. Instead, he has busied himself plugging market-oriented reforms such as private school vouchers and charter schools that have weak, if any, research support. He has even enthusiastically trumpeted for-profit failures like Education Alternatives, Inc., as successes.

There has to be an explanation for why a politician who has hitched his star to education reform would avoid taking credit for what has been widely hailed as one of the greatest achievements in the field. The most logical explanation is that reducing class size would demand a substantial investment in the public schools. It is a reform that reflects confidence that schools can be improved instead of dismantled. As Alexander no doubt knows, standing behind his initiative for smaller classes just because it works at a time when increasing the investment in education has been declared politically incorrect would make him a pariah among his market-oriented compatriots.

Reducing class size costs money—for more teachers and more space. The prevailing wisdom is that education reform can be accomplished with no additional funds. Reducing class size would represent an educational commitment to providing every child the right to learn in the best possible setting—

in other words, establishing an entitlement or right to be taught in a small class.

The claim among many of those who call themselves education reformers these days is that no one knows what the most effective learning environment for children may be, so they propose to "let a thousand flowers bloom." That's why they advocate the unregulated flow of public money into all sorts of market-based experiments and innovations. If the secret ever got out that plain old public schools with smaller classes might be the best investment of all, the visionaries-for-hire and high-tech innovators would be out of work.

So, mum was the word during Alexander's campaign for the Republican presidential nomination; no mention was made of the fact that he'd actually played a leading role in commissioning "one of the great experiments in education in United States history." Political expedience and alliances required that he instead promote much less substantive but more market-oriented school reforms.

The Hidden Agenda

Despite the educational rhetoric, a major motive behind private school voucher plans, for-profit management of public schools, and, to some extent, charter schools is to fend off the traditional role of the public schools in helping to redistribute power and economic opportunity. Some citizens are already beginning to understand just how little these reforms have to do with education. It's true that some polls show disaffection with the performance of the public schools and support for choice. But when people are asked about specifics, it is clear they do not support turning the schools over to some unregulated market. They want schools to have certified teachers, to publish test scores, to meet state academic, fiscal, and safety requirements—and they don't want voucher schools taking money out of the public school system.[7]

The prominence of market-oriented school reforms doesn't reflect the popular will so much as the ascendance of economic efficiency as the *ne plus ultra* of political and social decisionmaking. These reforms mark a radical attempt to destroy the social values built into public institutions such as schools, not an effort to improve the system. The destructive logic that drives them would put American society and culture in the service of the market rather than the other way around. Communities that have already felt the impact of the "creative destruction" of the market on jobs and families are now being invited to let the market work its wonders on their schools. The characteristics of the state of grace to be achieved when that process has drawn to its logical conclusion are left eerily undescribed.

Although there are mighty attempts to obscure it, the argument that no more money can be spent on schools is, at its root, really an argument that no more money can be spent on some groups of children. It is an attempt to replace the idea that all children have an equal claim on the educational resources of the community with the idea that some children are entitled to a better education because their parents can afford to pay for it. Some voucher advocates already are arguing that parents should be free to "supplement" the amount of money provided by tax dollars as proof of their commitment to their child's school.[8]

Market-oriented school reforms are similar to the current crop of so-called welfare reforms. The fight is not fundamentally about the absolute amount of money spent. Rather, it is a struggle over the relative division of wealth in our society. Neoconservatives who favor market-oriented education reforms reject the idea that the wealth of the United States will have to be apportioned much more equitably if poor and working-class children are to attend schools that are not falling down around them, as well as to have decent homes, adequate clothing, proper nutrition, and health care.

The evidence, unlike the power, is not on the neoconservative side. After fifteen years of market-oriented government policymaking, the United States can claim the dubious distinction of having the widest disparity in incomes in the industrial world.[9] No other industrial country spends its K–12 education resources so unequally. Poor children in the United States have the least amount of money spent on them; affluent children have the most.[10] Market enthusiasts have only one solution to that gap: more competition—which the rich have been winning and working-class Americans losing.

Market-oriented school reform proposals are part of a general unwillingness to directly confront the profound economic inequality in the United States and its social implications. The need to redistribute wealth is obscured by glib arguments: If bureaucracies were leaner and teachers' unions weaker, a golden age of student learning would emerge. If money were spent more wisely, there would be more than enough to provide a good education for every child. If parents could choose schools for their children, then good schools would flourish and bad ones would fail, resulting in the continuous creation of ever higher academic standards. If corporations could make a profit by either running the schools or running commercials in them, there would be no need for increased public tax dollars. Any suggestion that all too many public schools are starved for cash instead of awash in tax dollars sends neoconservative education reformers and their allies in the pundit class screaming onto op-ed pages and into radio microphones.

The market-loving reformers that populate organizations like the conservative American Legislative Exchange Council (ALEC) realize that increasing social spending on education would redistribute wealth downward. That's why ALEC issues report after report claiming to show that increased spending on education wouldn't do any good. Echoing the cataclysmic language of the Social Security "reform" debate, ALEC published a piece entitled "Projections for Education Spending Paint a Grim Picture of the Future."[11] The grim picture is that providing public education will require spending more money as more children continue to enter the K–12 system over the next decade.

ALEC attempts to steer the reform debate away from the forest (equal educational resources for all children) to focus on the trees (individual "failed" or "successful" schools). However, there is no reason why it shouldn't be possible to consider both issues simultaneously. What do we know about successful educational practices, and how do we ensure that they are used as widely as possible? How do we go about making sure that *all* children have equal resources devoted to providing them with the highest quality education? Unfortunately, the current vogue is to pretend theoretical platitudes about the market will lead to successful practices that will make an equitable division of resources unnecessary.

The Experience with Privatization

Market-oriented thinking has produced an international privatization boom. By the end of the 1980s, sales of state enterprises had exceeded $185 billion.[12] As of 1992, about 6,800 state-owned industries had been privatized in more than 80 countries—many of them in the old Eastern European Communist bloc and in the developing world.[13] The economic and social costs of privatization can be enormous. The saga of the Consolidated Rail Corporation (Conrail) in the United States illustrates how expensive the simplistic "public bad–private good" logic of free-market zealots can be. In the mid-1970s, the privately owned freight rail lines serving most of the eastern seaboard were on the verge of financial collapse. For years, Penn Central and the five other private freight lines that provided the bulk of the East Coast's hauling capacity had invested their profits in everything except keeping their equipment modernized and their roadbeds in good repair. In 1979, the federal government, unwilling to allow the freight rail system to collapse because of the widespread economic consequences that would have resulted, bought the operation. Over the next six years, the government invested $7 billion taxpayer dollars in Conrail.[14]

As a result of the government "throwing money" at the problem, Conrail was turning a profit by 1981. A practical person would have cheered and smiled as the government began to recoup its taxpayer-financed investment. The free-market policymakers in the Reagan administration, however, took the newly won profitability of Conrail as the signal to sell it back to private investors so that they, rather than taxpayers, could reap the benefits of the public's investment. In 1987, Conrail was privatized and sold off on the stock market for $1.65 billion[15]—a taxpayer subsidy of the "free" market of $5.4 billion.

In Great Britain, the Thatcher government sold off the state-owned power industry in 1988. The new privately owned regional distribution companies engaged in a costly race to build their own generating capacity and to convert from coal to gas power.[16] As a result, the British coal-mining industry, which had supplied the national power company, collapsed, throwing thousands of miners out of work and turning coal-mining towns into economic disaster areas. The costs—to individuals, society, and the national economy—have been enormous. The British government now has to provide for the social welfare of families that once were capable of providing for themselves. Meanwhile, in Argentina, where the economy is booming, the unemployment rate has risen sharply. That is, at least in part, the result of the widespread privatization program undertaken by the Argentinean government.[17]

In the United States, the divergence between the performance of the economy and the well-being of most workers is becoming increasingly difficult to conceal as the global market dictates the fate of America's workers. Over a decade of market-oriented social policy has created a bumper crop of billionaires at one end of the economic spectrum and wage stagnation, unemployment, and economic insecurity at the other end. Only people earning more than $80,000 a year have seen their incomes keep ahead of inflation.[18] By 1995, corporate CEOs were being paid 100 times more than the average worker, creating what one analyst called "an incredibly privileged class of people."[19]

The High Cost of the Free Market

Edward Luttwak, a senior fellow at the Center for Strategic and International Studies, argues that Americans are paying dearly for ignoring the social perspective in their political and economic decisionmaking. He has noted the difference in how Japan and the United States measure costs. In Japan, gasoline is very expensive by American standards. The government fixes fuel prices and prohibits self-service pumps, so Japanese gas stations compete for customers by providing high levels of service. In the United States, free-market economists brag that our self-service gas stations offer consumers much "cheaper" gas than in Japan.

In Luttwak's view, however, America's "cheap" gas carries a very high price tag. Although we don't pay dearly at the gas pump, we pay a price because of all the men and women who cannot find jobs servicing cars at gas stations. We get cheap gas and high-octane social problems. Our insurance rates are higher because of vandalism and thefts, and our taxes are higher because of court and prison costs. (California spends more money on its prison system than on its universities.[20]) Of course, that's just the dollars and cents of it. The social costs also are much higher in terms of the disruptions to family and community life caused by widespread unemployment and fear of crime. In Luttwak's view, the market that cuts prices by eliminating service and jobs does not provide such a bargain after all.[21]

Most Americans don't see what the "free" market costs them because they are encouraged to consider, for example, only the nominal cost of gasoline at the pump. However, they experience the consequences of such shortsighted market logic in their community when a neighbor becomes the latest victim of corporate downsizing or their local business district disappears because a Wal-Mart has opened just outside town.

Market-oriented education reforms such as private school vouchers, for-profit schools, and charter schools bring the same costly logic to the job of educating our young. They threaten to deliver the educational equivalent of "cheap" gas by creating a structural framework to separate the interests of the educational haves from those of the educational have-nots.

The New Separatism

The separation is similar to that of the approximately 900 "business improvement districts" established throughout the United States. Such districts are quasi-governmental entities that tax property owners within district boundaries for the provision of special services. Run by governing boards that are frequently weighted in favor of big property owners, these districts hark back to the eighteenth century when rights were attached to the ownership of property. Improvement districts effectively allow wealthy neighborhoods to provide for themselves while reducing their interest in addressing the needs of the broader community.[22] To be sure, poor neighborhoods have the formal right to form "improvement districts," but with little property value to tax, such districts can offer little hope of true improvement.

The separation of the destinies of the haves from that of the have-nots is becoming more obvious as market-driven educational reform continues to spread. In Wisconsin, local communities faced with a chronic shortage of tax revenue are now forming their own education foundations to raise and distribute private money to their schools.[23] Obviously, as in the case of "business improvement districts," the wealthiest communities have the most resources to draw upon for such supplemental benefits.

In Michigan, the State Board of Education adopted a secessionist reform in August 1995, labeled "autonomous" districts. These new districts could be created out of existing school districts by a vote of the local school board, the electors of the district, or the electors of a school's attendance area.[24] Michigan governor John Engler announced his support for the idea.

Autonomous district legislation would almost certainly provide a legal mechanism for wealthy neighborhoods to secede from less affluent neighborhoods in the same school district. It would also facilitate the establishment of racially homogeneous districts within racially diverse communities and, as a result, create the educational equivalent of private-gated communities—except the schools would be paid for by tax dollars.

If one or more wealthy attendance areas of a large school system formed autonomous districts, any remaining affluent neighborhoods would be under increasing financial pressure to do the same. As the number of affluent neighborhoods in a school district decreased, the financial burden on those remaining would necessarily intensify. The financial incentive for wealthy attendance areas to withdraw would make it harder and harder for them to remain part of the larger district even if they wished to do so.

Of course, poor neighborhoods could form autonomous districts just as they can form business improvement districts. However, the nominal right to do so would provide cold comfort. Autonomous districts in poor neighborhoods would consist of impoverished schools cut off from access to the resources of more affluent neighborhoods. They would be in worse financial shape than they were before. Although the Michigan autonomous district plan did not muster enough legislative support to pass in 1995, however, the proposal is expected to resurface.

Perversely, reforms such as the Michigan autonomous district proposal are often promoted as ways of "empowering" local communities. They do indeed empower wealthy communities to cut themselves off from any responsibility for poorer ones. Poor communities are merely empowered to struggle with their poverty alone. If there is a continued proliferation of plans that allow the winners in the global market to legally dissolve their social and political connections with the losers, the civic cost will be very high.

Paul Starr, a Princeton University sociology professor, argues that one of the main drawbacks of private school voucher plans is that they "could well drain much of the energy and life from local government" because for many people, their first taste of civic participation involves the education of their children. "Remove education to the marketplace," Starr says, "and the tendencies toward political uninvolvement, evident from declining voter participation, are only likely to be intensified."[25]

Proposals such as autonomous districts threaten to carry public education back to the dark days following *Brown* v. *the Board of Education* when "freedom of choice" plans sprang up all over the South in an attempt to avoid integration. Equally important, they are another way in which the inequality and self-interest of market relationships are spreading to civic culture and public policy. Instead of the government structuring the marketplace to ensure the general welfare, the market is allowed to reshape governmental institutions to serve special interests.

A Natural Self-Interest

AT&T ushered in 1996 with the announcement that it was putting 40,000 more workers on the street. The move is consistent with its corporate strategy to remain competitive in global markets. The stock market loved it, and stockholders may reap considerable financial benefits. However, the social costs in communities across the United States will be enormous.[26]

Corporate leaders, no matter how enlightened, are not in a position to address such social costs. Their interests are, by definition, much narrower. It is literally not in their job description to clean up the mess their decisions leave behind for the rest of society. Only governmental action can structure the boundaries for business activities to make sure corporations play by rules that don't tear civil society apart. If the market model is adopted in public education and other institutions of civil governance, there will be few practical ways left to promote the general welfare. Individuals will be, as they increasingly are already, left to the tender mercies of the global market.

When Governor William Weld of Massachusetts asked President Clinton to declare his state's fishing industry a natural disaster in March 1995,[27] he also was announcing the inability of an unregulated market to promote the common good. The Massachusetts fishing industry was failing not because of any "natural" disaster but because of chronic overfishing. In a self-destructive pursuit of profits, fishing boat operators were taking ever smaller fish in ever bigger catches to survive economically. Members of the fishing fleet, each pursuing his or her own economic survival, were incapable of halting the devastating race to the economic bottom. Recent scientific data show that the Georges Bank off Cape Cod, once one of the most productive fishing grounds in the world, may have to be closed to commercial fishing entirely for several years in order to replenish stocks of fish depleted primarily by overfishing.[28] It is a situation that even the most competent fishing operation can now do nothing to overcome.

The market left to itself inflicted a wound that scarred not just the Massachusetts economy but also the fabric of the state's social and cultural life. As one expert on New England fishing said: "If you no longer have a reason to go to sea, you are losing more than your economy, you are losing your character, you are losing your soul."[29]

The process that destroyed the Massachusetts fishing fleet has some of the characteristics of what economists Robert Frank of Cornell and Philip Cook of Duke call a "winner-take-all" market, that is, a market in which competition is both economically wasteful and socially destructive. Frank and Cook argue that it is much wiser to limit the rewards in "winner-take-all" markets and redistribute the surplus to others who lack either the skill or talent to enter the competition. In their view, this is not only more efficient, it is also more just.[30] In addition, it is more likely to promote social stability and long-term well-being.

Edward Luttwak sees another harmful consequence of allowing the market to structure civic life. He believes that "turbo-charged" capitalism is largely responsible for the growing climate of intolerance in contemporary American life. In his judgment, the global market has made the majority of Americans economically insecure. However, this majority "does not realize that the economy too can be subject to the will of the majority (it believes in Invisible Hands, in the unchallengeable sovereignty of the market, and in the primacy of economic efficiency), so it vents its anger and resentment by punishing, restricting, and prohibiting everything it can."[31]

Not surprisingly, this majority is particularly susceptible to the kind of hectoring, punishing approach to school reform that is suggested by the Center for Education Reform's Jeanne Allen: "The 'Nation-at-risk' report was a wake-up call that change within the system would not work unless you start holding kids accountable, holding schools accountable, holding educators accountable and putting consequences there for people who don't succeed."[32]

Allen doesn't say exactly what students, teachers, and schools should be accountable for or how they should be punished if they fail to meet her demands. And she does not reveal any understanding that, to be fair, the performance standards on which people are judged need to be clear and uniform—what the private sector calls competing on a level playing field.

On the contrary, critics like Allen deny that the educational terrain has any significance at all. References to inequality in the lives of children or in the resources of the schools they attend are brushed aside as excuses for a status quo that is not performing up to par. Allen and others like her seem intent on punishing people for failing without regard for the actual circumstances in which these people may find themselves. The rhetoric of punishment in the debate over school reform, as Luttwak's analysis suggests, finds a large audience among people who are themselves on shaky economic ground and who see few positive options for improving their own situations.

The Deteriorating Physical and Economic Infrastructure

In 1991, Jonathan Kozol documented the physical degradation of the schools poor children in America attend in *Savage Inequalities*.[33] In February 1995, the *New York Times* decried a New York City school system in which a second-grade class was taught in a stairwell, science classes were held in hallways, and one out of eleven children was without a desk.[34] The problems are not limited to New York. In December 1995, the General Accounting Office estimated that the nation's schools needed $112 billion to repair or rebuild them. The report detailed crumbling buildings and outdated technology at schools throughout the country.[35]

These circumstances cannot help but affect the ability of teachers to teach and children to learn effectively. They are not the result of student, teacher, or school failures. Threatening students and teachers with "consequences" will not alter these conditions. Unfortunately, rather than respond to the obvious need, school critics look for scapegoats and promote the nebulous magic of market forces while denying the need for anything so practical as money.

At a time when more and more people are in need of help to strengthen and stabilize their families, their schools, and their neighborhoods, the very idea of the government providing a framework of assistance is under attack. Instead, a bad case of nostalgia for the "good old days" of Victorian England and its alleged virtues seems to have broken out among conservative politicians, policymakers, and intellectuals.[36] Few seem willing to acknowledge that corporate decisions made in the name of economic efficiency and competitiveness are making it harder and harder for families to even survive, let alone solve the problems of their communities through grit and determination. Instead, conservative columnists such as Cal Thomas glibly mouth platitudes about "values." According to Thomas: "In the main, poverty is not caused by a lack of money. Poverty is caused by a lack of values."[37]

Actually, U.S. poverty is largely caused by economic and monetary policy. The policy of the Federal Reserve Board is to make sure that a certain percentage of Americans remain out of work to keep the economy from "overheating" and creating unacceptably high levels of inflation. Any sign that unemployment has dipped "too low" gives the financial markets the jitters, and the Federal Reserve Board notches up interest rates to cool things down (i.e., throw people out of work). As *New York Times* columnist Russell Baker has observed, paupers and welfare are essential to contemporary American capitalism.[38]

If, indeed, values cause poverty, then surely they are the values held by the occupants of corporate boardrooms, congressional offices, the White House, and Wall Street financial institutions. Laying off workers has become one of the major strategies used by profitable corporations to boost the bottom line. When Chemical Bank and Chase Manhattan Bank merged, news that their combined workforce would be reduced by 12,000 people (16 percent) sent their stock value up 11 percent. In other words, each fired worker increased the stock value of the two banks by about $216,000. One tongue-in-cheek commentator noted that if the banks had fired all their employees, they could have increased their share value another 53 percent.[39] Just as the best poem may be a blank page, perhaps the most profitable business of the future will have no employees at all.

The policies of the Federal Reserve and the U.S. government are no more "natural" than the "natural" disaster that overtook the Massachusetts fishing industry. They are the created disasters of government policies that serve the market instead of people. Americans are now being urged to place the education of their children—their entire futures, really—into the uncaring hands of the market.

Because market values so often define the boundaries of acceptable debate over public issues, alternatives that corporate America doesn't want to talk about are frequently ignored. For example, even when there is a sound economic reason to worry about inflationary economic "overheating," slowing the economy by raising interest rates is not the only possible response. As economist Robert Heilbroner has suggested, another way to accomplish the same result is to raise taxes. People will still lose their jobs when the economy slows, but the government will have the resources to soften the impact by spending the money on those who need help. An "anti-inflation" tax is, in Heilbroner's view, more consistent with democratic values than raising interest rates because the tax spreads the burden of fighting inflation broadly throughout the population rather than allowing a few to profit while many suffer.[40]

Heilbroner sees the market within the framework of a value-laden "political economy" that does not operate according to the dictates of objective "natural" laws. Since he doesn't see God's hand but rather human decisions at work in the market, Heilbroner is able to imagine ways of promoting the general welfare by making explicit political decisions to control the economy. That position is roundly rejected by the free-market zealots currently working their will in Washington and statehouses across the country.

As long as the market is allowed to shape American public life, schools will be asked to educate children living in poverty with fewer and fewer resources. Data released in 1995 in the Luxembourg Income Study, the most comprehensive evaluation available of the distribution of the wealth in eighteen industrial nations, found that U.S. children suffered higher levels of poverty than children in any of the other countries except Israel and Ireland. And in no other country was the gap between the most affluent households with children and the poorest households with children as wide as in the United States.[41]

Despite all the talk in the United States about welfare payments perpetuating poverty, somehow the governments of Western European countries are able to reduce the level of childhood poverty dramatically through social welfare programs. In 1991 in Great Britain, the childhood poverty rate was reduced from 27.9 percent to 8.4 percent after tax and transfer (social welfare) adjustments. In France, it was reduced from 21.2 percent to 4.6 percent; in West Germany, from 8.4 percent to 2.8 percent; and in Canada, from 15.7 percent to 9.3 percent. In the United States, on the other hand, the childhood poverty rate started at 22.3 percent and, after taking taxes and all welfare government programs into account, was reduced only slightly to 20.4 percent.[42]

The Real Bottom Line

Any number of education reforms would help not only the children behind the statistics on poverty but also children as a whole: universal child care available on demand, comprehensive early childhood education programs for every child, small classes taught in small schools close to home for elementary-age children, learning opportunities in a variety of settings for older children, and year-round education and free access to training and education throughout life, just for starters.

Many of these reforms, plus the diverse array of innovative ideas about school structure and educational content, are already being tried in individual school districts around the country. Some will, no doubt, improve student achievement. However, no isolated success will change the grim statistics on childhood poverty. And no single success will reverse the trend toward increasing economic inequality in American society. Market-oriented school reforms provide a simple unifying idea; however, they will never improve the distribution of educational resources. Markets, left to themselves, concentrate wealth; they don't apportion it in the most socially desirable way.

Equitable school reform can succeed only as part of a more general set of economic and social reforms that equalize opportunity and distribute the wealth in American society more broadly. Market values reside entirely in the buying and selling of *things*. Corporate school reformers may be faulted for making false claims for private school vouchers or charter schools as a result of blind faith, shallow analysis, or deliberate attempts to mislead. Certainly, someone should blow the whistle on the high-tech Music Men who promise River City High a computer in every pot and gleaming Tomorrowland space needles of learning as far as the eye can see—and then waltz out of town after diverting time, attention, and resources away from the task of improving the quality of education for all children.

The basic skills and the common body of knowledge we believe every child should have cannot be allowed to succumb to a cacophony of commercials and blatant corporate and political propaganda. Unfortunately, when the market perverts educational values, it is only doing what markets are supposed to do—providing opportunities for self-interested individuals to profit.

The market can offer no guidance on matters of justice and fairness that are at the heart of democratic civil society and that *should* be at the heart of its schools and other institutions. Left to its own devices, the market is as utterly incapable of making high-quality schools available to every child, regardless of economic circumstances, as it is of providing a job for every American who needs one.

Since the market is concerned with buying and selling, it cannot represent the interests of children. Turning children over to the market assures that they will be treated as an expense to be reduced or a resource to be harvested. In the process, some children and their families will necessarily be considered more valuable than others. For the market to produce winners, there always have to be losers.

Over time, market values have eroded and debased the humane values of democratic civil society. Listen closely to the language that already fills discussions about school reform. It is the language of commerce applied to human relationships. Children are defined as "future customers," "future workers," and "future taxpayers." There is little talk of the value of children in their own right—right now. There is lots of talk about "tough love" but little mention of any other kind of love. Costs are put in terms of "the bottom line," not what justice demands. When the logic of the market is allowed to dominate society, relationships are inevitably turned into commodities to be bought and sold. And every person can be assigned a material value, either great or small. The antithesis is the democratic ideal that all people are created equal.

The hallmark of America's advanced market economy is not universal well-being. It is universal advertising. The illusion of everything from happiness to fighting hunger to health care to political leadership is substituted for the real thing. The market leads toward a virtual world in which "P.R. armies have forged a new world of pseudo-events, video press releases, infomercials, letter writing campaigns, manufactured celebrities . . . all of which has made us disoriented and suspicious."[43]

In the United States, every available surface, from shopping carts to buses to computer Web pages to public schools, is now blanketed with commercials. Children are sold to advertisers from the time they are born, taught that possessions define their value, and blessed with lives filled with pseudo-events, pseudo-emotions, and pseudo-knowledge provided by marketers. Yet we expect these children to grow up capable of making independent judgments and effectively participating in democratic civic life.

The debate over public education reform cannot be understood by thinking only about schools. It is part of a much broader struggle: whether America will move in the direction of its democratic ideals or be further ensnared in the logic of the market. The outcome is by no means assured. As author Leslie Savan has written, in the United States there is now "no human emotion or concern—love, lust, war, childhood, innocence, social rebellion, spiritual enlightenment, even disgust with advertising—that cannot be turned into a sales pitch."[44]

The challenge facing American society and its children is not how to find ever more ingenious ways to speed the market on its way. The real challenge of the next century is to take control of our lives back from the market.

Appendix

Milwaukee Principles for Corporate Involvement in the Schools*

School-business relationships based on sound principles can contribute to high quality education. However, compulsory attendance confers on educators an obligation to protect the welfare of their students and the integrity of the learning environment. Therefore, when working together, schools and businesses must ensure that educational values are not distorted in the process. Positive school-business relationships should be ethical and structured in accordance with all eight of the following principles:

1. Corporate involvement shall not require students to observe, listen to, or read commercial advertising.
2. Selling or providing access to a captive audience in the classroom for commercial purposes is exploitation and a violation of the public trust.
3. Since school property and time are publicly funded, selling or providing free access to advertising on school property outside the classroom involves ethical and legal issues that must be addressed.
4. Corporate involvement must support the goals and objectives of the schools. Curriculum and instruction are within the purview of educators.
5. Programs of corporate involvement must be structured to meet an identified education need, not a commercial motive, and must be evaluated for educational effectiveness by the school/district on an ongoing basis.
6. Schools and educators should hold sponsored and donated materials to the same standards used for the selection and purchase of curriculum materials.

---

*These principles were developed at a meeting proposed by Alex Molnar and hosted by the School of Education, University of Wisconsin–Milwaukee, November 26–27, 1990.

They have been adopted by the following organizations:

Action for Children's Television
National Parent-Teachers Association
American Association of School Administrators
National Association of State Boards of Education
National Council for the Social Studies
National Education Association

They have been endorsed by the state superintendents of education in the following states: California, Georgia, Iowa, Louisiana, Maine, Massachusetts, Minnesota, Nevada, Pennsylvania, South Carolina.

7. Corporate involvement programs should not limit the discretion of schools and teachers in the use of sponsored materials.
8. Sponsor recognition and corporate logos should be for identification rather than commercial purposes.

The National Education Association

"The Preserve Classroom Integrity Pledge"
Any business program should:

- have real educational value and promote a love of learning
- reinforce basic classroom curricula, not contrived activities
- advance an educational goal, not merely a public relations purpose
- allow any decision to participate to be made at the school level
- be open to students who voluntarily choose to participate.

It should *not*:

- offer trips, gifts, or prizes in exchange for teachers pushing commercial products in their classrooms
- discriminate against any group of students
- impede or interfere with student instructional time
- require the purchase of a product by students or parents
- require teachers, students, or parents to promote a commercial product.

Society of Consumer Affairs Professionals in Business (SOCAP) Guidelines*

Consumer education and information materials should meet the following minimum standards:

Accuracy. Statements are consistent with established fact or with prevailing expert opinion on the subject. Information is easily verifiable. Information is current at the time the material is produced, and can be expected to remain current throughout the time the sponsor distributes it.

Objectivity. Points of view are fairly presented. If the subject is controversial, arguments are balanced. Any sponsor bias is clearly stated and references to differing views are made.

Completeness. The materials contain all relevant information and do not deceive or mislead by omission.

---

*As published in Consumers Union, *Captive Kids: Commercial Pressures on Kids at School* (Yonkers, N.Y.: Consumers Union Education Services, 1995).

Language. Materials are both interesting and understandable. Word choice, organization and sentence length are suited to the primary target audience. Technical terms are used sparingly and are fully defined.

Non-discrimination. The text and illustrations are free of any content that could be considered derogatory toward a particular group; for example, an ethnic group, an age group, a race, or sex. The diversity of our population should be recognized.

Non-commercial. The name or logo of the business sponsor is used to identify the source of the materials and, if applicable, to provide contacts for further information. Text and illustrations do not contain any of the sponsor's brand names, trademarks, related trade names, or corporate identification. The sponsor's legal copyright notice is used to designate ownership of presentation and date of production or revision. When appropriate, permission to reprint for nonprofit educational purposes should be noted.

International Organization of Consumers Unions (IOCU)

Code of Good Practice and Guidelines for Controlling Business-Sponsored Educational Materials Used in Schools*

All Business Sponsored Educational Materials (BSEM) should adhere to these minimum standards:

Accuracy. Statements must be consistent with established facts or accepted expert opinions on the subject. Information must be appropriately referenced so that it can be easily verified.

Objectivity. All major or relevant points of view are fairly presented. If the subject is controversial, arguments in favor must be balanced by arguments against. The sponsor bias must be clearly stated and references to opposing views must be made.

Completeness. The materials contain all relevant information and do not deceive or mislead by omission nor by commission.

Non-discriminatory. The text and illustrations are free of any references or characterizations that could be considered derogatory or stereotype a particular group; for example, an ethnic group, an age group, a race, or a sex.

Non-commercial. Sponsored material specifically designed for educational use should be clearly designated as such. Under no circumstances should promotional material be presented as "educational." Text and illustrations must not contain any of the sponsor's brand names, trademarks, related trade names, or corporate identification. Corporate identification, however, should be stated clearly and in a prominent place (for example, the front or back cover of publications or in the titles of videos or teaching packs). Such corporate identification should be used in these positions only to identify the sponsor with the material and to provide contacts for fur-

*As published in Consumers Union, *Captive Kids: Commercial Pressures on Kids at School* (Yonkers, N.Y.: Consumers Union Education Services, 1995).

ther information. No implied or explicit sales message, exhortation to buy a product or service, merchandising slogan or other attempts to influence the purchasing decisions of pupils, or their families, should be included. The sponsor may use the legal copyright notice to designate ownership of presentation and date of publication of BSEM.

Evaluative. The materials should encourage awareness among pupils about the subject as well as encourage cognitive evaluation of the said subject.

Distribution. No unsolicited BSEM should be distributed or direct-mailed to pupils or teachers.

Organizations Concerned with Commercialism

Center for Media Education
1511 K Street NW
Suite 518
Washington, D.C. 20005
phone: (202) 628-2620
fax: (202) 628-2654

Center for Science in the Public Interest
1875 Connecticut Avenue NW
Suite 300
Washington, D.C. 20009-5728
phone: (202) 332-9110

Citizens for Media Literacy
38½ Battery Park Avenue
Suite G
Asheville, N.C. 28001
phone: (704) 255-0182
fax: (704) 254-2286

Consumers Union
101 Truman Avenue
Yonkers, N.Y. 10703
phone: (914) 378-2000

Media Foundation
1243 W. 7th Avenue
Vancouver, BC V6H IB7
CANADA

National PTA
2000 L Street NW
Suite 600
Washington, D.C. 20036
phone: (202) 331-1380

UNPLUG
The Center for Commercial-Free Public Education
360 Grand Avenue, #385
Oakland, Calif. 94610
phone: (510) 268-1100   1-800 UNPLUG-1
fax: (510) 268-1277
e-mail: UNPLUG@igc.apc.org

Notes

Chapter One

1. National Commission on Excellence in Education, *A Nation at Risk: The Imperatives for Educational Reform* (Washington, D.C.: U.S. Department of Education, 1983), p. 1.

2. Michael Timpane and Laurie Miller McNeill, *Business Impact on Education and Child Development Reform* (New York: Committee for Economic Development, 1991), p. 9.

3. National Association of Partners in Education, Inc., *National School District Partnership Survey: Statistical Report* (Alexandria, Va.: National Association of Partners in Education, Inc., 1991), p. 3.

4. RJR Nabisco Foundation, *Next Century Schools* (Washington, D.C.: RJR Nabisco Foundation, 1989).

5. Interview with George R. Kaplan, a Washington, D.C., educational policy analyst, January 9, 1996.

6. Gary Putka, "Lacking Good Results, Corporations Rethink Aid to Public Schools," *Wall Street Journal*, June 27, 1989.

7. Ibid.

8. Douglas D. Noble, "New American Schools and the New World Order" (paper presented at the annual meeting of the American Educational Research Association, San Francisco, April 1992).

9. David T. Kearns, "Why I Got Involved," *Fortune* (Special Issue), Spring 1990, p. 46.

10. William B. Johnston, *Workforce 2000* (Indianapolis, Ind.: Hudson Institute, 1987).

11. William B. Johnston, "Global Work Force 2000: The New World Labor Market," *Harvard Business Review* 69, no. 2 (March-April 1991): 115–127.

12. Commission on the Skills of the American Workforce, *America's Choice: High Skills or Low Wages!* (Rochester, N.Y.: National Center on Education and the Economy, 1990), p. 25.

13. The Secretary's Commission on Achieving Necessary Skills, "Learning for Living: A Blueprint for High Performance," U.S. Department of Labor, April 1992.

14. Edward B. Fiske, "Impending U.S. Jobs 'Disaster': Workforce Unqualified to Work," *New York Times,* September 25, 1989.

15. Tamar Lewin, "Low Pay and Closed Doors Greet Young in Job Market," *New York Times,* March 10, 1994.

16. John Pawasarat and Lois M. Quinn, *Survey of Job Openings in the Milwaukee Metropolitan Area: Week of May 22, 1995* (Milwaukee: University of Wisconsin, Milwaukee Employment and Training Institute, 1995).

17. Nan Stone, "Does Business Have Any Business in Education?" *Harvard Business Review* 69, no. 2 (March-April 1991): 46–48 and passim.

18. Keith Bradsher, "Skilled Workers Watch Their Jobs Migrate Overseas," *New York Times,* August 28, 1995.

19. The National Alliance of Business, *The Business Roundtable Participation Guide: A Primer for Business on Education* (New York: Business Roundtable, 1991), pp. 43–49.

20. Jay Taylor, "Desperate for Dollars," *American School Board Journal* 178, no. 9 (September 1992): 23.

21. Richard Rothstein, *Where's the Money Gone?* (Washington, D.C.: Economic Policy Institute, 1995).

22. Janice Shamon, "Buying Low: Schools for Sale," *Z Magazine* 5, no. 5–6 (May 1992): 65.

23. Robert B. Reich, quoted in Kenneth Jost, "Business Role in Education," *CQ Researcher* 1, no. 27 (November 22, 1991): 889.

24. Michael Rosen, *Public Investment, Private Gain: A Review of Wisconsin's Tax Expenditure Budget from Fiscal Years 1974–1994* (Milwaukee: Institute for Wisconsin's Future, 1995).

25. Taylor, "Desperate for Dollars," p. 25.

26. Louis F. Miron and Robert K. Wimpelberg, "School/Business Partnerships and the Reform of Education," *Administrator's Notebook* 33, no. 9 (University of Chicago, 1989).

27. John E. Chubb and Terry Moe, *Politics, Markets and America's Schools* (Washington, D.C.: Brookings Institution, 1990).

28. Kevin B. Smith and Kenneth J. Meier, *The Case Against School Choice: Politics, Markets, and Fools* (Armonk, N.Y.: M. E. Sharpe, 1995).

29. David C. Berliner and Bruce J. Biddle, *The Manufactured Crisis* (Reading, Mass.: Addison-Wesley, 1995).

30. Louis V. Gerstner, "Our Schools Are Failing: Do We Care?" *New York Times,* May 27, 1994.

31. See, for example, Bruce Murphy and Terrence Falk, "A Loss of Trust," *Milwaukee Magazine,* November 1994, pp. 36–40 and passim.

32. John F. Witte, *First-Year Report: Milwaukee Parental Choice Program* (Madison: Robert M. La Follette Institute of Public Affairs, University of Wisconsin–Madison, 1991); John F. Witte, Andrea B. Bailey, and Christopher A. Thorn, *Second-Year Report: Milwaukee Parental Choice Program* (Madison: Robert M. La Follette Institute of Public Affairs, University of Wisconsin–Madison, 1992); John F. Witte, Andrea B. Bailey, and Christopher A. Thorn, *Third-Year Report: Milwaukee*

Parental Choice Program (Madison: Robert M. La Follette Institute of Public Affairs, University of Wisconsin–Madison, 1993); John F. Witte, Christopher A. Thorn, Kim Pritchard, and Michelle Claibourn, *Fourth-Year Report: Milwaukee Parental Choice Program* (Madison: Robert M. La Follette Institute of Public Affairs, University of Wisconsin–Madison, 1994); Geoffrey Whitty, "Creating Quasi-Markets in Education: A Review of Recent Research on Parental Choice and School Autonomy in Three Countries," in Michael Apple, ed., *Review of Research in Education,* vol. 22 (Washington, D.C.: American Educational Research Association, in press); J. Douglas Willms and Frank H. Echols, "The Scottish Experience of Parental School Choice," in Edith Rasell and Richard Rothstein, eds., *School Choice: Examining the Evidence* (Washington, D.C.: Economic Policy Institute, 1993), pp. 49–68; Bruce Fuller, *Who Gains, Who Loses from School Choice: A Research Summary*, policy brief (Denver: National Conference of State Legislatures, 1995); Martin Carnoy, "Is School Privatization the Answer?" *Education Week,* July 12, 1995; Smith and Meier, *The Case Against School Choice,* chap. 8.

33. Barbara Miner, "Who Owns the Wealth?" *Rethinking Schools* 9, no. 4 (Summer 1995): 27.

34. Interview with Kaplan.

35. Anne Curley, "No Wonder Democrats Control State," *Milwaukee Journal,* February 5, 1984.

36. Council of Small Business Executives, Independent Business Association of Wisconsin, and the Metropolitan Milwaukee Association of Commerce, *Choices* (Milwaukee: Metropolitan Milwaukee Association of Commerce, 1986).

37. Council of Small Business Executives, Independent Business Association of Wisconsin, Metropolitan Milwaukee Association of Commerce, and Wisconsin Manufacturers' Council, *Choices II* (Milwaukee: Metropolitan Milwaukee Association of Commerce, 1987).

38. Rosen, *Public Investment,* p. 8.

Chapter Two

1. Consumers Union, *Captive Kids: Commercial Pressures on Kids at School* (Yonkers, N.Y.: Consumers Union Education Services, 1995), p. 4.

2. Donald D. Burk, "Free Teaching Materials—Assets or Liabilities?" *School Executive* 76, no. 12 (August 1957): 55–57.

3. Ann De Rouffignac, "School Contests Help Concerns Promote Brand Names," *Wall Street Journal,* July 3, 1992.

4. "Courting the Corporates," *AASA Leadership News,* January 15, 1995, p. 1.

5. "Lake Bluff Earns Computers from Kohl's," *Shorewood (Wis.) School District Quarterly Bulletin,* Summer 1992, p. 3.

6. Maria E. Odum, "Middlemen Ring Up Profits in Food Chain's School Computer Programs," *Washington Post,* April 19, 1993.

7. Campbell Soup Company, *Campbell's Labels for Education Program 1990–1991 Merchandise Catalog* (Monticello, Minn.: Campbell Soup, 1990).

8. Copies of this and other corporate promotional materials quoted in this volume are in the author's possession. Due to the idiosyncratic nature of these materials, it is virtually impossible to cite most of them in a conventional manner.

9. "Apples for the Students Partnership for Education Program," information brochure, 1991.

10. Robert L. Martin, "Private Sector Help Critical for Success," *AASA Leadership News*, May 31, 1992, p. 5.

11. Lifetime Learning Systems, corporate promotional materials (Hinsdale, Ill.: Lifetime Learning Systems, 1995).

12. Richard Stenger, "Corporate Dumping," *Washington City Paper*, December 11, 1992, p. 22.

13. "Environmental Groups Charge That School Curriculum Produced by Procter and Gamble Is Deceptive," *Corporate Crime Reporter* 8, no. 4 (January 24, 1994).

14. Julie Vacho-Straubhaar, "The Health Hazards of BGH," *Milwaukee Journal*, January 4, 1994.

15. Mark Evens, "Education Marketing Basics," *Advertising Age*, October 10, 1988, p. 18.

16. "Experience the Power of Trust with Scholastic," company promotional brochure, published by Scholastic, Inc., New York.

17. Consumers Union, *Captive Kids*, p. 7.

18. Joan Dye Gussow, "Who Pays the Piper?" *Teachers College Record* 81, no. 4 (Summer 1980): 448–466.

19. Consumers Union, *Captive Kids*.

20. "Kiddie Corps," *Mother Jones*, July-August 1992, p. 14.

21. Peter Finn, "Whose History Is It Anyway?" *Inquirer: The Philadelphia Inquirer Magazine*, May 1, 1994, pp. 14–15 and passim.

22. Edwin C. Broome, "Report of the Committee on Propaganda in the Schools" (presented at the Atlanta meeting of the National Education Association, July 1929.)

23. ASCD Liaison Committee on Instructional Materials, *Using Free Materials in the Classroom* (Washington, D.C.: Association for Supervision and Curriculum Development, 1953). See also *Choosing Free Materials for Use in the Schools* (Washington, D.C.: American Association of School Administrators, 1955).

24. Burk, "Free Teaching Materials," pp. 55–57.

25. Sheila Harty, *Hucksters in the Classroom: A Review of Industry Propaganda in Schools* (Washington, D.C.: Center for Study of Responsive Law, 1979).

26. Consumers Union, *Selling America's Kids: Commercial Pressures on Kids of the 90's* (Yonkers, N.Y.: Consumers Union, 1990).

27. Consumers Union, *Captive Kids*.

28. Michael F. Jacobson and Laurie Ann Mazur, *Marketing Madness: A Survival Guide for a Consumer Society* (Boulder: Westview Press, 1995).

29. Consumers Union, *Captive Kids*, p. 63.

30. Dana Hawkins, "Johnny Can Read for Cash and Freebies: Is Bribery the Best Way to Get a Kid to Learn?" *U.S. News & World Report*, October 30, 1995, pp. 72–73.

31. Ibid.

32. Personal correspondence with the author, November 1995.

33. Ibid.

34. Ibid.

35. Fairness and Accuracy in Reporting, "A Word from the Sponsor," *EXTRA! Update*, October 1995, p. 3.

36. Ibid.

37. James E. Causey, "Beer Industry Upset with Poster Citing Alcohol as Nation's Top Drug," *Milwaukee Journal Sentinel*, August 14, 1995.

38. Ibid.

39. Ibid.

40. Paul Kane, "Beer Industry Fights for Its Best Interests," *Milwaukee Journal Sentinel*, August 14, 1995.

41. Jessica Porter, "Study Chides *Weekly Reader*'s Tobacco Coverage," *Education Week*, November 15, 1995, p. 10.

42. Geoffrey Cowley, "I'd Toddle a Mile for a Camel," *Newsweek*, December 23, 1991, p. 70.

43. Ibid.

44. Porter, "Study Chides *Weekly Reader*'s Tobacco Coverage."

Chapter Three

1. Jack Lail, "What's a Whittle?" *Washington Journalism Review*, November 1990, p. 45.

2. Ibid., p. 27.

3. Ibid., p. 110.

4. Patrick Reilly, "New Whittle Shocker," *Advertising Age*, January 16, 1989.

5. Thomas Moore, "The Blooding of Chris Whittle," *U.S. News and World Report*, November 6, 1989, p. 43.

6. John Birmingham, "Marketers—and Revisionists—Are Taking a Hard Look at Whittle," *AdWeek's Marketing Week*, April 9, 1990, p. 20.

7. Channel One ad, *New York Times*, June 7, 1989.

8. Channel One ad, *New York Times*, June 11, 1989.

9. *Channel One Chronology*, Channel One corporate document.

10. Editorial, "Zap the Commercials," *Christian Science Monitor*, March 6, 1989.

11. Scott Hume, "'Channel One' Ads Bug Adults, Survey Shows," *Advertising Age*, August 14, 1989.

12. Lillian N. Gerhardt, "Whittle's Ed-Tech Trojan Horse," *School Library Journal* 35, no. 8 (April 1989): 4.

13. "Is the Classroom for Blackboards or Billboards?" *Consumer Reports*, May 1989, p. 286.

14. Editorial, "A Classroom Intrusion," *Boston Globe*, May 31, 1989.

15. Bob George, "More to Channel One than Meets the Eye," *Rantoul (Ill.) Press*, November 22, 1989.

16. "Major School Groups Blast Plan for Commercial TV in Classes," *Education Week*, March 8, 1989.

17. "Classroom TV Ads Called 'Academic Acid Rain,'" *Communicator* 12, no. 10 (June 1989).

18. Gerhardt, "Whittle's Ed-Tech Trojan Horse."

19. Bill Carter, "Whittle Names a Board to Advise Channel One," *New York Times*, August 28, 1989.

20. Plaintiffs-appellants' brief, dated May 11, 1990, *State of North Carolina* v. *Whittle Communications* and *Davidson County Board of Education* v. *State of North Carolina*, case no. 164PA90.

21. Steve Behrens, "Channel One Chugs into 3rd Year," *Current* 11, no. 2 (February 3, 1992): 1. *State of North Carolina* v. *Whittle Communications* (1991), 402 S.E. 2d 556.

22. Clay Robison, "Channel 1 Fate Is Put in Hands of Local Boards," *Houston Chronicle*, March 14, 1992.

23. Joe Cutbirth, "PTA Criticizes Channel One Decision," *Fort Worth Star Telegram*, March 17, 1992.

24. Ibid.

25. Editorial, "TEA's 'Trade Secret,'" *Houston Post*, April 4, 1994.

26. Harris County Appraisal District records, dated 1/3/96, chart titled "Channel One Televised News Service—RCN Model."

27. Interview with Karen Miller, December 28, 1995.

28. Editorial, "Let Schools Choose 'Channel One,'" *New York Times*, June 16, 1989.

29. "Commercial In-School Television Report and Staff Recommendations," State Education Department, New York, June 16, 1989.

30. Editorial, "The Channel One Lynch Mob," *Advertising Age*, June 26, 1989.

31. Alex Molnar, "Whittle or Nothing?" *In These Times* 18, no. 14 (May 30, 1994): 26–27.

32. Ibid.

33. Interview with Jill Levy, executive vice president of the Council of Supervisors and Administrators of New York, January 27, 1996.

34. "Should 10th Grade Come with Compulsory Commercials?" ad placed by the California State Superintendent of Public Instruction, *New York Times*, June 18, 1990.

35. Memo from Jim Wilson, director of fiscal policy, planning, and analysis, to Joe Symkowick, chief counsel, Legal and Audits Branch, California Department of Education, "Revised Cost of Channel One Broadcast in Schools," May 25, 1989.

36. Joanne Lipman, "Future of Whittle's Channel One Unclear," *Wall Street Journal*, May 1, 1989.

37. Joanne Lipman, "Criticism of TV Show with Ads for Schools Is Scaring Sponsors," *Wall Street Journal*, March 2, 1989.

38. Patrick Reilly, "Whittle Sticks by 'Channel One' Rollout," *Advertising Age*, March 13, 1989.

39. Joanne Lipman, "Future of Whittle's Channel One Unclear," *Wall Street Journal*, May 1, 1989.

40. Jane Mayer, "How Chris Whittle Faltered on the Issue of TV Ads in Schools," *Wall Street Journal*, August 8, 1989.

41. Scott Donaton, "Whittle: 'Channel One' Is a Hit," *Advertising Age*, September 18, 1989.

42. "Channel One Gets Sponsors," *New York Times*, September 18, 1989.

43. Ana Arana and Aleta Watson, "Channel One Used Ethnic Divisions to Win Customers," *San Jose Mercury-News*, December 13, 1992.

44. "High School Official That Backed Whittle Is Paid by Company," *Wall Street Journal*, December 1, 1992.

45. William Trombley, "$640,000 Paid to Lobbyists by Classroom TV Firm," *Los Angeles Times*, September 1, 1991.

46. Patrick M. Reilly and Suzanne Alexander, "Whittle's Plan for Big Growth Runs into Snags," *Wall Street Journal*, August 6, 1993.

47. Editorial, "Channel One Rides Again," *Sacramento Bee*, July 10, 1993.

48. Suzanne Alexander, "Whittle Wins California Fight over School TV," *Wall Street Journal*, September 10, 1992.

49. Reilly and Alexander, "Whittle's Plan for Big Growth Runs into Snags.

50. Whittle Communications corporate materials. These are also the source of quotes in the following four paragraphs.

51. Hugh Rank, "Channel One/Misconceptions Three," *English Journal* 81, no. 4 (April 1992): 31.

52. Ibid.

53. Hugh Rank, *The Pitch* (Park Forest, Ill.: Counter Propaganda Press, 1991), chap. 11.

54. Saul Hansell, "A Shaky House of Plastic with No Quick Fix in Sight," *New York Times*, December 28, 1995.

55. "Group Sets Boycott of Pepsi over Ads on Channel One," *Wall Street Journal*, May 5, 1992.

56. "Fargo Board Debates Controversial Program," *Jamestown (N.D.) Sun*, October 22, 1990.

57. Susie Gran, "The Controversy over Channel One," *Albuquerque Tribune*, January 10, 1992.

58. "Tube Wars," *Insight*, May 18, 1992, pp. 26–27, included in documents from Woodhaven High School (Flat Rock, Mich.) and Woodhaven Education Association.

59. Jayne Schindler, "Channel One Is Junk," *Eagle Forum* 13, no. 1 (Spring 1992): 1, 19.

60. Cyndee Miller, "Teachers Fight Channel One; Two Advertisers Drop Out," *Marketing News*, August 17, 1992, and Joe Mandese, "Whittle Suffers New Woes as NEA Targets Sponsors," *Advertising Age*, July 11, 1994.

61. Bradley S. Greenberg and Jeffrey E. Brand, "Channel One: But What About the Advertising?" *Educational Leadership*, December 1993–January 1994, p. 57.

62. "Houston, Texas," in *Case Studies* (Oakland, Calif.: Unplug, 1995), pp. 1–2.

63. Thomas Moore, "The Blooding of Chris Whittle," *U.S. News and World Report*, November 6, 1989, p. 43.

64. Jerome Johnston and Evelyn Brzezinski, *Taking the Measure of Channel One: The First Year* (Ann Arbor: University of Michigan Institute for Social Research, 1992).

65. Jerome Johnston and Evelyn Brzezinski, *Channel One: A Three Year Perspective* (Ann Arbor: University of Michigan Institute for Social Research, 1994), p. 3.

66. Miller, "Teachers Fight Channel One; Two Advertisers Drop Out."

67. CBS, *60 Minutes* broadcast interview, October 10, 1993.

68. Tim Simmons, "TV News in Classroom Ineffective, Study Finds," *News Observer*, March 21, 1991.

69. Ana Arana and Aleta Watson, "Channel One Used Ethnic Divisions to Win Customers," *San Jose Mercury-News*, December 13, 1992.

70. Ibid.

71. Michael Morgan, *Channel One in the Public Schools: Widening the Gaps* (Oakland, Calif.: Unplug, 1993).

72. Terry Moe, "Keep Channel One in the Classroom," *San Francisco Business Times*, included in documents from Unplug (360 Grand Ave., Box 385, Oakland, Calif., 94610); complete citation unavailable.

73. Patrick M. Reilly, "Whittle's Sale of Channel One Completed by K-III," *Wall Street Journal*, October 3, 1994.

74. Patrick M. Reilly, "Phillips Electronics Says It Wrote Off Whittle Investment," *Wall Street Journal*, October 25, 1994.

75. Patrick M. Reilly, "A KKR Vehicle Finds Profit and Education a Rich but Uneasy Mix," *Wall Street Journal*, October 12, 1994.

76. James Dao, "School News Show with Ads Clears a Key Albany Panel," *New York Times*, May 24, 1995.

77. Memorandum to members of the New York Assembly and New York Senate from Gregory S. Nash, president of the National Education Association of New York, April 7, 1995.

78. Dao, "School News Show with Ads Clears a Key Albany Panel."

79. Statement released by Rhoda H. Karpatkin, president of Consumers Union, as Consumers Union's official position, May 25, 1995.

80. Interview with Jill Levy, executive vice president of the Council of Supervisors and Administrators of New York, January 27, 1996.

81. Sam Roberts, "Alone in the Vast Wasteland," *New York Times*, December 24, 1995.

82. Douglas D. Noble, "A Bill of Goods: The Early Marketing of Computer-Based Education and Its Implications for the Present Moment," in Bruce J. Biddle, Thomas L. Good, and Ivor F. Goodson, eds., *International Handbook of Teachers and Teaching* (Dordrecht, Netherlands: Kluwer Academic Publishers, in press).

83. Ibid.

Chapter Four

1. Peter Applebome, "Class Notes," *New York Times*, November, 16, 1994.

2. Martha M. McCarthy, "External Challenges to Public Education: Values in Conflict" (paper presented at the American Educational Research Association Annual Meeting, New Orleans, La., April 1994), p. 17.

3. Peter Schmidt, "Private Enterprise," *Education Week*, May 25, 1994, pp. 27–30.

4. M. William Salganik, "The Coming Scandal," *Baltimore Sun*, December 11, 1993.

5. G. H. Wohlferd, *Performance Contracting Overview*, 1972, ERIC document #EDO79339.

6. Office of Economic Opportunity, *An Experiment in Performance Contracting* (Washington, D.C.: Office of Planning, Research, and Evaluation, 1972); *The Evolution of Educational Performance Contracting in Five School Districts, 1971–72: A Working Note* (Santa Monica, Calif.: Rand Corporation, 1972).

7. J. Rosenthal, "Learning Plan Test Is Called a Failure," *New York Times*, February 1, 1972.

8. Keith Schneider, "U.S. Cites Waste in Its Contracts," *New York Times*, December 2, 1992.

9. Michael Winerip, "Billions for Schools Are Lost in Fraud, Waste and Abuse," *New York Times*, February 2, 1994.

10. David C. Berliner, "Mythology and the American System of Education," *Phi Delta Kappan* 74, no. 8 (April 1993): 633.

11. Ibid., p. 634.

12. Ibid.

13. David C. Berliner and Bruce J. Biddle, *The Manufactured Crisis* (Reading, Mass.: Addison-Wesley, 1995).

14. Berliner, "Mythology and the American System of Education," p. 637.

15. Ibid.

16. Ibid., p. 638.

17. Richard Rothstein, *Where's the Money Gone?* (Washington, D.C.: Economic Policy Institute, 1995).

18. C. C. Carson, R. M. Huelskamp, and T. D. Woodall, "Perspectives on Educa-

tion in America: An Annotated Briefing," *Journal of Educational Research* 86, no. 5 (May-June, 1993): 259–311.

19. Ibid.

20. E. A. Hanushek, "Throwing Money at Schools," *Journal of Policy Analysis and Management* 1, no. 1 (1981): 19–41; E. A. Hanushek, "The Economics of Schooling: Production and Efficiency in Public Schools," *Journal of Economic Literature* 24, no. 3 (September 1986): 1141–1177; E. A. Hanushek, "The Impact of Differential Expenditures on School Performance," *Educational Researcher* 18, no. 4 (May 1989): 45–65; E. A. Hanushek, "When School Finance 'Reform' May Not Be a Good Policy," *Harvard Journal on Legislation* 28, no. 2 (Summer 1991): 423–456.

21. Eric A. Hanushek, with Charles S. Benson et al., *Making Schools Work: Improving Performance and Controlling Costs* (Washington, D.C.: Brookings Institution, 1990).

22. Hanushek, "The Impact of Differential Expenditures on School Performance."

23. Larry V. Hedges, Richard D. Laine, and Rob Greenwald, "Does Money Matter? A Meta-Analysis of Studies of the Effects of Differential School Inputs on Student Outcomes," *Educational Researcher* 23, no. 3 (April 1994): 5–14.

24. "Accept 'Enlightened Commercialism'; Get 'High-Tech Educational Tools,' Communications Entrepreneur Advises," *TEA News* 20, no. 6 (December 1988): 12.

25. "Tennessee Fails to Head Off RA's Channel 1 Opposition," *TEA News* 21, no. 2 (August 1989): 9.

26. "Whittle Would Nominate Alexander to Design 'New American School,'" *TEA News* 21, no. 5 (November 1989): 6.

27. "Naisbitt: Next 'Megatrend' May Be School Privatization," *TEA News* 21, no. 10 (April 1990): 1.

28. "Alexander & Whittle: American Education Needs Reinventing," *TEA News* 21, no. 10 (April 1990): 5.

29. Kenneth Jost, "Private Management of Public Schools," *CQ Researcher* 4, no. 12 (March 25, 1994): 275.

30. *Whittle Schools & Laboratories* (Knoxville, Tenn.: Whittle Communications, L.P., May 16, 1991), p. 8.

31. Ibid., p. 10.

32. John S. Friedman, "Big Business Goes to School," *The Nation* 254, no. 6 (February 17, 1992): 188–192.

33. "Panel Is Chosen to Design Better, Cheaper Schools," *New York Times*, February 28, 1992.

34. Deborah Sontag, "Yale President Quitting to Lead National Private-School System," *New York Times*, May 26, 1992.

35. Suzanne Alexander, "Whittle's Hiring of Yale President Adds New Credibility to For-Profit School Plan," *Wall Street Journal*, May 27, 1992.

36. Richard Bernstein, "The Yale Schmidt Leaves Behind," *New York Times Magazine*, June 14, 1992, p. 33.

37. Ibid.

38. Tom McNichol, "Chris Whittle's Big Test," *USA Weekend*, September 18–20, 1992.

39. Jesse Kornbluth, "Chris and Benno's Excellent Adventure," *Vanity Fair*, August 1992, p. 147.

40. Tim Lott, "AISD Officials to Discuss Privatization with Company; Bishop Says School Managers—Like the Edison Project—Are Inevitable in Texas," *Austin-American Statesman*, May 4, 1994.

41. Kornbluth, "Chris and Benno's Excellent Adventure."

42. Carol Jouzaitis, "Preppy Pitchman," *Chicago Tribune*, September 17, 1992.

43. McNichol, "Chris Whittle's Big Test," p. 4.

44. Sara Mosle, "Dim Bulb," *New Republic* 208, no. 3 (January 18, 1993): 16.

45. Ibid., p. 20.

46. Marilee C. Rist, "Here Comes 'McSchool,'" *American School Board Journal* 178, no. 9 (September 1991): 31.

47. Patrick M. Reilly, "Whittle Seeks Edison Funding of $750 Million," *Wall Street Journal*, May 5, 1993.

48. Geraldine Fabrikant, "Whittle Said to Scale Back Its For-Profit Schools Plan," *New York Times*, July 30, 1993.

49. Patrick M. Reilly, "Whittle to Launch Leaner School Project After Failing to Attract Outside Investors," *Wall Street Journal*, August 2, 1993.

50. "Whittle Secures Financing for Edison School Project," *Wall Street Journal*, August 3, 1993.

51. Patrick M. Reilly and Suzanne Alexander, "Whittle's Plan for Big Growth Runs into Snags," *Wall Street Journal*, August 6, 1993.

52. "Whittle's Edison Project to Focus on Public School Management," *School Board News* 13, no. 15 (August 17, 1993): 5.

53. Thomas Toch, "Whittling the Future School," *U.S. News and World Report*, August 1993, p. 76.

54. Ibid.

55. Reilly and Alexander, "Whittle's Plan for Big Growth Runs into Snags."

56. Gary Putka and Suzanne Alexander, "Whittle Exceeded Time for Ads Twice in School Programs," *Wall Street Journal*, May 20, 1993.

57. Reilly and Alexander, "Whittle's Plan for Big Growth Runs into Snags."

58. Jolie Solomon, "Mr. Vision, Meet Mr. Reality," *Newsweek*, August 16, 1993, p. 62.

59. "An Education Dream Hits Reality," *New York Times*, August 9, 1993.

60. Solomon, "Mr. Vision, Meet Mr. Reality," p. 63.

61. Patrick M. Reilly, "Whittle Plans to Largely End Print Business," *Wall Street Journal*, May 13, 1992.

62. Patrick M. Reilly, "Whittle Is Facing Big Battle to Retain Drug Advertisers for Medical Network," *Wall Street Journal*, November 15, 1993.

63. Suzanne Alexander Ryan, "Some Big Advertisers Fail to Show for Whittle's Classroom News," *Wall Street Journal*, December 1, 1993.

64. Patrick M. Reilly, "Whittle Prepares to Close Network for Doctors' Offices," *Wall Street Journal*, March 1, 1994.

65. Patrick M. Reilly, "Whittle to Shut Its Book Unit for Lack of Ads," *Wall Street Journal*, March 18, 1994.

66. Skip Wollenberg, "Whittle Cuts Back as Revenues Drop," Associated Press wire report, May 13, 1994.

67. Geraldine Fabrikant, "Whittle Said to Scale Back Its For-Profit Schools Plan."

68. Mark Landler, David Greising, and Maria Mallory, "Is This the Last Hurrah for Chris Whittle?" *Business Week*, August 22, 1994, pp. 66–69.

69. Keith J. Kelly, "Whittle's Bridges Falling Down," *Advertising Age*, July 18, 1994.

70. "Whittle Said to Agree to Sale of School Channel," *New York Times*, August 10, 1994.

71. Dinitia Smith, "An Acerbic Encounter with Chris Whittle," *GQ*, December 1994, p. 239.

72. Peter Applebome, "Whittle's School Venture Needs Cash, Faces Cave-In," *(Memphis) Commercial Appeal*, November 26, 1994.

73. James B. Stewart, "Grand Illusion," *New Yorker*, October 31, 1994, pp. 64–68, 70–76, 78–81.

74. Jennet Conant, "The Whittle of Oz," *Vanity Fair*, November 1994, pp. 205–210, 244–247.

75. Smith, "An Acerbic Encounter With Chris Whittle," pp. 238–241, 271–272.

76. "Channeling Whittle's Thoughts," *Boston Globe*, August 16, 1994.

77. Editorial, "Edison Could Illuminate What a School Can Do," *Greensboro (N.C.) News and Record*, November 1, 1994.

78. Adam Tanner, "Edison Project's Future Hinges on Financing," *Christian Science Monitor*, December 22, 1994.

79. "Edison Project Secures $30 Million for Privatization Effort," *Education Daily*, March 17, 1995.

80. "Whittle Building to Be U.S. Courthouse," *(Memphis) Commercial Appeal*, January 12, 1995.

81. Curtis Lawrence, "Firms Face a Hard Sell in Seeking to Run Schools for MPS," *Milwaukee Journal*, August 11, 1993.

82. Walter C. Farrell, James H. Johnson, Cloyzelle K. Jones, and Marty Sapp, "'Edisonscam': Exposing the Edison Project," *Milwaukee Courier*, May 21, 1994.

83. Mike Lee, "Edison Project Draws Criticism," *Lubbock (Tex.) Avalanche-Journal*, August 25, 1994.

84. Janet Bingham, "Free-Market School Plan Hits Brick Wall; State Districts Get Too Little Money for Edison Project," *Denver Post*, November 6, 1994.

85. Nina Reyes, "No Agreement Near Between Edison, AISD," *Austin American-Statesman*, November 11, 1994.

86. Jeff Ortega, "Future Bleak for Project; Company's Cost Too High, Worthington School District Says," *Columbus Dispatch*, November 29, 1994.

87. Christine Dorsey, "Battle Lines Drawn on Edison Project," *Sherman (Tex.) Democrat*, February 24, 1995.

88. Fox Butterfield, "Governor of Massachusetts Says He Will Challenge Senator Kerry in 1996," *New York Times*, November 30, 1995.

89. David I. Rubin, "Whittle School Is Questionable Investment," *Boston Sunday Globe*, April 2, 1995.

90. Karen Avenoso, "Charter School's Hopes Collide with Reality," *Boston Globe*, December 28, 1995.

91. Gary Putka, "Do For-Profit Schools Work? They Seem to for One Entrepreneur," *Wall Street Journal*, June 8, 1994.

92. Joe Rigert and Carol Command, "Education Firm Oversells Its Record," *Minneapolis Star Tribune*, June 4, 1994.

93. Ibid.

94. James Bock, "'Sweetheart Deal of a Lifetime' Has a Price Tag," *Baltimore Sun*, June 5, 1995.

95. Malethia Armstrong, *Education Alternatives, Inc. (EAI) and Tesseract Schools: A Briefing Paper* (Baltimore: Maryland State Teachers Association, 1993).

96. Rigert and Command, "Education Firm Oversells Its Record."

97. "Bad Prediction," *Rethinking Schools* 10, no. 3 (Spring 1996): 21.

98. Rigert and Command, "Education Firm Oversells Its Record."

99. Franklin L. Smith, "The Outside Option," *American School Board Journal* 181, no. 4 (April 1994): 40–42.

100. "Commentary—Reality Check," *Education Investor* 2, no. 3 (March 1994): 1.

101. Rigert and Command, "Education Firm Oversells Its Record."

102. Barbara Miner, "Education for Sale?" *Rethinking Schools* 7, no. 4 (Summer 1993): 14.

103. Jost, "Private Management of Public Schools," p. 279.

104. "Dade County Says Good-Bye to EAI," *American School Board Journal* 182, no. 7 (July 1995): p. 8.

105. Rigert and Command, "Education Firm Oversells Its Record."

106. Miner, "Education for Sale."

107. Gene G. Marcial, "A Very Bad School Report," *Business Week*, February 28, 1994, p. 94.

108. Peter Schmidt, "E.A.I. Fiscal Health at Issue in Suit by 2 Stockholders," *Education Week*, March 9, 1994, p. 6.

109. Christopher Georges, "Dick and Jane Sell Short," *Washington Post*, March 13, 1994.

110. Judith Yates Borger, "Suit Against EAI Dropped," *Saint Paul Pioneer Press*, February 2, 1995.

111. News item, *Minneapolis Star Tribune*, October 10, 1993.

112. News item, *Minneapolis Star Tribune*, November 22, 1993.

113. Gary Gately and Ian Johnson, "EAI, Schools Narrow Differences on Enrollment," *Baltimore Sun*, January 27, 1994.

114. Scott Willis, "Public Schools, Private Managers," *ASCD Update* 36, no. 3 (March 1994): 3.

115. Rigert and Command, "Education Firm Oversells Its Record."

116. Putka, "Do For-Profit Schools Work?"

117. Lee Schafer, "Tough Lesson," *Corporate Report Minnesota* 25, no. 2 (May 1994): p. 56.

118. Jo Anna Natale, "Sector Shifters," *Executive Educator* 16, no. 9 (September 1994): p. 21.

119. Ibid., p. 22.

120. Ibid., p. 21.

121. Robert J. Samuelson, "The Boss as Welfare Cheat," *Newsweek*, November 11, 1991, p. 55.

122. Steven Burke, "Louis Gerstner No. 6—He's Got IBM in the Black but the Next Phase Will Be His Toughest Assignment Yet," *Computer Reseller News*, November 13, 1995, p. 130.

123. Mark Bomster, "Contract Plan for City Schools Given Support," *Baltimore Sun*, May 17, 1991.

124. Mark Bomster, "Minn. Firm to Run Nine City Public Schools," *Baltimore Sun*, June 10, 1992.

125. John Rivera, "Schools Plan Greeted with Optimism," *Baltimore Sun*, June 11, 1992.

126. Mark Bomster, "Amprey Wants to Widen Firm's Role in Schools," *Baltimore Sun*, June 17, 1993.

127. Editorial, "Tesseract: Proceed with Care," *Baltimore Sun*, July 9, 1995.

128. Gary Gately and Joan Jacobson, "Probe of EAI Sought," *Baltimore Sun*, December 4, 1993.

129. Gary Gately, "Give All Schools As Much Funding As Those EAI Runs, Clarke Urges," *Baltimore Sun*, March 4, 1994.

130. Gary Gately, "Teachers Union Asks for Federal EAI Investigation," *Baltimore Sun*, March 31, 1994.

131. Rick Green, "Amprey Says He Wants EAI to Run All Schools," *Hartford (Conn.) Courant*, May 5, 1994.

132. Bock, "'Sweetheart Deal of a Lifetime' Has a Price Tag."

133. Olivia S. Reusing, *A Report of Observations in Three Tesseract Schools* (Baltimore: Maryland State Teachers Association, 1994), p. 11.

134. "Report Shows Private Manager's Profits Hinge on Less Instruction and Larger Classes in Public Schools," American Federation of Teachers news release, March 30, 1994, p. 3.

135. *The Private Management of Public Schools: An Analysis of the EAI Experience in Baltimore*, prepublication copy (Washington, D.C.: American Federation of Teachers, 1994), p. 1.

136. Rigert and Command, "Education Firm Oversells Its Record."

137. *EAI's Mismanagement of Federal Education Programs: The Special Education*

and Chapter 1 Track Records in Baltimore (Washington, D.C.: American Federation of Teachers, 1994).

138. Gary Gately, "Md. Cites 3 EAI Schools for Special Education Violations," *Baltimore Sun*, July 18, 1995.

139. Rigert and Command, "Education Firm Oversells Its Record."

140. Gary Gately, "Amprey Drops Plan to Spend More City Funds to Expand EAI," *Baltimore Sun*, June 11, 1994.

141. Gary Gately, "Amprey Trips Paid for by EAI," *Baltimore Sun*, October 27, 1994.

142. Gary Gately and JoAnna Daemmrich, "EAI Fails to Improve Test Scores," *Baltimore Sun*, June 17, 1994.

143. Gary Gately, "Md. Cites 3 EAI Schools for Special Education Violations."

144. Gary Gately, "EAI Schools' Test Scores Fall Short," *Baltimore Sun*, October 18, 1994.

145. Gary Gately and JoAnna Daemmrich, "Pressure Grows to Terminate EAI Experiment," *Baltimore Sun*, October 19, 1994.

146. Gary Gately and JoAnna Daemmrich, "EAI Schools Fail to Match Citywide Attendance Gains," *Baltimore Sun*, October 26, 1994.

147. Gary Gately, "Amprey Trips Paid for by EAI."

148. Editorial, "A Can of Worms at North Ave." *Baltimore Sun*, October 19, 1994.

149. Peter Schmidt, "Flap in Baltimore Spurs Calls for Revisions in E.A.I. Pact," *Education Week*, October 26, 1994, p. 13.

150. David Bennett, "Entrepreneurship: The Road to Salvation for Public Schools," *Educational Leadership* 52, no. 1 (September 1994): p. 76.

151. "First in U.S. History: Hartford's Board Cedes District Management to Private Firm," *American School Board Journal* 16, no. 11 (November 1994): 8, 12.

152. Eric D. Randall, "Education Alternatives Makes Grade," *USA Today*, October 14, 1994.

153. Peter Schmidt, "Hartford Hires E.A.I. to Run Entire District," *Education Week*, October 12, 1994, p. 14.

154. "First in U.S. History," p. 12.

155. Rick Green, "Parents, Staff Criticize City School Board," *Hartford (Conn.) Courant*, February 8, 1995.

156. Rick Green, "City to Put Price on School Reform," *Hartford (Conn.) Courant*, May 11, 1995.

157. Rick Green, "School Administrators Question Spending Plan," *Hartford (Conn.) Courant*, May 10, 1995.

158. Rick Green, "EAI's Bill to Hartford: $1.2 Million, and Growing," *Hartford (Conn.) Courant*, May 16, 1995.

159. Rick Green, "Debate on EAI Tearing City's Soul" *Hartford (Conn.) Courant*, May 22, 1995.

160. Rick Green, "Mayor, City Leaders Order Major EAI Role," *Hartford (Conn.) Courant*, May 25, 1995.

161. "Golle Speaks," *The Education Industry Report*, November 1995, p. 1.

162. "EAI Proposes Change in Hartford," *Executive Educator* 17, no. 7 July 1995, p. 8.

163. "EAI Head Speaks: School Critics Must Be 'Blind, Deaf and Dumb,'" *Baltimore Sun*, June 4, 1995.

164. Bock, "'Sweetheart Deal of a Lifetime' Has a Price Tag."

165. James Bock, Mike Bowler, and Gary Gately, "Wary Schmoke Mulls Future of 'Experiment,'" *Baltimore Sun*, June 6, 1995.

166. Lois C. Williams and Lawrence E. Leak, *The UMBC Evaluation of the Tesseract Program in Baltimore City* (Baltimore: University of Maryland Center for Educational Research, 1995).

167. George Judson, "Baltimore Ends Education Experiment," *New York Times*, November 23, 1995.

168. Peter Schmidt, "Private Enterprise," *Education Week*, May 25, 1994, p. 29.

169. George Judson, "For Education Company, a Shift in Vision," *New York Times*, December 7, 1995.

170. Peter Applebome, "Lure of the Education Market Remains Strong for Business," *New York Times*, January 31, 1996, pp. A1, B8.

171. George Judson, "School Consultant Job Is Company's 2d Chance," *New York Times*, February 14, 1996.

172. Editorial, *Hartford (Conn.) Business Journal*, May 23, 1994, p. 4.

173. Communication by author with the Milwaukee Public Schools Office of Governmental Relations, December 1, 1995.

174. *Education Alternatives, Inc. Annual Report 1993* (Minneapolis: Education Alternatives, Inc., 1993).

175. *Partnership School Design* (New York: The Edison Project, 1994), p. 100.

176. Walter Farrell, "The Likely Impacts of Privatizing MPS: Can We Afford Them?" *Milwaukee Courier*, March 5, 1995, p. 4.

177. Sari Horwitz, "School Privatization Shelved," *Washington Post*, March 4, 1994.

178. "Answers from the Edison Project to Questions Raised by the Milwaukee Public Schools," March 18, 1994, see answer to question 15.

179. *The Education Industry Report* 3, no. 8 (September 1995): 1.

180. Bruce S. Cooper and Denis P. Doyle, "Education Supply: Will It Create Demand?" *Education Week*, March 20, 1996.

Chapter Five

1. W. Van Vliet and J. A. Smyth, "A Nineteenth-Century French Proposal to Use School Vouchers," *Comparative Education Review* 26, no. 1 (February 1982): 95–103.

2. Jeffrey R. Henig, *Rethinking School Choice: Limits of the Market Metaphor* (Princeton: Princeton University Press, 1993), p. 104.

3. "In the New South, New Racism Is Seen," *International Herald Tribune*, April 2, 1984.

4. David Tyack, *The One Best System: A History of American Urban Education* (Cambridge, Mass.: Harvard University Press, 1974).

5. Ivan Illich, *Deschooling Society* (New York: Harper and Row, 1971).

6. Allen Graubard, *Free the Children: Radical Reform and the Free School Movement* (New York: Pantheon, 1972). See also the letter from Herb Kohl to Mario Fantini printed in the appendix to Mario D. Fantini, *Free Schools of Choice* (New York: Simon and Schuster, 1973).

7. Paul Goodman, *The New Reformation: Notes of a Neolithic Conservative* (New York: Random House, 1970).

8. *Education Vouchers: A Report on Financing Elementary Education by Grants to Parents* (Cambridge, Mass.: Center for the Study of Public Policy, 1970), as cited in Richard F. Elmore, *Choice in Public Education* (Santa Monica, Calif.: Rand Corporation, 1986), p. 9.

9. Amy Stuart Wells, *Time to Choose: America at the Crossroads of School Choice Policy* (New York: Hill and Wang, 1993), p. 152.

10. Editorial, "Harmful Monopoly: The Public School System Should Be Broken Up," *Barron's National Business and Financial Weekly*, September 11, 1967, p. 1.

11. Wells, *Time to Choose,*" p. 174; Charles J. Russo and Michael P. Orsi, "The Supreme Court and the Breachable Wall," *Momentum* 23, no. 3 (September 1992): 42–45.

12. Thomas W. Lyons, "Parochiaid? Yes!" *Educational Leadership* 27, no. 8 (November 1971): 102–104, and Glenn L. Archer, "Parochiaid? No!" *Educational Leadership* 27, no. 8 (November 1971): 105–107. See also Grace Graham, "Can the Public School Survive Another Ten Years?" *Educational Leadership*, May 1970, pp. 800–803.

13. "Justice and Excellence: The Case for Choice in Chapter 1," U.S. Department of Education, November 15, 1985, as cited in Richard F. Elmore, *Choice in Public Education* (Santa Monica, Calif.: Rand Corporation, 1986), p. 9.

14. Henig, *Rethinking School Choice,* chap. 4.

15. Education Commission of the States, "Legislative Activities Involving Open Enrollment (Choice)," *Clearinghouse Notes*, December 1994.

16. Ibid., p. 91.

17. 166 Wis. 2d, 501, 480 N.W. 2d, 460 (1992)

18. John F. Witte, *First-Year Report: Milwaukee Parental Choice Program* (Madison: Robert M. La Follette Institute of Public Affairs, University of Wisconsin–Madison, 1991); John F. Witte, Andrea B. Bailey, and Christopher A. Thorn, *Second-Year Report: Milwaukee Parental Choice Program* (Madison: Robert M. La Follette Institute of Public Affairs, University of Wisconsin–Madison, 1992); John F. Witte, Andrea B. Bailey, and Christopher A. Thorn, *Third-Year Report: Milwaukee Parental Choice Program* (Madison: Robert La Follette Institute of Public Affairs, University of Wisconsin–Madison, 1993); John F. Witte, Christopher A. Thorn,

Kim Pritchard, and Michelle Claibourn, *Fourth-Year Report: Milwaukee Parental Choice Program* (Madison: Robert La Follette Institute of Public Affairs, University of Wisconsin–Madison, 1994).

19. Geoffrey Whitty, "Creating Quasi-Markets in Education: A Review of Recent Research on Parental Choice and School Autonomy in Three Countries," in Michael W. Apple, ed., *Review of Research in Education,* vol. 22 (Washington, D.C.: American Educational Research Association, in press); J. Douglas Willms and Frank H. Echols, "The Scottish Experience of Parental School Choice," in Edith Rasell and Richard Rothstein, eds., *School Choice: Examining the Evidence* (Washington, D.C.: Economic Policy Institute, 1993), pp. 49–68; Bruce Fuller, *Who Gains, Who Loses from School Choice: A Research Summary,* policy brief (Denver: National Conference of State Legislatures, 1995); Martin Carnoy, "Is School Privatization the Answer?" *Education Week,* July 12, 1995; Kevin B. Smith and Kenneth J. Meier, *The Case Against School Choice: Politics, Markets, and Fools* (Armonk, N.Y.: M. E. Sharpe, 1995), chap. 8.

20. Paul E. Peterson, *A Critique of the Witte Evaluation of Milwaukee's School Choice Program,* Occasional Paper 95-2 (Cambridge, Mass.: Harvard University Center for American Political Studies, 1995).

21. Interview with John Witte, January 29, 1996.

22. Letter from Timothy Sheehy, president of the Metropolitan Milwaukee Association of Commerce, to all members of the Wisconsin legislature, January 28, 1995.

23. *Milwaukee Parental Choice Program,* Wisconsin Legislative Audit Bureau Audit Summary Report 95-3 (Madison: Wisconsin Legislative Audit Bureau, 1995).

24. Letter from John F. Witte, Department of Political Science, University of Wisconsin–Madison, to members of the Wisconsin legislature, February 13, 1995.

25. *Milwaukee Parental Choice Program.*

26. Interview with Chris Ahmuty, executive director of the ACLU of Wisconsin, January 29, 1996.

27. Richard P. Jones, "Split Keeps Religious Schools Out of Choice Plan, for Now," *Milwaukee Journal Sentinel,* Saturday, March 30, 1996.

28. *"The California Voucher—Parental Choice in Education" Constitutional Amendment Initiated by Petition* (Denver: Education Commission of the States, 1993).

29. Henig, *Rethinking School Choice,* p. 67.

30. Jost, "Private Management of Public Schools."

31. Drew Lindsay, "With Voters Lukewarm, Calif. Group Shelves Voucher Initiative Until 1998 Election," *Education Week,* September 6, 1995, p. 17.

32. Mark Walsh, "N.J. Governor Agrees to Delay School Voucher Legislation," *Education Week,* January 18, 1995, p. 11.

33. Drew Lindsay, "PepsiCo Backs Off Voucher Plan in Jersey City," *Education Week,* November 15, 1995, p. 3.

34. *A Summary of Focus Group Findings in Chicago and Cleveland, on Behalf of Alliance for Better Schools* (Fairfax, Va.: Public Opinion Strategies, 1993).

35. Larry Rohter, "Puerto Rico Takes Lead with School Vouchers, and Feels the Arrows," *New York Times*, October 27, 1993.

36. Mark Walsh, "Court Strikes Down Puerto Rico's Private-School Voucher Program," *Education Week*, December 14, 1994, p. 17.

37. *1994–95 State Issues Report* (Denver: Education Commission of the States, 1995), pp. 65–68.

38. Joanna Richardson, "Minn. Governor Unveils Private School Voucher Plan," *Education Week*, November 29, 1995, p. 13.

39. *1994–95 State Issues Report*, p. 66.

40. Memo from John Goff, Ohio superintendent of public instruction, to BEST board of directors, October 30, 1995; Bert Holt, Cleveland Scholarship and Tutoring Program, reading from an official memo from the Ohio Department of Education's legal representation, January 29, 1996.

41. Drew Lindsay, "Pa. Governor Puts His Reform Plan on Back Burner," *Education Week*, January 10, 1996, p. 20.

42. Jost, "Private Management of Public Schools."

43. Jason DeParle, "Sheila Burke Is the Militant Feminist Commie Peacenik Who's Telling Bob Dole What to Think," *New York Times Magazine*, November 12, 1995, p. 37.

44. Barbara Miner, "Conservative Foundations Support Voucher Plans," in Robert Lowe and Barbara Miner, eds., *False Choices*, 2d ed. (Milwaukee: Rethinking Schools, 1993), pp. 36–37.

45. John E. Chubb and Terry Moe, *Politics, Markets and America's Schools* (Washington, D.C.: Brookings Institution, 1990).

46. David Callahan, "Liberal Policy's Weak Foundations," *The Nation*, November 13, 1995, p. 569.

47. Donald L. Barlett and James B. Steele, *America: What Went Wrong?* (Kansas City: Andrews and McMeel, 1992).

48. Bruce Murphy, "The Right Stuff," *Milwaukee Magazine*, December 1988, p. 56.

49. Ibid., p. 58.

50. Barbara Miner, "The Bradley Foundation and Milwaukee," *Rethinking Schools* 8, no. 3 (Spring 1994): 18.

51. Robert Lowe, "Offering Simple Solutions to Complex Problems: Why Susan Mitchell's Critique of MPS Doesn't Work," *Rethinking Schools* 8, no. 3 (Spring 1994): 15.

52. Barbara Miner, "The Power and the Money," *Rethinking Schools* 8, no. 3 (Spring 1994): 17–18.

53. Daniel Bice, "Private Funds Pay for Choice Defense," *Milwaukee Journal Sentinel*, December 1, 1995.

54. "Bradley Foundation Announces $1 Million Gift to PAVE Emergency Fund," Bradley Foundation press release, August 30, 1995.

55. Barbara Miner, "New Directions for the Bradley Foundation," *Rethinking Schools* 8, no. 3 (Spring 1994): 19.

56. "Bradley Foundation Announces $1 Million Gift to PAVE Emergency Fund."

57. "Media Advisory," PAVE, Milwaukee, September 4, 1995; Alan J. Borsuk, "Heavy Hitters Come to Push School Choice," *Milwaukee Journal Sentinel,* September 6, 1995.

58. David S. Broder, "Shameful Silence on School Vouchers," *Washington Post,* October 27, 1993.

59. "California Governor Seeks School Voucher Program," *New York Times,* January 10, 1996.

60. David C. Berliner and Bruce J. Biddle, *The Manufactured Crisis: Myths, Frauds, and the Attack on America's Public Schools* (Reading, Mass.: Addison-Wesley, 1995), pp. 180–181.

61. Charlotte Allen, "Choice: A Burkean Dissent," *American Spectator,* November 1993, pp. 62–63.

62. Drew Lindsay, "GOP Not Walking in Lock Step on School Issues," *Education Week,* March 20, 1996.

63. Bruce Murphy and Terrence Falk, "A Loss of Trust," *Milwaukee Magazine,* November 1994, p. 38.

64. Ibid.

65. Ibid.

66. Ibid.

67. Ibid.

68. Bruce Murphy, "The Right Stuff," *Milwaukee Magazine,* December 1988, p. 55.

69. David C. Berliner, "Mythology and the American System of Education," *Phi Delta Kappan* 74, no. 8 (April 1993).

70. Ibid.

71. Walter C. Farrell, James H. Johnson, Cloyzelle K. Jones, and Marty Sapp, "The Farrell Report: Privatization: Larger Negative Impacts," *Milwaukee Courier,* June 4, 1994, p. 4.

72. Howard Fuller and Sammis White, "Expanded School Choice in Milwaukee," *Wisconsin Policy Research Institute Report* 8, no. 5 (July 1995).

73. Curtis Lawrence, "State Dropout Rate Hits a Low," *Milwaukee Journal Sentinel,* January 20, 1996.

74. John Pawasarat and Lois M. Quinn, *Survey of Job Openings in the Milwaukee Metropolitan Area: Week of May 22, 1995* (Milwaukee: University of Wisconsin-Milwaukee Employment and Training Institute, 1995).

75. Kenneth R. Lamke, "Chvala Says Hospital Rate Unit Needed," *Milwaukee Sentinel,* July 30, 1994.

76. John Norquist, "Milwaukee Mayor John Norquist," in William D. Eggers, ed., *Revitalizing Our Cities: Perspectives from America's New Breed of Mayors,* policy study no. 186 (Los Angeles: Reason Foundation, 1995), pp. 1–3.

77. Allen Graubard, *Free the Children: Radical Reform and the Free School Movement* (New York: Pantheon Books, 1972), p. 300.

78. Douglas S. Massey and Nancy A. Denton, *American Apartheid: Segregation and the Making of an Underclass* (Cambridge, MA: Harvard University Press, 1993), p. 76.

79. Walter C. Farrell, Jr. and James H. Johnson, Jr., "Milwaukee's Racial Divide: Limited Opportunity," *The Milwaukee Courier,* April 6, 1996.

80. Richard Rhodes, "Victims of Family Values," *New York Times*, December 1, 1995.

81. Richard J. Herrnstein and Charles Murray, *The Bell Curve: Intelligence and Class Structure in American Life* (New York: Free Press, 1994). See also Charles Murray, *Losing Ground: American Social Policy 1950–1980* (New York: Basic Books, 1984).

82. Louis Menand, "The Trashing of Professionalism," *New York Times Magazine*, March 5, 1995, p. 42.

83. Paul N. DeWeese, letter on TEACH Michigan Education Fund (913 W. Holmes, Suite 265, Lansing, Mich. 48910-4490) letterhead addressed "Dear friend," Christmas 1994.

84. Charles Sykes, "Wisconsin's Best, Brightest, Dimmest and Dullest Legislators," *Milwaukee Magazine*, March 1986, pp. 69–79.

85. Milton Friedman, *Capitalism and Freedom* (Chicago: University of Chicago Press, 1963), p. 89.

86. Denis Doyle, *Where Connoisseurs Send Their Children to School: An Analysis of 1990 Census Data to Determine Where School Teachers Send Their Children to School* (Washington, D.C.: Center for Educational Reform, 1995), p. 7.

87. Ibid., p. 29.

88. Gerald W. Bracey, "The Fifth Bracey Report on the Condition of Public Education," *Phi Delta Kappan* 77, no. 2 (October 1995): 149–160.

89. Salim Muwakkil, "Face the Nation," *In These Times* 19, no. 25 (October 30, 1995): 15–18.

90. John-David Morgan, "Expresso," *(Milwaukee) Shepherd Express,* September 14, 1995.

91. Carol Innerst, "Polly Williams: School Choice's Independent Icon," *Washington Times* (national weekly edition), October 2–8, 1995, p. 31.

92. Curtis Lawrence, "Choice Schools' Fees Draw Fire," *Milwaukee Journal Sentinel*, August 22, 1995.

93. Curtis Lawrence, "Choice Debate Expands to Fees, Fund-Raising," *Milwaukee Journal Sentinel*, December 24, 1995.

94. Ann Bradley, "Christian Coalition Offers Tips on Promoting Vouchers," *Education Week*, September 20, 1995, p. 7.

95. Marilee Rist, "Parochial Schools Set Out to Win Their Share of the Market," *Executive Educator* 13, no. 9 (September 1991): 24.

96. Daniel M. McKinley, "Crisis and Opportunity in Milwaukee," *Momentum* 23, no. 3 (September 1992): 18–20.

97. Ibid., p. 20.

98. Drew Lindsay, "PepsiCo Backs Off Voucher Plan in Jersey City," *Education Week*, November 15, 1995, p. 3.

99. Blant Hurt, "Leadership, Walton Style," *Arkansas Business*, May 1, 1995, reprinted in *The Voucher Voice*, Spring 1995, p. 3.

100. John Judis, "TRB: The Gold Standard," *New Republic*, November 6, 1995, p. 4.

101. Robert Dreyfuss and Peter Stone, "Medikill," *Mother Jones*, January-February 1996, pp. 22–27 and passim.

102. Robert Pear, "Democrats Object to a Health Plan by G.O.P. in House," *New York Times*, March 29, 1996.

103. J. Patrick Rooney, "Golden Rule—Living Up to Its Name," *Momentum* 23, no. 3 (September 1992): 29.

104. Barbara Miner, "Conservatives Push Privately Funded Vouchers," in Robert Lowe and Barbara Miner, eds., *False Choices*, 2d ed. (Milwaukee: Rethinking Schools, 1993), pp. 33–35.

105. Lindsay, "PepsiCo Backs Off Voucher Plan in Jersey City."

106. Marie Rohde, "Minority Test Scores at Catholic Schools Mirror Lag in City," *Milwaukee Journal*, August 1, 1991.

107. Ernst-Ulrich Franzen, "Archdiocese Abolishes School System," *Milwaukee Sentinel*, January 27, 1994; correspondence, Milwaukee Public Schools Governmental Relations Office to the author, December 1 and 6, 1995.

108. Emily Koczela, Timothy J. McElhatton, and Jean B. Tyler, *Public and Private School Costs: A Local Analysis* (Milwaukee: Public Policy Forum, 1994).

109. Denise M. Topolnicki, "Why Private Schools Are Rarely Worth the Money," *Money*, October 1994, p. 100.

Chapter Six

1. Claudia Wallis, "A Class of Their Own," *Time*, October 31, 1994, pp. 53–61.

2. "Free at Last," *The Economist*, July 2, 1994, pp. 26, 31.

3. Tom Mirga, "Rebels with a Cause," *New Democrat* 6, no. 2 (April-May 1994): 17–22.

4. Peter Applebome, "Latest 'Best Hope' in U.S. Education: Chartered Schools," *New York Times*, October 12, 1994.

5. R. Craig Sautter, *Charter Schools: A New Breed of Public Schools*, policy briefs, report 2 (Oak Brook, Ill.: North Central Regional Educational Laboratory, 1993), p. 17.

6. Tom Watkins, "So You Want to Start a Charter School," *Education Week*, September 6, 1995, p. 40.

7. *Charter Schools: New Model for Public Schools Provides Opportunities and Challenges* (Washington, D.C.: United States General Accounting Office, 1995), p. 2.

8. Sage McCotter, *Charter Schools*, Clearinghouse issue brief (Denver: Education Commission of the States, 1995), p. 1.

9. University of Minnesota Humphrey Institute of Public Affairs and Education Commission of the States, *Charter Schools: What Are They Up To? A 1995 Survey* (Denver: Education Commission of the States, 1995).

10. Louann A. Bierlein and Lori A. Mulholland, *Charter School Update and Observations Regarding Initial Trends and Impacts*, Morrison Institute for Public Policy policy brief (Tempe: Arizona State University, 1995), p. 1.

11. *Charter Schools: New Model for Public Schools Provides Opportunities and Challenges*, p. 3.

12. Ibid., p. 4.

13. Louann A. Bierlein and Lori Mulholland, *Comparing Charter School Laws: The Issue of Autonomy*, Morrison Institute for Public Policy policy brief (Tempe: Arizona State University, 1994), p. 6.

14. *ERS Bulletin* 23, no. 7 (March 1996).

15. Sue Urahn and Dan Stewart, *Minnesota Charter Schools: A Research Report* (St. Paul: Research Department, Minnesota House of Representatives, 1994).

16. University of Minnesota Humphrey Institute, *Charter Schools*, pp. 27–28.

17. Urahn and Stewart, *Minnesota Charter Schools*, p. 55.

18. Interview with Carl Stokes, chair of the Baltimore City Council Education Committee, November 20, 1994.

19. "U.S. Gives $829,000 to Charter Schools," *Boston Globe*, September 1, 1995.

20. Peter Schmidt, "Citing Doubts, L.A. Board Revokes School's Charter," *Education Week*, December 14, 1994, p. 3. See also "Edutrain Charter Revoked," *Connections*, California Network of Educational Charters, January 1995, p. 4.

21. Louis V. Gerstner Jr., "Our Schools Are Failing: Do We Care?" *New York Times*, May 27, 1994.

22. Jeanne Allen, with Angela Dale, *The School Reform Handbook* (Washington, D.C: Center for Education Reform, 1995), p. 48.

23. Marcella R. Dianda and Ronald G. Corwin, "Vision and Reality: A First-Year Look at California's Charter Schools," *Southwest Regional Laboratory Metro Educator*, April 1994, p. 3.

24. Ruth E. Randall, "What Comes After Choice?" *Executive Educator* 14, no. 19 (October 1992): 35.

25. "Edventures 95," conference flyer distributed by the American Association of Teachers in Private Practice.

26. Janet R. Beales, *Teacher, Inc.: A Private-Practice Option for Educators* (Midland, Mich.: Mackinac Center for Public Policy and the Reason Foundation, 1995).

27. George Judson, "Yale Student Strike Points to Decline in Tenured Jobs," *New York Times*, January 17, 1996.

28. Lisa Davis, "You, Too, Can Open a School! In Arizona, It's Just Like Any Other Business," *Phoenix New Times*, March 30–April 5, 1995, p. 16.

29. Lonnie Harp, "American Visionaries: Educators and Entrepreneurs Alike Go Searching for a Pot of Gold to Finance Their Dream Schools," *Education Week*, November 29, 1995, pp. 12–15.

30. Hal Mattern, "Money Woes Rekindle Charter-School Debate," *Arizona Republic*, December 17, 1995.

Chapter Seven

1. Elizabeth R. Word, John Johnston, Helen Pate Bain, B. DeWayne Fulton, Jayne Boyd Zaharias, Charles M. Achilles, Martha Nanette Lintz, John Folger, and Carolyn Breda, *The State of Tennessee's Student/Teacher Achievement Ratio (STAR) Project Technical Report 1985–1990* (Nashville: Tennessee Department of Education, 1990).

2. Jeremy D. Finn and Charles M. Achilles, "Answers and Questions About Class Size: A Statewide Experiment," *American Education Research Journal* 27, no. 3 (Fall 1990): 557–577.

3. C. Steven Bingham, *White-Minority Achievement Gap Reduction and Small Class Size: A Research and Literature Review*, publication #TSU-95-0025-(B)-3-531308 (Nashville: Tennessee State University Center of Excellence for Research and Policy on Basic Skills, 1995).

4. Barbara A. Nye, Jayne Boyd-Zaharias, B. DeWayne Fulton, C. M. Achilles, Van A. Cain, and Dana A. Tollett, *The Lasting Benefits Study 8th Grade Technical Report* (Nashville: Tennessee State University Center of Excellence for Research and Policy on Basic Skills, 1995); Barbara A. Nye, Jayne Boyd-Zaharias, B. DeWayne Fulton, C. M. Achilles, and Van A. Cain, *The Lasting Benefits Study 6th Grade Technical Report* (Nashville: Tennessee State University Center of Excellence for Research and Policy on Basic Skills, 1993).

5. Jeremy D. Finn and Deborah Cox, "Participation and Withdrawal Among Fourth-Grade Pupils," *American Educational Research Journal* 29, no. 1 (Spring 1992): 141–162.

6. Frederick Mosteller, "The Tennessee Study of Class Size in the Early School Grades," *The Future of Children: Critical Issues for Children and Youths* 5, no. 2 (Summer-Fall 1995): 113–127.

7. *Does the U.S. Still Want a Public Education System?* Education Writers Association backgrounder (Washington, D.C.: Education Writers Association, 1994).

8. Paul R. Peterson, "Vouching for a Religious Education," *Wall Street Journal*, December 28, 1995.

9. Keith Bradsher, "Widest Gap in Incomes? Research Points to U.S.," *New York Times*, October 27, 1995.

10. Gerald W. Bracey, "The Third Bracey Report on the Condition of Education," *Phi Delta Kappan* 75, no. 2 (October 1993): 104–117.

11. American Legislative Exchange Council (910 17th Street NW, Washington, D.C., 20006) news release, "Report Card on American Education 1994," September 20, 1994.

12. John B. Goodman and Gary W. Loveman, "Does Privatization Serve the Public Interest?" *Harvard Business Review* 69, no. 6 (November-December 1991): 26.

13. Dani Sandbery, "The Pirate Privateers," *New Internationalist*, no. 259, September 1994, p. 14.

14. "Conrail for Sale," *Time*, June 13, 1983, p. 51.

15. Richard I. Worsnop, "Privatization," *CQ Researcher* 2, no. 42 (November 13, 1992): 987.

16. William E. Schmidt, "Britain Now Seeks Market for Coal," *New York Times*, October 22, 1992.

17. Calvin Sims, "Argentina Booming, Bypassing Jobless," *New York Times*, February 5, 1995.

18. Louis Uchitelle, "Wage Stagnation Is Seen As a Major Issue in the 1996 Election Campaign," *New York Times*, August 13, 1995.

19. Louis Uchitelle, "1995 Was Good for Companies, and Better for Alot of C.E.O.'s," *New York Times,* March 29, 1996.

20. Fox Butterfield, "Prison-Building Binge in California Casts Shadow on Higher Education," *New York Times*, April 2, 1995.

21. Edward N. Luttwak, "If the Economy Is So Good, Why Do We Feel So Bad?" *Milwaukee Journal*, December 18, 1994.

22. Doug Lasdon and Sue Halpern, "When Neighborhoods Are Privatized," *New York Times*, November 30, 1995.

23. Karen Herzog, "Network of Fund-Raising Groups Eyed to Boost Public Schools," *Milwaukee Sentinel*, January 17, 1995.

24. *Michigan Public School Governance* (Lansing: Michigan State Board of Education, 1995).

25. Richard I. Worsnop, "Privatization," *CQ Researcher* 2, no. 42 (November 13, 1992): 988.

26. Robert B. Reich, "How to Avoid These Layoffs?" *New York Times*, January 4, 1996.

27. "Massachusetts Seeks to Designate Fishing Industry Natural Disaster," *New York Times*, March 22, 1995.

28. Ibid.

29. Ibid.

30. Peter Passell, "Lonely, and Rich, at the Top," *New York Times*, August 27, 1995.

31. Edward Luttwak, "The Middle-Class Backlash," *Harper's*, January 1996, pp. 15–16.

32. Peter Applebome, "Have Schools Failed? Revisionists Use Army of Statistics to Argue No." *New York Times*, December 13, 1995.

33. Jonathan Kozol, *Savage Inequalities* (New York: Crown, 1991).

34. Editorial, "Students Without Desks," *New York Times*, February 5, 1995.

35. Peter Applebome, "Record Cost Cited to Fix or Rebuild Nation's Schools," *New York Times*, December 26, 1995.

36. See, for example, Gertrude Himmelfarb, "The Victorians Get a Bad Rap," *New York Times*, January 9, 1995, and Katherine Q. Seelye, "Gingrich Looks to Victorian Age to Cure Today's Social Failings," *New York Times*, March 14, 1995.

37. Cal Thomas, "The Surest Route out of Poverty Lies in Regaining Sense of Values," *Milwaukee Journal*, December 18, 1994.

38. Russell Baker, "Those Vital Paupers," *New York Times*, January 17, 1995.

39. Floyd Norris, "You're Fired! (But Your Stock Is Way Up)," *New York Times*, September 3, 1995.

40. Robert Heilbroner, "Weighing the Human Interest Rate," *Harper's,* March 1995, pp. 18–22.

41. Keith Bradsher, "Low Ranking for Poor American Children," *New York Times*, August 14, 1995.

42. Gerald Bracey, *Transforming America's Schools: An Rx for Getting Past the Blame* (Arlington, Va.: American Association of School Administrators, 1994).

43. Neal Gabler, "The Fathers of P.R.," *New York Times Magazine*, December 31, 1995, p. 29.

44. Leslie Savan, "The Bribed Soul," *Advice*, no. 18 (Summer 1995):1.

About the Book and Author

The commercialization of public education is upon us. With much fanfare and plenty of controversy, plans to cash in on our public schools are popping up all over the country. Educator and award-winning commentator Alex Molnar has written the first book to both document the commercial invasion of public education and explain its alarming consequences.

Giving Kids the Business explains why hot-button proposals like Channel One, an advertising-riddled television program for schools; for-profit public schools run by companies such as the Edison Project and Education Alternatives, Inc.; taxpayer-financed vouchers for private schools; market-driven charter schools; and the relentless interference of corporations in the school curriculum spell trouble for America's future.

Imagine that the tobacco industry may be helping to shape what your son and daughter learn about smoking. Imagine that your son is given a Gushers fruit snack, told to burst it between his teeth, and asked by his teacher to compare the sensation to a geothermal eruption (compliments of General Mills). Imagine your daughter is taught a lesson about self-esteem by being asked to think about "good hair days" and "bad hair days" (compliments of Revlon). Imagine that to cap off a day of world-class learning, your child's teacher shows a videotape explaining that the Valdez oil spill wasn't so bad after all (compliments of Exxon). Anyone curious about how schools are being turned into marketing vehicles, how education is being recast as a commercial transaction, and how children are being cultivated as a cash crop will want to read *Giving Kids the Business*.

Alex Molnar is considered one of the nation's leading experts on the commercialization of public education. His views have been widely reported in newspaper and magazine articles, and he has been a frequent guest on radio and television programs. Molnar is professor of education at the University of Wisconsin–Milwaukee.

Index

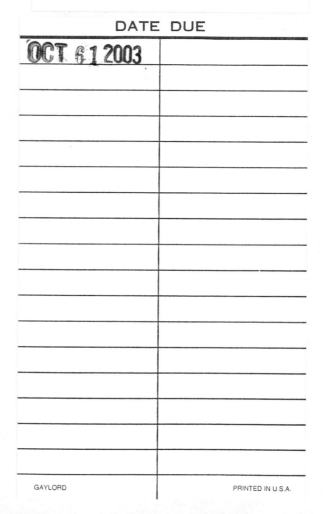